THE ARCHAEOLOGY OF ROMAN SURVEILLANCE IN THE CENTRAL ALENTEJO, PORTUGAL

CALIFORNIA CLASSICAL STUDIES

NUMBER 5

Editorial Board Chair: Donald Mastronarde

Editorial Board: Alessandro Barchiesi, Todd Hickey, Emily Mackil, Richard Martin, Robert Morstein-Marx, J. Theodore Peña, Kim Shelton

California Classical Studies publishes peer-reviewed long-form scholarship with online open access and print-on-demand availability. The primary aim of the series is to disseminate basic research (editing and analysis of primary materials both textual and physical), data-heavy research, and highly specialized research of the kind that is either hard to place with the leading publishers in Classics or extremely expensive for libraries and individuals when produced by a leading academic publisher. In addition to promoting archaeological publications, papyrological and epigraphic studies, technical textual studies, and the like, the series will also produce selected titles of a more general profile.

The startup phase of this project (2013–2017) is supported by a grant from the Andrew W. Mellon Foundation.

Also in the series:

Number 1: Leslie Kurke, *The Traffic in Praise: Pindar and the Poetics of Social Economy*, 2013

Number 2: Edward Courtney, *A Commentary on the Satires of Juvenal*, 2013

Number 3: Mark Griffith, *Greek Satyr Play: Five Studies*, 2015

Number 4: Mirjam Kotwick, *Alexander of Aphrodisias and the Text of Aristotle's* Metaphysics, 2016

THE ARCHAEOLOGY OF ROMAN SURVEILLANCE IN THE CENTRAL ALENTEJO, PORTUGAL

Joey Williams

CALIFORNIA CLASSICAL STUDIES

Berkeley, California

© 2017 by Joey Williams.

California Classical Studies
c/o Department of Classics
University of California
Berkeley, California 94720–2520
USA
http://calclassicalstudies.org
email: ccseditorial@berkeley.edu

ISBN 9781939926081

Library of Congress Control Number: 2016963103

CONTENTS

Acknowledgments ix
List of Figures and Illustrations xi

1. The Archaeology of Surveillance Landscapes 1
    Archaeological applications of visibility analysis 5
    The study of Alentejan *fortins* and *recintos-torre* 10
    Organization of chapters 12
    Living between empire and resistance: negotiating a contested landscape 15
2. The Early Roman Alentejo in Context 17
    The landscape and its natural resources 18
        Locating the landscape 18
        Natural resources 20
    A history of the region from a Roman perspective 23
        The Roman conquest of western Iberia 24
        From Viriathus to Augustus: the formation of Roman Lusitania 29
    The archaeology of the early Roman Alentejo 36
        Indigenous sites in the central Alentejo 37
        The Roman presence in the Alentejo: the first century BCE to the first century CE 39
3. Surveillance Structures in Ancient Art, Literature, and Archaeology 45
    Surveillance structures in Roman art 45
    Watchtowers, observation posts, and fortified villas in ancient texts 47

4. A Catalogue of Watchtowers in Early Roman Central Portugal	54
Catalogue of *fortins* and *recintos-torre* in the central Alentejo	55
Defining *fortins* and *recintos-torre*	55
Format of the entries	57
Fortins	59
Recintos-torre	72
Surveillance structures after the first century BCE	77
5. The First Century BCE Watchtower at Caladinho	80
The archaeological remains	82
Dating the structure	85
Ceramic classes	88
Ceramic fabrics	91
Analysis of the ceramic assemblage	94
Other materials from Caladinho	100
Towards an understanding of *fortins* and *recintos-torre*	101
The identity of Caladinho's inhabitants	102
6. Visibility Analysis of a Roman Colonial Landscape	108
Geographic information systems and visibility analysis: building a database	108
Methodology and sources of information	108
Defining the entries	109
Estimating height of observers	111
Visibility analysis of the central Alentejo in the first century BCE	112
7. Toward a Theory of Surveillance in a Roman Colonial Landscape	121
Archaeological remains of surveillance structures	123
Villas and their towers: an archaeology of exploitation	123
Static defenses of the Hadrianic frontier, northern England	125
Surveillance and the quarries at Mons Claudianus, Egypt	127
Toward a typology of surveillance	128
Border control	128
Oversight	129
Borderless surveillance	130

Defining surveillance in ancient colonial landscapes 131
   Entangled landscapes 132
   Empire and surveillance beyond the panopticon 135
Conclusions and future directions 138

Select Figures and Illustrations 141
Bibliography and Abbreviations 147
Index 167

ACKNOWLEDGMENTS

This book would not have been possible without the encouragement, assistance, and generosity of numerous institutions and individuals. First and foremost, I must thank the faculty at the University at Buffalo, especially my advisor Prof. Bradley Ault, for shepherding this project from inception to dissertation. Much of my perspective on archaeological materials was shaped by Prof. J. Theodore Peña and Prof. Archer Martin. They have both offered abundant encouragement and guidance, and they are greatly appreciated. The PortAnta Archaeological Cooperative and the National Museum of Archaeology in Lisbon have supported my work since I first visited Portugal as a field school student. Without their generosity this project would never have been conceived.

The support of the municipality of Redondo continues to be essential to the excavation at Caladinho and other archaeological projects in Alentejo. I must offer profound thanks especially to Rui Mataloto. Our work together provided the stimulus for this project, and I am forever grateful that he agreed to excavate a little hilltop called Caladinho with me. Caladinho has grown significantly since those first days, and I have many people to thank for bringing that fieldwork to fruition. The staff, volunteers, and friends of the Caladinho Archaeological Project—Catarina Alves, Brandi Bethke, Rui "Josué" Clemente, Inês Conde, Andrew Donnelly, José Inverno, Michael Kat, Emma Ljung, Mark Nakahara, Mark Pawlowski, Karilyn Sheldon, and Rhodora Vennarucci—were instrumental in completing the four seasons of excavation that anchor this book. I must also thank our field school students, too numerous to mention individually, whose hard work in difficult conditions made all this possible.

I am also grateful to my excavation colleagues for allowing me to publish here their photos and drawings related to Caladinho and other sites in Portugal. Specific credits are included in the captions. Please note that only a few select Figures are printed in this book, while the entire set is freely available online at eScholarship.org, the website that provides open-access viewing of this work.

The anonymous referees and the editorial board of California Classical Studies were indispensable in reshaping this project from dissertation to publication

Donald Mastronarde read and commented on multiple drafts of this book, and it has improved a great deal thanks to his guidance. I am also thankful for the editorial assistance provided by Elizabeth Ditmars in the final stages of the manuscript's preparation. Any remaining errors in the text are mine alone.

This book was made possible by several institutions. The Department of Classics at the University at Buffalo supported my work in its doctoral program through fellowships, summer research funds, and teaching assistantships. The University at Buffalo also provided the software necessary for the chapter on visibility analysis. Financial support for some of the fieldwork was also provided by the Mark Diamond Research Fund of the University at Buffalo's Graduate Student Association. Over many summers, Rui Boaventura and Maia Langley of the PortAnta Research Cooperative provided me with food, shelter, and good company (the three primary needs of any archaeological research). I must thank them both for introducing me to the archaeology of Portugal. The completion of this research was made possible by a doctoral exchange fellowship offered by the Faculté des Lettres at the University of Lausanne, Switzerland.

My deepest gratitude goes to Brandi Bethke. She has enthusiastically supported and patiently endured the writing of my dissertation and the writing of this book. There are no words sufficient to express the depth of my affection. Thank you.

Finally, this book is dedicated to my grandmother, Ava Crossno, who was an excellent storyteller.

Joey Williams
Norman, December 2016

LIST OF FIGURES AND ILLUSTRATIONS

NOTE: The entire set of figures is available in open access online at eScholarship.org (search for the title of this book to locate the page for this book, which will have a link to the Supplement of images). Only a select set of figures (those marked with an asterisk below) are printed in this book (following Chapter 7) for the convenience of the reader.

*Fig. 1.1.   The central Alentejo, Portugal
*Fig. 1.2.   Map of small fortified structures in the central Alentejo
Fig. 1.3.   Defensive tower from the walls of the Roman town of Ammaia
Fig. 2.1.   The Serra d'Ossa viewed from near Alandroal, Portugal
Fig. 2.2.   Cities and settlements of the first century BCE central Alentejo
Fig. 2.3.   Marks of ancient tools from the quarries near Vila Viçosa, Portugal
Fig. 2.4.   An unnamed Roman mine near the site of Castelinhos do Rosário, Portugal
Fig. 2.5.   First century BCE structures from Rocha da Mina
Fig. 2.6.   Granite wine or olive press weight reused as a sundial at Santa Susana
*Fig. 3.1.   Watchtower on the Column of Trajan
*Fig. 3.2.   Watchtowers on the Column of Trajan
Fig. 4.1.   Visible schist walls from the *fortim* at Beiçudos (F2)
Fig. 4.2.   View of the *fortim* of Cortes (F5) from the north
Fig. 4.3.   Hydraulic feature encountered near Outeiro Pintado (F6)
Fig. 4.4.   Extant wall from the *fortim* at Três Moinhos (F7)
Fig. 4.5.   View from Monte do Almo (F8) toward the western pass over the Serra d'Ossa
Fig. 4.6.   View of Caladinho (F9) from the northwest
Fig. 4.7.   Castelinho (F10) from the north with the Ribeira de Lucefécit in the foreground
Fig. 4.8.   Castelinhos do Rosário (F12) from the air
Fig. 4.9.   Northern external wall from Castelinhos do Rosário (F12)
Fig. 4.10.   Interior of the cistern from Castelinhos do Rosário (F12)
Fig. 4.11.   View of the interior of the *recinto-torre* at Mariano (R17)
Fig. 4.12.   Ceramics recorded at Mariano (R17) during survey

Fig. 4.13.   Amphora sherd from Outeiro da Mina (R18) stamped with the name *Silvi(i)*
Fig. 4.14.   View of the artificial platform at Castelo do Mau Vizinho (R20)
Fig. 4.15.   Plan of Castelo dos Mouros (R23)
Fig. 4.16.   Corner of the *recinto-torre* known as Castelo dos Mouros (R23)
Fig. 4.17.   Lusitanian and Baetican amphorae from Castelo dos Mouros (R23)
Fig. 4.18.   Local common wares from Castelo dos Mouros (R23)
Fig. 4.19.   View of the hill holding Val d'El-Rei de Cima *recinto-torre* (R24)
Fig. 4.20.   Roman villas south of the Serra d'Ossa
Fig. 5.1.   Ceramics recovered from Caladinho (F9) during initial survey
*Fig. 5.2.   Plan of the tower at Caladinho (F9), Sector 1, as of 2010
Fig. 5.3.   Plan of Caladinho (F9), Sectors 1 and 3, as of 2013
Fig. 5.4.   Sector 2, CAL[202]
Fig. 5.5.   Caladinho Harris Matrix, Sector 1
Fig. 5.6.   A selection of Chalcolithic artifacts recovered from Caladinho (F9)
Fig. 5.7.   Caladinho (F9), Sector 1, at the end of the 2012 season
Fig. 5.8.   CAL[59], a fallen mud brick wall with its bonding clay preserved
Fig. 5.9.   Caladinho (F9), Sector 1: leaning interior walls and hallway
Fig. 5.10.   Late 19th–early 20th century Alentejan construction
Fig. 5.11.   CAL[99], the stone paving at the entrance to the tower
Fig. 5.12.   CAL[93], fallen staircase inside the Sector 1 storeroom
Fig. 5.13.   CAL[96]3, a bronze door handle from Caladinho (F9)
Fig. 5.14.   Bedrock outcrop to the west of the tower at Caladinho (F9)
Fig. 5.15.   Caladinho (F9), Sector 1: large room from the tower from the western corner
Fig. 5.16.   Caladinho (F9), Sector 3: remains of a hearth against the southeastern wall
Fig. 5.17.   CAL[23]1, base of an Italian terra sigillata platter
Fig. 5.18.   CAL[19]1, Italian terra sigillata base with *Camurius F(ecit)* stamp
Fig. 5.19.   CAL[8]1, Italian terra sigillata base with *Dar/eus* stamp
Fig. 5.20.   CAL[8]1, detail of *Dar/eus* stamp
Fig. 5.21.   CAL[17]1, small Italian terra sigillata cup with *Avil(i) / fig(uli)* stamp
Fig. 5.22.   CAL[23]3, Italian terra sigillata fragment with *Ḍio(medes) / Ṣcro(fula)* stamp
Fig. 5.23.   CAL[70]1, a large Campanian black gloss platter of form Lamboglia 7
Fig. 5.24.   CAL[314]1, Campanian black gloss base with an internal stamp
Fig. 5.25.   CAL[94]1, a plain-rimmed bowl of form *Consp.* 7.1
Fig. 5.26.   CAL[100]7, mouth of a Haltern 70 amphora
Fig. 5.27.   Comparison of ceramic classes from Caladinho (F9) by sherd count
Fig. 5.28.   Comparison of ceramic classes from Caladinho (F9) by sherd weight

Fig. 5.29. Comparison of ceramic provenance from Caladinho (F9) by sherd count
Fig. 5.30. Comparison of ceramic provenance from Caladinho (F9) by sherd weight
Fig. 5.31. Selection of Italian terra sigillata cups and bowls from Caladinho (F9)
Fig. 5.32. Selection of Italian terra sigillata platters from Caladinho (F9)
Fig. 5.33. CAL[100]10-14, 24, 27, *orlo bifido* baking tray with inscribed interior base
Fig. 5.34. Selection of diagnostic amphorae recovered from Caladinho
Fig. 5.35. Total amphorae sherd count from Caladinho (F9)
Fig. 5.36. Total amphorae sherd weight from Caladinho (F9)
Fig. 5.37. CAL[34]5, Baetican *mortaria* similar to form Emporiae 36, 2
Fig. 5.38. CAL[94]3, loom weight with worn corners
Fig. 5.39. CAL[71]1 and CAL[93]3, loom weights with inscribed decoration
Fig. 5.40. CAL[301]4, fragment of an iron agricultural tool
Fig. 5.41. CAL[66]1, bronze *fibula*
Fig. 6.1. Inherent viewshed from F1
Fig. 6.2. Inherent viewshed from F2
Fig. 6.3. Cumulative viewshed from R17 and R18
Fig. 6.4. Inherent viewshed from F3
Fig. 6.5. Inherent viewshed from R19
Fig. 6.6. Cumulative viewshed from F6 and F7
Fig. 6.7. Cumulative viewshed from F1, F2, F3, F6, F7, R17, R18, and R19 south of Ammaia 314
Fig. 6.8. Inherent viewshed from F4
Fig. 6.9. Cumulative viewshed from R20, R21, R22, R23, and R24 north of Évora
Fig. 6.10. Inherent viewshed from F9
Fig. 6.11. Inherent viewshed from F8
Fig. 6.12. Inherent viewshed from F5
Fig. 6.13. Cumulative viewshed from F5, F8, F9, and F10
Fig. 6.14. Inherent viewshed from F10
Fig. 6.15. Inherent viewshed from F12
Fig. 6.16. Inherent viewshed from F13
Fig. 6.17. Inherent viewshed from F14
Fig. 6.18. Inherent viewshed from F15
Fig. 6.19. Cumulative viewshed from F11, F12, F13, F14, and F15
Fig. 6.20. Inherent viewshed from F11
Fig. 6.21. Inherent viewshed from F16
Fig. 6.22. Cumulative viewshed of all *fortins* and *recintos-torre* in the study area
Fig. 7.1. Cumulative viewshed of Roman villas south of the Serra d'Ossa

The Archaeology of Roman Surveillance in the Central Alentejo, Portugal

CHAPTER 1

THE ARCHAEOLOGY OF SURVEILLANCE LANDSCAPES

The historian Appian, writing of the culmination of nearly two centuries of war, rebellion, and resistance in ancient Iberia, notes that Julius Caesar "brought under subjection by force and arms all of those Iberians who were doubtful in their allegiance, or had not yet submitted to the Romans" (*Hisp.* 102).[1] This short passage implies the final acts, initiated by Caesar, of a process of conquest and colonization in a cultural landscape which still lay outside of the sphere of the nascent Roman Empire. The landscape—and the peoples, locales, and concerns within it—provide an opportunity to approach the colonial encounter in one of the first regions to experience, and to resist for almost two hundred years, Roman imperial ambition.

Central Portugal in the first century BCE was a region caught between various cultural forces. Indigenous peoples waged recurrent rebellions against Rome, and reports of banditry and unrest in the region come to us from a number of ancient sources (Appian, *Hisp.* 71; Dio Cassius 37.52.1–4; Florus 1.33.15–17; Livy 28.32.9; Plutarch, *Mar.* 6.1, *Sert.* 14.1; Strabo 3.3.8; Valerius Maximus 9.1.5; Varro, *Rust.* 1.16.2).[2] The independent tribes of northwestern Iberia, settled around their *castros*, largely retained control over their ancestral territories and maintained their centuries-old trade with Mediterranean cultures.[3] In the south, the Roman conquest of both Carthaginian and indigenous centers had been ongoing since the Second Punic War.[4] By the first century BCE, the agricultural and mineral wealth

---

[1] ...ὅσα τῶν Ἰβήρων ἐσαλεύετο ἢ Ῥωμαίοις ἔτι ἔλειπε, πολέμῳ συνηνάγκασε πάντα ὑπακούειν.

[2] Keay (2001: 126–27) argues against the direct effects of warfare on the majority of the ancient Iberian population despite the numerous Greek and Latin sources that suggest the conquest of the peninsula was particularly bloody, at least for the Romans.

[3] Queiroga 2003.

[4] The Roman colonization of the Iberian littoral and inland areas may be understood as a part of a long series of colonial encounters in the peninsula. See Castro Martínez et al. 1996; Ruiz and Molinos

of the formerly Punic-controlled area was increasingly exploited by Roman colonists and trading companies, known as *societates*. The Alentejo region, a geographically distinct area of central Portugal located between the Tejo and Guadiana rivers, was incorporated into the new Roman territory of *Hispania Ulterior* at the end of the second century BCE following the military defeat of the Lusitanians and Celtiberians.[5] Yet while the Roman state may have claimed control over the region at the close of these wars, the actual projection of colonial power into the central Alentejo was not to begin in earnest until the first century BCE. Even then control over this territory was contested as factions within Rome itself struggled for dominance.

Given the interest of ancient historians in battles, the dispositions of armies, and the deeds of Roman generals in the Iberian Peninsula, it would be simple enough to explain the colonization of this region as the Roman military domination of the peoples of ancient Spain and Portugal. And, indeed, Iberia was the scene of some of the most dramatic and violent events of the Second Punic War, the Celtiberian and Lusitanian Wars, and Rome's own civil wars. Such a reading fails to recognize the individual and community agency possessed by all actors, both foreign and indigenous, who were taking part in this colonial encounter. From this perspective, violence represents an expression of power or a reaction to it, and past cultural responses to insecurity, unrest, and violence may be found in the material record. The course of the Roman conquest, reorganization, and settlement in the ancient Alentejo was, as with any colonial encounter, a negotiated process between numerous factions. As M. Dietler points out, only a broad consideration of multiple perspectives can adequately illuminate the unforeseen cultural consequences of colonialism.[6] Thus a consideration of the complexities of the ancient Alentejan social and political landscape provides an important step towards an understanding of the Roman colonial encounter in this region and perhaps others as well.

The study of Roman Portugal has intensified in the last decade thanks to the numerous salvage excavations undertaken in response to the building of the Alqueva Dam.[7] While the dam brought modernization to the most rural parts of

---

1998; Moret 2000; Aubet 2001; Domínguez 2002; González-Ruibal 2006; Sanmartí 2009.

[5] Both Richardson (1986) and Keay (2001: 127) have argued that the terms *Hispania Citerior* and *Hispania Ulterior* do not originally represent demarcations of provincial territories but rather geographical regions of consular or proconsular responsibility. It was not until the first century BCE, perhaps not until the reforms under Augustus, that Rome's overseas provinces were organized into distinct territorial units (Nicolet 1991: 189–207). Before this change in both legal and perceived status, Roman policies treated Iberian communities as if they were organized along the lines of city-states with which Rome could build a powerful confederacy like the one it had forged in Italy (Knapp 1977: 81–118).

[6] Dietler 2010: 56.

[7] For an example, see the report of the excavation of Castelo da Lousa recently published by Alarcão et al. (2010c). Many hundreds of sites were surveyed and excavated as part of the *Plano de*

Portugal, concomitant archaeological projects revealed numerous new facets of the region's ancient past. In particular, the *Instituto Português de Arqueologia*, the *Instituto de Gestão do Património Arquitectónico e Arqueológico* (IGESPAR), and the *Direção-Geral do Património Cultural* supported both single-site excavations and large regional surveys. This work has culminated in the production of archaeological maps for each of the country's municipal territories.[8] Alongside these, a new generation of professionals and academics has worked to revolutionize the archaeology of Portugal, to introduce new methodologies, and to reinvigorate the study of prehistoric, protohistoric, and Roman occupations.

The central Alentejo region (Fig. 1.1), now home to the Alqueva Dam, possesses a landscape of rolling hills, steep ravines, and arable plains. The Guadiana River forms the eastern boundary and served as the main route or transport in this region. Numerous *arroios*, dry stream beds or washes, meander around the hills. The nature of the central Alentejo, its relative isolation from the major centers of both the ancient and modern worlds, and its lack of monumental architecture have given impetus to the study of the rural landscape and its inhabitants. Numerous projects have examined the growth of villas in Roman Portugal and their economic and social positions during the empire.[9] Other scholars have examined the pre-Roman Iron Age occupation of the region.[10] Despite the extensive body of work exploring the late Iron Age and Roman periods in the Alentejo, archaeologists have only recently begun to consider the transition, both materially and culturally, from the sparsely populated Alentejo of the Iron Age to the more settled and intensely exploited Alentejo of the first century CE. Numerous rural sites from the late first century BCE and early first century CE have been identified in the last two decades. Of these, most are small, isolated, and fortified, and many are equipped with towers.

These small fortified towers or tower enclosures (Fig. 1.2), known in Portuguese scholarship as *fortins* or *recintos-torre*, are among the most enigmatic structures uncovered in the Alentejo. They appear in a broad swath in the central Alentejo and have predecessors in the similar structures far to the south and west. These sites have been variously defined as military, commercial, agricultural, or domestic in purpose, and their inhabitants identified as Lusitanian, Carthaginian, and

---

Minimização do Impacto Arqueológico do Regolfo da Barragem de Alqueva (EDIA 1999).

[8] The *Carta Arqueológica do Alandroal* (Calado 1993), the *Carta Arqueológica do Concelho de Évora* (Calado 1996a), and the *Carta Arqueológica do Concelho do Redondo* (Calado and Mataloto 2001) provide the locations of many sites mentioned in this text.

[9] Among these excavations, the ongoing work at the villa of Torre de Palma, near Monforte in the Alto Alentejo, has received a great deal of attention from scholars. See Maloney and Hale 1996; Fugate 2000; Maloney and Hoffstot 2002; Langley 2006; and Boaventura and Banha 2006.

[10] See especially Calado and Rocha 1997; Fabião 1998; Burgess et al. 1999; Álvarez-Sanchís 2000; Mataloto 2004b; Mataloto et al. 2007; Langley et al. 2008; Mataloto and Alves 2008; Mataloto 2010: 60–70.

Roman. Their positions in the landscape, however, suggest that they represent an important repositioning in the struggle for control over the region. Many of these structures are associated with the surveillance of important trade routes, mines, quarries, or fertile agricultural areas. This utilization of vision and visibility played a crucial role in the negotiation of territorial control and the reorganization of the landscape under colonial rule.

Larger fortified sites occupying positions similar to the *fortins* and *recintos-torre*, such as Castelo da Lousa and Castelinhos do Rosário, also sought control of the region's resources and trade routes. Unlike the *fortins* and *recintos-torre*, from which these larger settlements may have grown, Castelo da Lousa and Castelinhos do Rosário remained occupied and active well into the Imperial period.[11] In addition to these larger sites, previous studies of the role of intelligence gathering in ancient military and administrative operations have suggested a wide variety of surveillance options available to Roman commanders.[12] Textual evidence indicates that Roman *exploratores* and *speculatores*, scouts and spies, were attached to each legion.[13] Knowledge of the landscape would have been of supreme importance for Roman military commanders, and similar knowledge would have benefited any attempts at reorganizing or exploiting conquered territory even on an *ad hoc* basis. Military itineraries from Iberia, scratched into simple clay tablets, indicate the army's route through the north of the peninsula, which allowed them to observe wide areas. An example of one such tablet from northern Iberia reads:

> The 7th Gemina Legion to Portus Blendius. To Rhama, seven miles. Amaia, eighteen. Villegia, five. Legio [...], five. Octaviolca, five. Iuliobriga, ten. Aracillum, five. To Portus Blendius, [...]. Gaius Lepidus M[...] duumvir (*AE* 1921, 6; *AE* 1924, 62).[14]

Similar patrol routes may have been established in the central Alentejo. Larger forts, camps, and garrisons, only a few of which have been found in Alentejo, may have also provided some local surveillance.[15]

By the end of the first century BCE, as Augustus pacified the last holdouts of Iberian resistance in the north, some large Roman villas in the Alentejo were equipped with towers, perhaps to keep check on gangs of slaves working in the

---

[11] Castelinhos do Rosário remains largely unexplored and unpublished, although its architectural remains were completely uncovered in the 1970s by the owner of the hill where the site is located. For Castelo da Lousa, see Paço and Leal 1966; Wahl 1985; Fabião 1996; Gonçalves and Carvalho 2002; and Alarcão et al. 2010c.

[12] Leighton 1969; Sherk 1974; Donaldson 1988; Gichon 1989; Ferrill 1992; Lee 2006.

[13] Speidel 1970, 1983; Austin 1987; Austin and Rankov 1995; Sheldon 2002, 2005.

[14] [...] l(egio) VII Gemina ad portu[m] / Ble(n)dium / Rhama VII milias / Amaia XVIII /5 Villegia V / Legio I[...] V / Octaviolca V / Iuliobriga X / Aracillum V /10 p[or]tus Blen[dium ...] / C. Lep[idus] M[...] IIvir. The translation assumes that p[or]tus on the tablet is a scribal error for p[or]tum.

[15] Fabião 2006.

fields or to watch for bandits. High walls and towers were also established at new Roman settlements in the area, like *Civitas Ammaiensis* (Ammaia), and offered the inhabitants of these new cities a command of the visual landscape around them as well as spreading a potent symbolic message of the new colonies' strength and permanence (Fig. 1.3).[16] While the Roman colonization of the Alentejo in the first century CE brought about significant changes in settlement, the new *villae* and *coloniae* continued to make use of surveillance structures in the now peaceful, reorganized landscape. The different uses of these structures represent a significant departure from how vision and visibility were utilized in the previous century, and signal the changes wrought in the region by Roman imperialism.

ARCHAEOLOGICAL APPLICATIONS OF VISIBILITY ANALYSIS

Over the last two decades archaeologists have increasingly interpreted the spaces, places, and regions where human activity occurs as elements of the built and natural landscape. Defining the concept of "landscape" has remained elusive. R. E. Witcher notes that in order for archaeologists to analyze landscape effectively, we must accept that landscapes are "socially constructed, subjectively experienced, and polysemic in nature."[17] Even so, analyses of landscape may derive conclusions from economic data as readily as they do from experiential, humanistic, or phenomenological approaches. In this way studies of landscape bridge the divide between qualitative and quantitative analyses of culture.[18] Landscape, then, represents the space, both real and figurative, where human activities occur. It is both the realm of the social and the economic, yet it is also closely linked to memory, power, conflict, and their expressions. As human activities leave their material expressions on even the smallest archaeological sites, those same material remains mark both the social construction of a landscape and our interpretation of it.

The archaeology of landscape offers a broad, regional view of a variety of sociocultural phenomena. For example, its analysis permits us to contextualize studies of changing settlement patterns within the natural environment as well as the broader political economy. P. A. Shackel, in the introduction to a special volume of *Historical Archaeology* devoted to landscapes of conflict, reviews the potential of landscape archaeology for our understanding of the organization of power and its material expression.[19] By framing landscapes as the spaces within which rela-

---

[16] Abascal and Espinosa 1989; Corsi 2014; Corsi and Vermeulen 2009: 3; Corsi and Vermeulen 2012: 41–44; Vermeulen and Taelman 2010. Some of these new settlements proved to be quite impermanent. See Fabião and Guerra 2010.

[17] Witcher 1999: 13. See also Green 1990: 358; Bender 1993: 3; Boaz and Uleberg 1995: 252.

[18] Tilley 1994: 8.

[19] Shackel 2003: 5–6.

tionships of power, inequality, and conflict may be negotiated, we may begin to recognize the material remains of those relationships. This is particularly true for colonized regions, zones of contact, or other spaces where an imperialist power encounters indigenous peoples. Analysis of the material impact of empire on a landscape can reveal much about power, conflict, and cultural entanglement that may arise from a colonial encounter.

Surveillance represents one such expression of power within a landscape. The use of surveillance has long been understood as the domain of an empowered individual or group, and most commonly as an apparatus of the state itself. J. Bentham, in the late eighteenth century, proposed a design for a prison which he called the panopticon.[20] His prison would allow the inmates to be observed at all times and thereby limit their agency. In the 1970s, Michel Foucault, in his essays on power and knowledge, expanded the concept beyond prisons and into other relationships of power and subjugation.[21] Foucault posited the panopticon as the state's preferred method of social control, or the potential for observation exercised by an authority on a subject person or group. The panopticon controls the subject of its gaze not by the gaze itself but by the knowledge of its presence. Those subjected to the panopticon alter their behavior in response to the possibility of being under surveillance. The panopticon provides an excellent interpretive framework for particular contexts, such as the observation of prisoners or coerced labor, but in colonial settings, where power relationships are uncertain and entangled, the social role of surveillance must be reconsidered.[22]

The landscape of the Iberian interior represents one such region where surveillance may be understood as entangled within larger processes of colonization. Surveillance over borders, such as that imposed by the German-Raetian *limes* or by the towers on and beyond Hadrian's Wall, represents a mode of surveillance—"border control"—that is familiar to modern audiences. Border surveillance in an ancient context relied on surveillance to control access to border crossings but also to project the power of the Roman state on those that lived outside of it. The subjects of border surveillance knew that they were being watched, and that attempts at brigandage or other illegal border crossing risked a punitive response from the Roman military. In the interior of western Iberia, however, surveillance had no foreign territory as the subjects of its gaze. The territory was borderless, and the subjects of surveillance in a colonial landscape are the landscape's own potentially restive inhabitants. Thus surveillance in a colonial context must be embedded and widespread within the landscape in order effectively to express control over the surveilled.

---

[20] Bentham 1787.

[21] Foucault 1980; 1991: 187, 200–201.

[22] For a review of the concepts of entanglement and agency in the archaeology of colonial contexts, see Dietler 1998; 2010: 55–74.

Previous studies of surveillance archaeology have regularly sought to use the panopticon as an interpretive framework. In some archaeological contexts, such as H. Friedman's study of carceral oversight and its control of slaves involved in mining and metal production, the panopticon provides a useful means of understanding the function of surveillance and the means of its application.[23] Slaves, prisoners, and the condemned were largely powerless to escape surveillance by masters, wardens, and overseers, and thus they were powerless to escape their bondage. Roman systems of carceral oversight in the context of forced labor approach Bentham's panopticon. In a colonized landscape, however, power was not expressed without resistance, and control over territory, resources, and populations relied on negotiation. In this colonial arena, the panopticon does not provide an adequate interpretive model for understanding surveillance. A theory of surveillance in this borderless zone is one that recognizes that watching and being watched, and controlling others through the threat of being watched, is entangled in colonial processes. Instead of the unidirectional application of power in the form of the panopticon, this study emphasizes that surveillance was one tool used to control, negotiate, and subdue the colonial landscape.

By embedding the concept of surveillance in the archaeological study of a colonized landscape, this book offers a new perspective on the negotiation of territorial control and sheds new light on the history of the early Roman Alentejo. The application of geographic information systems (GIS) to archaeology allows the visualization of the precise areas potentially under surveillance from any given point or site. Viewshed analysis—the projection of total areas of intervisibility from a given point or points—offers an excellent tool for the analysis of vision and visibility in the Alentejan landscape. Other incorporations of GIS-based visibility analysis into archaeological research have sometimes lacked a robust theoretical framework, being characterized at times as "a method in search of a theory."[24] Yet such a theory seems all the more essential given the potential for this mode of analysis to untangle some elements of colonial contact in the ancient world.

Visibility analysis, particularly viewshed analysis, has increasingly been used in the interpretation of archaeological sites and landscapes in the last twenty years.[25] Through visibility analysis, the territory under surveillance can be effectively projected, lines of sight can be clearly understood, and the potential for communication between points or routes in the landscape can be seen.[26] By recognizing the importance of vision and visibility in the central Alentejo, this work seeks more

[23] Friedman 2008: 196–229, 2009a: 7–10. See also Yekutieli 2006.
[24] Conolly and Lake 2006: 232–33. Recent work has challenged this analysis. See especially Llobera 2003, 2007.
[25] See Kvamme 1989; Wheatley 1995; Christopherson and Guertin 1996; Loots 1997; Woodman 2000; Ruestes 2008a, 2008b; Friedman 2008: 196–229, 2009b.
[26] Christopherson and Guertin (1996), Malm (1999), and Llobera (2001) approach the use of vision and its opposition in GIS and archaeological research.

fully to engage these concepts with archaeological discussions of the negotiation of colonial landscapes.

Viewshed analysis is the algorithmic attempt at computing the intervisibility of points within a landscape. Calculating intervisibility requires a relatively high-resolution topographic map, usually in the form of a digital elevation map (DEM). The DEM is projected as a raster, a type of digital image where individual points of data are represented by squares which make up the image. On this raster, the landscape is divided into a grid of uniform squares. Each square in the grid is assigned a value which corresponds to its relative height. Using GIS software, various visibility analyses, including inherent viewshed, cumulative viewshed, and total viewshed, can be calculated from the raster data. Thus viewsheds may provide a map of those areas within a landscape that are visible or invisible depending on one's location.[27] Archaeological remains within the landscape, such as towers, can provide additional height to any individual square within the raster and so influence the resulting viewshed. Those archaeological sites which are topographically prominent will, in most cases, have a greater degree of intervisibility than those which are located elsewhere. Inherent viewshed analysis (sometimes referred to as "simple viewshed analysis") is the calculation of the visual structure of a landscape. When taken as part of a larger analysis of settlement, inherent viewshed analysis may reveal the role of surveillance and visibility in the placement of sites, particularly those for which visual control over the landscape was an essential function.[28] Those sites with little intervisibility between themselves and the rest of their landscape are likewise important as their locations may be the result of the conscious choice to remain invisible at the cost of limiting their own ability to surveil.

Cumulative viewshed analysis provides a more complex method of analyzing a landscape, and is a natural progression from inherent viewshed analysis. In a cumulative viewshed, the results of some or all inherent viewsheds are summed, and the complete area visible from the chosen points, including any overlap between their areas of visibility, is displayed on the map layer.[29] Cumulative viewshed analysis is particularly useful for identifying locations which provide the best degree of visibility of a target area.[30] Analyses of the areas under surveillance and of the intensity of that surveillance are useful for understanding the role of surveillance structures in a particular landscape.[31]

Various problems of both method and theory complicate the utility of viewshed analysis. First, it is practically impossible to reconstruct precisely an individual's degree of vision at any given point in the past. The factors limiting such a

[27] Wheatley and Gillings 2002: 204.
[28] Conolly and Lake 2006: 224.
[29] Wheatley 1995: 173.
[30] Llobera 2003: 33.
[31] For an excellent example see Friedman 2008: 206–28, 2009b.

reconstruction are numerous, including variation in the height of the observer, differences between present and past vegetation, built or natural objects which are no longer extant, and the weather at any given time.[32] Thus, viewshed analyses should best be taken as a general, aggregate representation of vision and visibility rather than a particular one.

Archaeological studies of viewsheds have received criticism for their privileging of vision over other sensory experiences of place and space.[33] While this critique may encourage us to explore more phenomenological approaches to landscape, these approaches are best understood as complementary rather than contradictory.[34] Additionally, the "alleged obsession with vision" which has been the focus of criticisms of visibility analysis has been called into question by T. Ingold.[35] Nevertheless, the availability of powerful analytical tools, such as GIS, and the existence of numerous types of ancient surveillance place questions of space, settlement patterning, and vision at the center of analyses of past landscapes. While other sensory experiences may provide additional valuable avenues of research, vision remains an essential element for our understanding of ancient landscapes.

Assessing the degree of visual interference caused by vegetation in the paleo-landscape is one of the most common concerns in determining intervisibility. In the central Alentejo, the hot, dry climate appears to have persisted even during the Iron Age and Roman periods.[36] Large stands of eucalyptus trees, which greatly obscure visibility in some areas today, were only introduced in the middle of the twentieth century. We may surmise that the number of indigenous trees was perhaps even more limited than it is today. These trees would have provided the primary impediments to vision that are no longer extant today. Even so, their overall impact on visual acuity would have been minor.

In previous studies of visibility within a landscape, scholars have estimated the average distance at which the human eye may recognize and distinguish objects at 6.2 km.[37] H. Friedman, in her recent study of surveillance structures in Roman Jordan, estimated human visual acuity in that landscape at only 4 km owing to local environmental factors.[38] Given the clarity of the air in the Alentejo, the lack of blowing sand, and the sparse vegetation in most seasons, I have here chosen to follow the upward estimate of 6.2 km. This choice is largely based on personal

---

[32] Gillings and Wheatley 2001: 32; Friedman 2008: 199.
[33] Witcher 1999; Tschan et al. 2000: 43–45; Wheatley and Gillings 2000; Conolly and Lake 2006: 233.
[34] Llobera et al. 2010: 146; Tilley (1994) provides the most widely read phenomenological exploration of archaeological landscapes.
[35] Ingold 2000: 246.
[36] López García 1986; Carrión et al. 2000; López Sáez and López Merino 2005; López Merino et al. 2010: 275–78.
[37] Wheatley and Gillings 2000: 15–20.
[38] Friedman 2008: 200.

experience in the central Alentejo after seven years of fieldwork at a variety of sites. The recognition of groups of humans or animals within the landscape would necessarily be easier than the recognition of individuals regardless of the visual distance between observer and target(s).

The varying height of observers provides another complication for the accurate modeling of surveillance.[39] M. Gillings and D. Wheatley estimate the average height of observers at 1.75 m.[40] Prehistoric human remains have been excavated from Alentejan sites, but their applicability to populations of the first century BCE and first century CE are questionable. Thus, the standard of 1.75 m as the average height of an observer provides the best available estimate. The relative height of surveillance structures within the central Alentejan landscape also influences the results of any visibility analysis. The excavation of the tower at Caladinho suggests a structure of multiple stories. The extant walls of the tower rise to a height of 2.5 m in some places, and the upper stories appear to have been constructed from lighter mud brick rather than schist.[41] A stone outcrop next to the tower rises to a height of over 6 m above the base of the structure and so provides a useful gauge for estimating the height of the tower itself.[42] With the addition of the height of the observer, an offset of 7.75 m is included in the calculation of viewsheds from these structures. The height of these small fortified structures—many identified as towers or tower-enclosures—is considered in further detail in subsequent chapters.

THE STUDY OF ALENTEJAN *FORTINS* AND *RECINTOS-TORRE*

The small fortified Alentejan structures have been given a variety of names in a variety of languages, including *atalayas, casas fuertes, castella, fortins, tours d'Hannibal, turres,* and *recintos-torre* among other things. The terms *fortim* and *recinto-torre*, translated as "small fort" and "tower enclosure" respectively, possess the widest usage among Portuguese scholars and represent the most general description of these structures, and so best leave open the interpretation of their nature and purpose. The identity of their inhabitants, however, has proven far more difficult to establish. C. Fabião has recently reviewed the numerous possible identities for the occupants of the *fortins* and *recintos-torre*.[43] Given their artifact

---

[39] Conolly and Lake 2006: 232.
[40] Gillings and Wheatley 2001: 33.
[41] Mataloto and Williams 2012: 5–6.
[42] Friedman (2008: 205) also estimates free-standing towers to be 6 m tall. Those towers were incorporated into structures she estimates to be 10 m in height. Some of the more substantial surveillance structures in the central Alentejo may have reached heights of 10 m or more, but the lack of well-preserved examples necessitates a more conservative estimate. Estimates of tower heights which differ from 6 m are clearly indicated where those structures are discussed below.
[43] Fabião 2012.

assemblages, positions within the landscape, and dates of occupation, he posits connections to domestic, agricultural, industrial, and military uses, and so a variety of different inhabitants. Indeed, differentiating between these activities may not be of use for understanding the occupants of these sites. Observation posts and watchtowers in the Roman East, for example, appear to have been operated by civilians even though their purpose was connected to the military occupation of their respective locations.[44] This comparative evidence is discussed in detail below.

By situating these small fortified structures within the growing body of research on ancient peasants, we may more readily theorize their social and economic roles within the landscape.[45] The peasants who lived in the small fortified settlements of the central Alentejo, whether indigenous peoples or first-generation colonists, were not the most powerful actors within their landscape. They are, to judge by the architectural and material remains, best categorized by their apparent vulnerability. They may very well have supported the causes of rebellious factions, but the material culture of these sites suggests an interest in the consumption of both imported and locally produced Roman wares. Their agency within the contested, colonial landscape of the first century BCE Alentejo was confined to their response to outside forces. They chose where and how to situate their fortified farmsteads, and in doing so reveal their attempts at negotiating between the multiple competing forces operating within this colonized region. Some sought refuge in hard-to-find, even hidden, places, like the shrine of Rocha da Mina (discussed in Chapter 2). Others sought locations that offered commanding views of the countryside, but whether this was to lay claim to the area or simply to see what was coming is unclear. The best locations for settlement, perhaps, offered reasonable expectations of seclusion but also permitted a degree of vision over the landscape.

Yet evidence from other *fortins* and *recintos-torre* beyond the Alentejo suggests that at least some of these small fortifications were also occupied by elements of the Roman military. Recent work on a *fortim* near the mouth of the Tejo River near Santarém, called Altos dos Cacos, has recovered a *pilum*, numerous lead *glandes*, a *ballista* ball, and other examples of Roman *militaria* alongside a domestic assemblage.[46] Monteró, a small "outpost" in the northeast of Spain

---

[44] Peacock and Maxfield (1997: 255) suggest that civilians operated the surveillance structures around Mons Claudianus based on evidence derived from *ostraka* found at the site. Friedman (2008: 202–203), building from this example, suggests that the same might have been true for the watchtowers in Roman Jordan.

[45] In fact, they share many material similarities with the small, poor, isolated farmsteads of republican Italy. Lloyd (1991), Gros (2001: 271–75), Bowes (2012), and Terrenato and Motta (2012) provide several relevant examples.

[46] Pimenta et al. 2012: 71–76. Various *militaria*—including *pila, glandes*, and pieces of bronze armor—were also recovered from Castelo da Lousa. See Ruivo 2010: 498–503, 514–15. Some have argued for the military occupation of some or all *recintos-torre*. See Almeida 1945; Maia 1974b, 1978, 1986; Kalb and Hock 1984; Berrocal 1996; Alonso Sánchez and Corrales 2000. Additionally, Alonso Sánchez (1988) and Heras Mora (2009, 2010) have offered comparative studies of Roman military fortifications

which dates from 125–75 BCE, possesses a similarly mixed assemblage. T. Ñaco del Hoyo and J. Principal suggest that Monteró (and perhaps other small fortified sites in Iberia) was a *castellum* which housed a garrison of native *auxilia*.[47] Given that many *fortins* and *recintos-torre* are situated overlooking important routes of communication or installations for extractive industries, this interpretation may indeed have merit. As with small farmers seeking out defensive positions within the landscape, joining the Roman auxiliaries represents a conscious response to the new demands of colonization. Stationing these Iberian allies in the *fortins* and *recintos-torre* likewise represents a conscious response, in this case one made by the Roman imperial authority in the region.[48] The ascent of Roman control over the central Alentejo entangled natives, colonists, and soldiers alike. By examining the individual responses to cultural contact and the social disruption of colonization, we may piece together some of the consequences, both social and political, of Roman imperialism in this region and beyond. The purpose of the *fortins* and *recintos-torre* and the identities of their inhabitants are considered in greater detail below.

ORGANIZATION OF CHAPTERS

The following chapter examines the history and environment of Iberia. The topography of the central Alentejo, of particular importance for a study of surveillance, is given close attention. Similarly, the natural resources available in the ancient Alentejo provide an important facet of the local context. For a better understanding of the sociopolitical setting, this chapter also includes a summary history of western Iberia from the late Iron Age through the formation of the Roman province of Lusitania. Special attention is paid to episodes of indigenous resistance, the impact of the Roman civil wars on the peninsula, and the reorganization and incorporation of the central Alentejo as part of an imperial province under Augustus. Taken together, these elements give necessary context and definition to

---

in Extremadura, the western part of Spain that was once a part of Lusitania. Diosono (2005) suggests that a similar structure that he refers to as a *castellum* was part of a Roman system of territorial control emplaced around the modern city of Granada. Moret (1995; 1999; 2010: 18–25) argues against the military occupation of these small fortified structures. See also Berrocal 1992; Ortiz Romero 1995; Alarcão et al. 2010a: 28–33. Many fortified farmsteads and rural towers exist in other Mediterranean contexts. For examples see Ober 1985; Carter et al. 2000; Morris 2001; Morris and Papadopoulos 2005; Decker 2006. Friedman (2008: 202), in her analysis of towers in Roman Jordan, disputes the identification of these structures as fortified farms, but suggests that civilians may have played a role in the surveillance of the surrounding region. The difficult issue of defining the towers' functions and their occupants is explored further in chapters 3 and 4.

[47] Ñaco del Hoyo and Principal 2012: 165–68. See also Alonso Sánchez and Corrales 2000.

[48] For a thorough exploration of the role of commanders' independent decision-making on Roman foreign policy see Eckstein 1987.

the region.

The remainder of Chapter 2 turns to a survey of the archaeology of Roman Portugal, particularly those sites dating to the first century BCE in the Alentejo region. This survey focuses on the sites and materials important for an understanding of the period of conquest and provincial organization in western Roman Iberia. *Coloniae* and *municipia*, such as *Pax Iulia, Liberalitas Iulia Ebora*, and *Civitas Ammaiensis*, are examined for their relevance in understanding the growing Roman influence in the region during the first century BCE. Attention is also paid to the scattered and fragmentary evidence of the Roman military presence in the Alentejo. Among the sites considered are the late republican army camp at Cáceres el Viejo, the remains of Castelo da Lousa, and the Roman-occupied hillforts at Cabeço de Vaiamonte and Mesas do Castelinho, among others. This chapter also explores the archaeological evidence for early Roman industry and agriculture in the Alentejo, especially villas, mines, quarries, field systems, and transportation routes.

Chapter 3 surveys the evidence for surveillance systems presented in ancient art and textual sources the better to contextualize this archaeological data. Ancient authors such as Appian, Livy, and Pliny the Younger each comment on the different roles of watchtowers in ancient structures. Epigraphic sources, while scattered and fragmentary, provide insights into the purposes behind the establishment of towers in certain regions, as does the early Christian treatise *De Duobus Montibus Sina et Sion*.[49] Images of watchtowers and other surveillance structures, such as seasonal treehouses meant for the observation of slaves, are also examined in this chapter. While depictions of watchtowers are relatively rare in ancient art, these images provide us not only additional context for interpretation but also examples of structures comparable to those seen in the archaeological record.

Focus shifts in Chapter 4 to the archaeological remains of surveillance structures in the first century BCE Alentejo. The main part of chapter is dedicated to collating and presenting the evidence for the numerous small fortified towers, *fortins* and *recintos-torre*, in the Alentejo. These are each detailed in a comprehensive catalogue that updates previous work on these sites.[50] The location and dating of each site is given, and when possible the artifact assemblage is considered. This chapter also considers the role of surveillance structures after the first century BCE, particularly the construction of observation towers at villas.

The archaeological remains of Caladinho, one of the Alentejan *fortins*, are described in Chapter 5. The excavation of Caladinho is the first of the central Alentejan *fortins* to be systematically and comprehensively investigated. This site pro-

[49] The epigraphic evidence for the surveillance structures around Mons Claudianus in Egypt are covered at the end of Chapter 5 in order to compare more fully these observation posts with the *fortim* of Caladinho.

[50] Moret 1990, 1995, 1999, 2010; Calado and Mataloto 2001; Mataloto 2002, 2004a, 2010; Moret and Chapa 2004; Mayoral Herrera and Celestino Pérez 2010; Mataloto et al. 2014.

vides a useful case study for understanding the role of surveillance structures in this landscape. Chapter 5 first considers the excavated remains of the site and its artifact assemblage. An abbreviated catalogue of pottery from the site, including only artifacts essential to understand the site's inhabitants, is provided. The rest of the chapter is dedicated to the analysis of the ceramic data, the interpretation of the site and its inhabitants, and a consideration of the role of Caladinho in understanding the other *fortins* and *recintos-torre* located in the first century BCE central Alentejo. This chapter argues that the site of Caladinho currently represents our best example of a first century BCE surveillance structure embedded in the contested colonial landscape of the central Alentejo. Caladinho holds implications for the study of the *fortins* and *recintos-torre* presented here as well as for our understanding of landscape, settlement organization, and the colonization of the western Iberia in the first century BCE. The information garnered from this research has already greatly expanded our understanding of the role of these tower enclosures in the landscape, the nature of their inhabitants, and the longevity of their occupation.

The sixth chapter offers a visibility analysis of surveillance structures from the first century BCE and first century CE in the central Alentejo. First, this chapter details the specific sources and types of data used in the creation of the GIS database as well as the categorization of the sites presented. The main part of this chapter, however, deals with the visibility analysis of sites in the study area and its interpretation. The relative topographic prominence of each site is examined, synthesized, and related to the established archaeological remains at Caladinho and other sites in the region. The surveilled landscape of the first-century BCE central Alentejo is then compared to the same landscape a century later, as well as with other surveilled landscapes around Roman quarries in Egypt and along the imperial frontier in northern England.

A theory of surveillance in Roman colonial contexts, one that goes beyond Foucault's panopticon to recognize the agency of multiple actors to surveil and to avoid surveillance, is explored in the seventh and final chapter.[51] Given that surveillance networks appear to be common throughout the Roman world—especially in those areas with histories of indigenous resistance or with significant numbers of individuals pressed into industrial activity—this seventh chapter argues for the value of surveillance theory for our understanding of colonial encounters under the Roman Empire. By drawing on the data presented in previous chapters, this chapter proposes a typology of surveillance landscapes present in the Roman world, particularly in colonial contexts. This typology incorporates surveillance landscapes in several different zones of colonial contact during the late Republic and early Empire. The primary aim of this chapter is to provide an

---

[51] This book also engages in the ongoing debate over surveillance theory. See Lyon (2006) for an overview of recent approaches.

improved, theoretically grounded understanding of the early Romano-Alentejan cultural landscape, and by doing so to suggest a potential model for other colonial encounters in the ancient Mediterranean and beyond.

LIVING BETWEEN EMPIRE AND RESISTANCE:- NEGOTIATING A CONTESTED LANDSCAPE

Ultimately, this book develops an archaeology of the people living between the forces of empire and resistance. The inhabitants of the Roman Alentejo in the first century BCE, as with those living in any colonized region, were caught between multiple competing factions. They existed in a context of sociopolitical uncertainty. Their shared landscape was populated with violence, unrest, and insecurity. Guerillas, under the bandit-turned-revolutionary Viriathus, had waged a long and brutal struggle against foreign occupation of the region a century earlier. The renegade general Quintus Sertorius led a similar coalition against Roman forces in the second quarter of the first century BCE. Still further insurrections threatened to erupt even in the last half of that century.[52] Roman military units were garrisoned not only in their own camps but among indigenous settlements as well—an effective means of curtailing further rebellion—but these forces were also often caught up in civil strife between the factions of Roman government. New settlers claimed access to natural resources, and the territories of many groups were in flux, ultimately to be redistributed, reorganized, and annexed by colonial interests by the beginning of the first century CE.

Entangled in such uncertainty, the inhabitants of the early Roman Alentejo responded to this contested landscape in a number of ways. Distinct among these was the establishment of small settlements in locations chosen specifically for their topographic prominence. These structures first appeared in the Alentejo during the middle decades of the first century BCE. These small structures, while all fortified to varying degrees, are relatively poor in both their construction materials and artifact assemblages, especially when compared to the villas established around the time of their abandonment.[53] They provided surveillance over routes of passage and communication in the local landscape, and monitored the approaches between large indigenous settlements, new Roman colonial cities, and valuable natural resources. They existed to guard this colonized landscape as much as to claim it through the use of surveillance. With some notable exceptions, they were

---

[52] García y Bellido 1945.

[53] Lowe (2009: 54–115) provides a useful summary of the villas established in Iberia during the late Republic and early Empire. Alarcão (1988) gives an overview of the villas in the Alto Alentejo, although the last two decades of fieldwork have revealed numerous sites not mentioned in his gazetteer of Roman Portugal. Gorges (1990) edited a useful volume that, while now over two decades old, continues to orient discussion of Roman villa culture in western Iberia.

all abandoned or incorporated into new Roman villas less than a century later as control over the region was decided.

The last two decades have seen remarkable changes in our understanding of the archaeology of the Alto Alentejo. As the region has strengthened economically, new construction projects have given impetus to new archaeological research. New foreign projects, most often with the assistance of local archaeologists, have shed light on the important cultural heritage of this region of Portugal. Despite all these efforts, however, the Alentejo remains in many ways ignored and understudied by English-speaking scholars, and resources for even small-scale excavations are now quite limited. The significance that this region and its archaeology can play in our understanding of the dynamics of Roman conquest and the archaeologies of colonialism should be ignored no longer. As we grapple in our own era with the implications of empire, colonialism, and the rise of both the surveillance state and radical responses to it, there are lessons for us in the humble crumbling *fortins* of the central Alentejo.

CHAPTER 2

THE EARLY ROMAN ALENTEJO IN CONTEXT

Defining the early Roman Alentejo requires careful attention to topography, environment, and the vast natural resources of the region in the context of its complex history as a landscape of conflict. The region existed as a borderland between numerous groups and cultures for several centuries, even before the rupture of Roman imperial conquest. It was inhabited by competing Iberian peoples, among them the *Lusitanii* and the *Celtici* tribes, and was host to traders and settlers from powerful groups to the south, including Phoenicians and Tartessians.[1] Romans first record their presence in the region during the Second Punic War and ostensibly conquered the Alentejo at the close of that conflict.[2] Ongoing resistance to Rome, however, required the involved parties to navigate the difficult cultural terrain of colonization within this shared landscape. By the period of civil wars, colonial investment in the landscape had made it a valuable prize to Rome's contending political factions. Mineralogical resources, farmland, and the earliest colonial settlements were linked to the wider Mediterranean economy through natural routes of transport as well as newly built road systems.[3] The built and natural aspects of the Alentejan landscape lend necessary context to the multifaceted events that shaped this region between the first century BCE and the first century CE.

This chapter offers a survey of this Romano-Alentejan landscape, its specific geographic location, natural resources, environmental factors, and topography. This last element will prove to be very significant in later chapters as this discussion moves into discussions of visibility, surveillance, and their roles in a colonized region. The natural resources of this region, particularly in the area between the Tejo and Guadiana rivers, also provide essential context since the changing methods of their exploitation and of their administration suggest significant so-

---

[1] Fabião 1998; Álvarez-Sanchís 2000; González-Ruibal 2006.
[2] González Román 1981; Curchin 1991.
[3] Roldán 1975; Blázquez Martínez 2002: 493–94; Vermeulen 2006.

ciocultural transformations. Next, this chapter also engages with the primary historical sources for the Alentejo during this early Roman period. The lion's share of attention is devoted to the historical events which characterize the nature of the colonial encounter during the periods in question. Despite this focus, the biases of these ancient authors, none of whom self-identify as Iberian, requires a careful delineation between the ideology of empire and the social and physical reality of the encounter itself.

The final element that gives context to the central Alentejo is the archaeological record, both indigenous and Roman, of the region. The majority of archaeological sites in the Alentejo have received scant attention in the wider realm of Mediterranean archaeology, yet a growing body of Portuguese scholarship continues to provide new insights into this otherwise understudied corner of the ancient world. This chapter offers a review of the most compelling and essential sites from the first century BCE and first century CE in the central Alentejo. These archaeological remains, which have sometimes received little prior scholarly attention, give necessary context to the surveillance landscape. They indicate, materially, the processes of the colonial encounter and hint at the wider social, political, and economic implications of the Roman presence in the region. When understood together, the central Alentejo's environmental, historical, and archaeological data offer context to a region that provides a robust framework for the study of ancient colonialism in Iberia and beyond.

THE LANDSCAPE AND ITS NATURAL RESOURCES
Locating the landscape

The geographic location of the archaeological landscape considered below is best defined by topographic features and natural geographic areas, although the modern political geography is also influential given that archaeological data are variously available region to region. The south and south-central region of modern Portugal, not including the Mediterranean coastal Algarve, is a historic, geographic, and cultural region known as the Alentejo. It lies between the Tejo River in the north and Guadiana River in the east, and is generally subdivided into two geographic regions, the northern Alto Alentejo and southern Baixo Alentejo.[4] In the recent past it has been subdivided into three municipal districts located around Portalegre in the north, Évora in the center, and Beja in the south. Since 2009 the Évora district has been coterminous with an intraregional administrative unit known as the *Comunidade Intermunicipal do Alentejo Central* (CIMAC), although the *Alentejo Central* region is not yet commonly marked on modern political maps. The political division of the Alentejo into northern, central, and

---

[4] Daveu et al. 1987.

southern regions is roughly contiguous with numerous natural geographic and topographic features, such as the Estremoz Anticline and Serra d'Ossa range in the north, the Serra de Monfurado in the west, the Guadiana River in the east, and the Serra de Portel in the south.[5] These natural features do not, in each case, represent the precise borders of the modern political unit, yet they do serve to bound a generally central geographic region within the Alentejo. The geographic area under study here includes sites that are largely located within this central Alentejan region, although a few lie just outside its borders. The central Alentejo is often recognized in modern scholarship on Alentejan archaeology, and the present study seeks to treat this region as a specific geographically distinct area in the same manner.

The landscape of the Alentejo itself is best described as gently rolling plains and hills, cut by small streams and washes, and featuring higher elevations in the northeast. It shares much in common with the geography of Extremadura, the Spanish autonomous community to the east which, with most of Portugal, originally formed a large part of the Roman province of *Lusitania*.[6] The Alentejo's topography is rugged, despite being dominated by rolling plains. The terrain is often rocky and difficult to traverse. Some areas are passable only by following the winding paths of streams or washes. The limited routes of communication through the central and northern Alentejo provided ample opportunity for their control by surveillance and carefully located defensive structures.

Known in both Spanish and Latin as the *Tagus*, the Tejo River follows its long course east to west until it eventually flows through Lisbon and into the Atlantic. It forms the northern border of the Alentejo region. The Guadiana, which the Romans called the *Anas* for its many ducks, has its source in the south of the Iberian Peninsula. It runs east to west for much of its course, but abruptly turns south after it enters Portugal. This segment forms the southwestern boundary of the landscape examined here. The river, while not navigable by boat, provided an essential route for trade and transport through this landscape. Now, however, the Alqueva Dam Project, while providing us with valuable data from many salvage excavations in the last two decades, has inundated a large part of the Guadiana river valley. Many relevant archaeological sites, including Castelo da Lousa, are situated along this river, but now they lie beneath the lake formed with the dam's completion.

The present study area is also bordered by mountains. The landscape north of the Tejo rises slowly until it forms the Serra da Lousã and Serra de Estrela ranges in central Portugal. To the southeast, the Sierra Morena range lies beyond the Guadiana river valley and separates it from the Guadalquivir river basin. The

---

[5] CIMAC 2014: http://www.cimac.pt/pt/site-alentejo-central/caraterizacao/Paginas/Ambiente.aspx
[6] Rodríguez Díaz (1998) provides a useful exploration of Spanish Extremadura during the late Iron Age and early Roman periods.

Serra d'Ossa, a relatively small range of mountains, is situated within the Alentejo between the modern towns of Estremoz and Redondo. Many of the sites in this study are situated around it. It rises from the low hills of the Alentejo, and presents the most difficult part of the landscape to traverse (Fig. 2.1). The Serra de Caldeirão range rises just beyond the modern city of Beja and forms the southern boundary of the present study area.

The study area is also defined by the presence of a cluster of specific archaeological sites, known in Portuguese as *fortins* and *recintos-torre* (Fig. 2.2). Twenty-four have so far been identified in the Alto Alentejo. This number is increased with the inclusion of similar but substantially larger and longer-lived sites such as Castelo da Lousa. Together with the region's ancient cities, including *Pax Iulia*, Évora, and Ammaia, and its many villas, these sites represent responses to the Roman colonization of the region over the course of the first century BCE and into the early first century CE.[7]

Natural resources

Iberia, especially the southern and western parts of the peninsula, is famed for its mineralogical resources, many of which have been exploited on an industrial scale since even before the Roman conquest. The area is dotted with ancient quarries and mines of a variety of sizes and scales, and numerous Roman villas in the area boast significant extant industrial spaces and equipment that supported their abundant agricultural production. The region remains famous for its olives, wine, and animal products, and although the soil is poor or rocky in many areas, the Alentejo nevertheless produces a significant amount of grain.

Ancient sources also discuss the precious metals present in the sands of Iberia's rivers, particularly the Tejo. Both Catullus and Ovid use the same adjective, *aurifer*, meaning "gold-bearing," to describe the river (Cat. 29.19; Ov. *Amores*, 1.15.34). Catullus writes concerning the result of Rome's colonial activities, "First our father's estate was torn apart, next the Pontic plunder, and third the Iberian spoils, as the gold-bearing river Tejo knows well" (29.17–19).[8] Juvenal, in his *Satires*, also remarks on the wealth in the river, "Let not the sands of the cloudy Tejo and the gold it rolls into the sea be so precious to you that you lose sleep and, sorrowful, accept gifts that will one day be surrendered" (3.54–57).[9] These ancient authors are correct in their characterization of the Tejo River as a source for gold, and archaeological evidence suggests that mines were established as far upstream

---

[7] Alarcão 1990a.

[8] *Paterna prima lancinata sunt bona / Secunda praeda Pontica inde tertia / Hibera, quam scit amnis aurifer Tagus.*

[9] *...Tanti tibi non sit opaci / omnis harena Tagi quodque in mare volvitur aurum, / ut somno careas ponendaque praemia sumas / tristis....*

as the Roman town of Ammaia.¹⁰

Western Iberia remains noted for its high quality marble quarries even today, and many of these sources for decorative and building stone have been exploited since before the Roman occupation.¹¹ The most productive of these quarries exist between the Tejo and Guadiana rivers near the cities of Beja, Estremoz, Évora, and Vila Viçosa.¹² The region between Estremoz and Vila Viçosa, located in the districts of Évora and Portalegre, contains a very large deposit of high quality marble known as the Estremoz Anticline (Fig. 2.2). While modern activity has obscured the archaeological record of ancient quarries in the Estremoz Anticline, there remains evidence for a significant industrial presence particularly during the first century CE (Fig. 2.3).¹³ The marble quarried from the Estremoz Anticline was used in the construction and ornamentation of Roman colonies and settlements throughout the Alentejo and beyond.¹⁴ The intensive Roman exploitation of the Estremoz Anticline quarries suggests that control over them was an important part of the Roman colonization of the region.

The mines of the Alentejo are minor in comparison to the massive metallurgical installations in the north and south of the Iberian Peninsula. The mines of Las Médulas in the province of León represent one of the largest industrial activities in the ancient world. Pliny the Elder, once *procurator metallorum* of the region, tells us that they produced somewhere around 6,500 kg of gold per year through the use of hydraulic mining (*HN* 33.78). Vast amounts of silver, iron, and lead were likewise produced in the Sierra Morena range south of the Guadiana. In the northern and central Alentejo, however, relatively few mines were established, and none of them on the same scale as the imperial mines in the rest of Iberia. The mining areas near the ancient cities of Ammaia and *Pax Iulia*, while significant, are dwarfed by the scale of industrial activity elsewhere in the peninsula, although the mines of Ammaia extracted gold through techniques similar to those used at Las Médulas.¹⁵ The copper mines of Aljustrel, known in antiquity as the *Metallum Vipascense*, lie within the territory of *Pax Iulia*, and are famous for the two bronze tablets, the *lex metalli Vipascensis* and the *lex metallis dicta*, discovered there in the nineteenth and twentieth centuries.¹⁶ The tablets provide the legal context for working the mines under a *societas publicanorum* and have long been of interest to scholars seeking to understand the organization of Roman imperial industry

---

[10] Deprez et al. 2007: 33–41; Taelman et al. 2010: 63–64. For the more plentiful mines in the southern Alentejo, see Rego 1996.

[11] Fusco and Mañas Romero 2006: 19; Lamberto and Caetano 2008: 472.

[12] Nogales Basarrate et al. 2008: 422–23.

[13] Romero and Fusco 2008: 490–91.

[14] Alarcão 1988: 135–36; Rodà de Llanza 1999: 124.

[15] Deprez et al. 2007; Taelman et al. 2010.

[16] Domergue 1990, 1987: 495–508.

and mining.[17] The products of the mines at Aljustrel no doubt fed the urban center of *Pax Iulia* as it grew to prominence in the region during the first century BCE and first century CE. It is likely that the mining area's valuable products also involved the settlement with wider economic concerns in the Mediterranean as well as demanding an increased scrutiny of the local landscape particularly when that landscape remained unsettled and potentially insecure.

Some small mining and metallurgical installations have been identified in Alentejo (Fig. 2.4). They appear to have been established during the first century BCE and the first century CE and many are associated with the fortified structures that are the focus of this book. In some cases, such as with the small mines around Castelinhos do Rosário, it appears that the fortified structures served to provide control over the mines through surveillance. None of these mines have been adequately explored by archaeologists, and their precise relationship with other sites remains in question. But by locating these small mines within the cumulative viewsheds of the nearby *fortins* and *recintos-torre*, the connections between them may become more evident.

The mines in the Alentejo may represent the periphery activities of the "gold rush" described by Diodorus (5.36). According to his account, many Italians migrated to southern Iberia after the Second Punic War, and particularly in the first century BCE, to take advantage of the mineral resources of the newly conquered regions. J. S. Richardson suggests that these early settlers operated on public lands and paid rents, *vectigalia*, to the Roman state.[18] Antonio Mateo's review of the legal sources concerning Roman mining expands on Richardson's interpretation with a more nuanced approach. He posits that small-scale miners paid a *vectigal* for the right to mine, but that the scale of these mining interests reflected the relative abundance of metals in the region. In those areas where metals were not as abundant or were more difficult to access, individuals or small groups would mine in simple pits.[19] Larger, richer deposits which required substantial investment were exploited by *societates publicanorum* in both opencast and deep-vein mines.[20] The small mines near sites like Castelinhos do Rosário perhaps provide examples of the work of these individual prospectors in the Alentejan landscape during the first century BCE. As the mineral deposits in the south of the peninsula became occupied by both individual miners and *societates publicanorum*, it is no surprise that some struck out for the interior of Iberia. The small scale and short occupation of most mines in the central Alentejo suggests that these ventures were not always profitable.

---

[17] Domergue (1983) and Lazzarini (2001) cover the mines at Aljustrel and the two Vipasca tablets. But see also the discussion of the tablets by Edmondson (1987), Curchin (2004: 144–50), and Hirt (2010: 262–68) as well as discussion of the legal organization of Roman mining on public lands by Mateo (2001).

[18] Richardson 1996: 137.

[19] Mateo 2001: 58–65.

[20] Mateo 2001: 43–55.

The soils of western Iberia were noted by many ancient authors as particularly poor. Strabo's characterization of the region's agricultural potential, for example, is quite negative (*Geog.* 3.1.2). Additionally, poor soils are blamed by ancient authors as the source for revolts in western Iberia. Appian's account of Rome's war against the Lusitanians (*Hisp.* 59) contains an excellent example. In it, the praetor Servius Sulpicius Galba pretends to sympathize with the Lusitanians, and suggests that the region's poor soil had driven them to break their treaty with Rome when their own crops failed. Yet the admitted poverty of the Lusitanians does not keep Galba from deceiving and massacring thousands. After acknowledging the infertility of the territory granted to the Lusitanians under the original treaty, Galba promises to allot the Lusitanians new, more fertile ground. Once the Lusitanians have left their homes, presumably with their families, in the hopes of being granted arable land, the Roman soldiers surround and massacre the crowd, leaving only a few survivors (*Hisp.* 10.59–60). This episode suggests that Roman commanders were working to reorganize and assert control over western Iberia even during the earliest moments of colonial interaction in the region.[21] Natural resources, from metals and stones to the Alentejo's sparse fertile agricultural land, drew the attention of both colonizer and colonized. The various attempts at seizing and controlling these specific resources are elements of the negotiation of power within the newly colonized landscape.

A HISTORY OF THE REGION FROM A ROMAN PERSPECTIVE

A number of ancient historians record the history of western Iberia, yet none of these historians write from the perspective of the region's indigenous peoples. No Iberian historian's work survives for us, and our knowledge of the pre-Latin languages of the peninsula is fragmentary. Nevertheless, while these Greek and Roman historians provide an account biased by their connection with colonial power, they are our only textual sources of information. Their biases are often recognizable, but their histories can provide a useful window into this region that archaeology has not or cannot provide alone.

The Roman historian Livy is foremost among the historians who discuss the peoples of western Iberia. He records, with some useful details, the earliest stages of Roman colonization of Iberia, the first attempts by Iberian cultures to resist Roman hegemony, and his descriptions of the Lusitanians and their culture. Few other ancient sources provide in-depth commentary on the history of Iberia

[21] Athenaeus (8.330C–331B) records that the now fragmentary book thirty-four of Polybius' *Histories* (34.8.4–5) characterizes Lusitania as fertile, favorable province, in contrast with the descriptions given by Strabo and Appian and counter to our understanding of the region's past and present environmental conditions.

during the late Iron Age. The peninsula's connection to the Punic Wars, however, gives Livy ample reason and opportunity to discuss the region and its conquest and colonization by the Romans. Livy's treatment of the peoples of western Iberia is profoundly negative. This discourse is likely part of Livy's attempt to justify the Roman military presence in the peninsula which had not yet, by Livy's time, been successful at eliminating the last holdouts of resistance.

The Alexandrian historian Appian, who wrote in the first half of the second century CE, is particularly useful for understanding the wars between Romans and indigenous Iberians during the first century BCE. The sixth book of his *Roman History*, known as the *Hispanica* or the *Iberica*, chronicles the Roman conquest of Spain's Mediterranean coast during the Second Punic War through the final annexation of the northwest of the Iberian Peninsula under Augustus. Yet, as G. S. Bucher notes, "where we can check it, Appian's text contains a perplexing mixture of good data and errors."[22] Appian's history is meant as criticism of the violence endemic to the Roman Republic. By focusing on the strife and bloodshed of the Republic's final two centuries, he intends for the Roman Empire to appear superior to its predecessor in comparison.[23] Appian advocates for Roman imperial hegemony because it promises to bring peace, and so his focus on the wars, and the atrocities, that occurred during the Republic's conquest of western Iberia may betray his bias. Nevertheless, despite his inaccuracies and his bias, Appian remains essential to the study of the history of early Roman Iberia simply because so few other extant ancient authors deal comprehensively with the region during this period.

Other authors provide additional contextualization to western Iberia in the early Roman period. A great number of these recount the career of Viriathus, a successful guerilla commander in the mid-second-century BCE. Lusitanian War. Plutarch's biography of Sertorius is also useful for the study of the Roman presence in western Iberia during the first half of the first century BCE. The *De Bello Hispaniensi*, most likely written by one of Julius Caesar's lieutenants, characterizes the effects of the war between Caesar and the sons of Pompey the Great in the peninsula. Although the majority of military actions during the campaign occur in the south of the peninsula, numerous *Lusitanii* take part in the conflict. The willingness of the Lusitanians to fight for Caesar or the Pompeians reflects the dynamism of identity and sociopolitical relationships during the colonial encounter between indigenous Iberians and Romans.

The Roman conquest of western Iberia

After the Second Punic War, Rome asserted control over the coastal regions of

---

[22] Bucher 2000: 412.
[23] Bucher 2000: 442–43.

Iberia, particularly in the east and south of the peninsula. The eastern coast was given the name *Hispania Citerior* and was, after Cato's successful campaign there in the first decade of the second century BCE, largely pacified up to the boundary of the Ebro River (Livy 34.11–21).[24] While Cato had faced rebellion in all corners of the peninsula, the resistance to Roman hegemony appears to have been conducted by individual tribal or ethnic groups rather than as an organized pan-Iberian rebellion. Cato was received in Rome as a *triumphator*, and the senate again sent two praetors to govern the provinces of *Hispania* (Appian, *Hisp.* 39–41).

Following Cato's return to Rome with an immense amount of plunder (Livy 34.46), other Roman generals appear eager to wage war in Iberia (Livy 34.1.1–2; 35.1). At the end of 194 BCE—only a year after Cato had supposedly ended organized resistance—P. Cornelius Scipio Nasica, then *propraetor* of *Hispania Ulterior*, was faced with a counterinvasion of his province by an army of Lusitanians. The Lusitanians had left the central Alentejo, crossed the Guadalquivir, and entered Roman controlled territory with the intent to plunder. After doing so and succeeding, Scipio's army appears to have ambushed and defeated them near the Guadalquivir (Livy 35.1.9–11).[25] In the following year, M. Fulvius Nobilior defeated a combined army of at least four different Iberian tribal groups, Celtiberians, Oretani, Vaccaei, and Vettones, near Toletum (Livy 35.7.6–8; 35.22.5–8). The Oretani were likewise routed by G. Flaminius during a battle between the Guadiana and Guadalquivir rivers (Livy 34.55.6). The conquest of this region opened the Guadiana and Tejo rivers to the Romans, and the first incursions into the central Alentejo were made possible.

The proconsul Lucius Aemilius Paulus, circa 189 BCE, subdued over two hundred Iberian settlements according to Plutarch (*Aem. Paul.* 6.7.4). While this number is likely inflated, epigraphic evidence from Baetica (specifically from Alcalá de los Gazules on the southern tip of the peninsula) suggests that Paulus did conquer some regions formerly outside of the Roman sphere of influence.[26] An inscription on a bronze tessera suggests the means by which Paulus added at least one indigenous settlement's territory to *Hispania Ulterior*. The inscription reads:

> L. Aimilius, son of Lucius, commander, decreed that the slaves of the Hastenses,

---

[24] Keay 1988: 29–31. While Cato's efforts appear to have been met with a great measure of success, other areas of the peninsula remained very much in revolt. For example, the subsequent governor of *Hispania Citerior*, Sextus Digitius, lost half of his garrison to a rebellion in the northeast. Only the intervention of P. Cornelius Scipio Nasica, then the governor of *Hispania Ulterior*, kept the eastern part of the peninsula from erupting in violence (Livy 35.1.3–4).

[25] The precise location of this battle is unclear, but the site is thought to be the town of Ilipa mentioned by Pliny the Elder (*HN* 3.4). This episode marks the first involvement of the Lusitanians in the Iberian resistance to Roman colonization of the peninsula. Interestingly, it appears that Lusitanian territory was not considered a part of *Hispania Ulterior* until Roman military actions against the *Lusitanii* pushed them northward.

[26] Stylow 2005: 258.

who live in *Turris Lascutana*, should be freed.[27] They shall continue to possess and hold the land and the *oppidum* which they currently possess so long as the Roman people and senate wish it to be so. Done in camp on the twelfth day before the Kalends of February (CIL 1² 2.614).[28]

By freeing the slaves and turning the town and its agricultural land over to them, Paulus had created a new and potentially enthusiastic Roman ally in the region. The fate of the slaves' former masters remains unknown.

After the first two decades of the second century BCE, Roman power encompassed nearly the entirety of the eastern and southern coasts and the nearby regions. But this control was hard won. As praetor, Tiberius Sempronius Gracchus conducted one of the most successful campaigns against the inhabitants of the central Spanish *mesetas* while his counterpart, L. Postumius Albinus, invaded the territory of the *Lusitanii* for the first time (Livy 40.35.2-9).[29] As previous governors of the Iberian provinces had done a decade earlier, Gracchus and Albinus "prepared to conduct the affair with a common purpose and plan" (Livy 39.30.1).[30] Gracchus had captured a great number of Celtiberian towns by 179 BCE, and Albinus led a Roman army into Lusitania that same year. J. L. de Vasconcelos conjectures that Albinus' route took him through the central Alentejo between the Guadiana and Tejo rivers.[31] His campaign against the *Vaccaei* and *Lusitanii* met with great success. Both commanders were awarded triumphs (Livy, *Per.* 41.3-4). These actions against the inhabitants of Lusitania mark the first substantive expression of Roman military power in the region. They were not, however, wars of conquest, and little territory appears to have changed hands after Albinus' campaign. Instead, Gracchus and Albinus had lessened the threat that the Celtiberians and Lusitanians posed to the Roman coastal possessions in *Hispania Citerior* and *Hispania Ulterior*.

Ancient historians report that Iberian resistance was so fierce that few Roman commanders desired to be appointed military tribune or legate in the two Spains in the first half of the second century BCE (Livy, *Per.* 48.17-18). New recruits were

---

[27] The name of the settlement, *Turris Lascutana*, implies the presence of a tower. The nature and purpose of such a structure, should it have existed at this site, is unknown. Given the connection with slaves, it may have been intended as a vantage point for surveillance over slave labor. Or, as Morris and Papadopoulos (2005: 206) suggest, this tower may have been associated with overseeing a mine. Pliny the Elder (*HN* 3.1.15) also mentions *Turris Lascutana*, but its precise location in southwestern Iberia remains unknown.

[28] *L(ucius) Aimilius L(uci) f(ilius) inpeirator decreivit / utei quei Hastensium servei / in turri Lascutana habitarent / leiberei essent agrum oppidumqu(e) / quod ea tempestate posedisent / item possidere habereque / iuosit dum poplus senatusque / Romanus vellet act(um) in castreis / a(nte) d(iem) XII K(alendas) Febr(uarias).*

[29] Keay 1988: 32.

[30] *...communi animo consilioque parati rem gerere.*

[31] Vasconcelos 1913: 111. Alarcão (1988: 27) posits instead that Albinus took a more northerly route through Beira Baixa.

equally terrified of the prospect of serving in *Hispania Ulterior* thanks to the tales told by returning veterans (Polybius 35.4.3). These stories came, perhaps, as a result of the attacks carried out by the Lusitanians and other Iberian groups between 160 and 153 BCE. Evidence for this unrest comes to us only in summary form in the *Periochae* of Livy:

> In addition, [Book 47 of Livy] contains an account of the unsuccessful campaigns waged in Hispania by various commanders. The consuls, in the five hundred and ninety-eighth year after the founding of the city, began to enter their office on the Kalends of January. The date of the election was changed because the *Hispani* were in revolt (Livy, *Per.* 47.12).[32]

That such a change in the procedures of the Roman Republic was made on the account of unrest in Iberia is remarkable. It suggests that matters in *Hispania* were so extreme that the fundamental processes of the Roman republican government were disrupted.

By the 150s BCE, the Roman military had expanded its reach into the heart of *Hispania* in response to numerous uprisings among the Celtiberian, Turdetanian, Lusitanian, and other Iberian groups mentioned above. Indeed, the Roman conquest in the peninsula appears to have been based on reaction to crises rather than a carefully planned strategy of military domination. These new territories would again come under attack by the Lusitanians under the command of Punicus in circa 155 BCE. Although his name suggests that he was descended from a Carthaginian family, he was at the fore of a Lusitanian army that made raids into that group's former territory. Whether their ultimate goal was reconquest or simply plunder, the Lusitanians under Punicus were remarkably successful. Punicus succeeded in routing both praetors and killing around 6,000 soldiers and officers.[33] As his troops marched toward the southern coast of Iberia, he joined forces with the Vettones and laid siege to an allied city. During this siege Punicus was struck with a stone and killed (Appian, *Hisp.* 56).

Punicus provides the first successful example of the leader of Iberian resistance later embodied by Viriathus (and, arguably, Q. Sertorius). As villains, these men provide ample fodder for ancient historians to discuss the virtues idealized by the Romans as well as their intrinsic otherness. Punicus is a particularly good example since he represents through his very name the threat of a renewed, resurgent

---

[32] *Praeterea res in Hispania a compluribus parum prospere gestas continet. Consules anno quingentesimo nonagesimo octavo ab urbe condita magistratum Kal. Ian. inire coeperunt. Mutandi comitia causa fuit quod Hispani rebellabant.*

[33] According to Polybius (35.4), these disasters and setbacks would be reversed. The *Periochae* of Livy (48.17–21) credits P. Cornelius Scipio Aemilianus as the reason that the Romans continued prosecuting war in the Iberian Peninsula. When others balked at serving in *Hispania*, P. Cornelius Scipio Aemilianus volunteered for any post in any province. He was assigned the tribuneship in Iberia and took part in the fighting there.

Carthage. His unceremonious defeat merely paves the way for Roman authors to characterize the next great Iberian leader, Viriathus, as an even more dangerous foe. Indeed, as is discussed below, Viriathus is called the *Hispaniae Romulus*, suggesting that he was, in defeat, seen as the leader of a power equivalent to Rome itself (Florus 1.33.15).

Punicus was succeeded by his lieutenant, Caesarus. In 153 BCE, Caesarus led his army of *Lusitanii* and *Vettones* against the praetor of *Hispania Ulterior*, L. Mummius, who would eventually go on to destroy Corinth. According to Appian, Caesarus succeeded in capturing the standards from Mummius' legions, and the Iberians paraded these around Celtiberia (*Hisp.* 56). The parading of the legionary standards by the Lusitanians and Vettones was perhaps meant as mockery not only of the Roman practice of carrying standards but also of the Roman presence in the peninsula itself. Since Roman settlements during this early period were largely isolated on the coasts, the indigenous experience of Roman culture was limited to imported products and encounters with invading armies on the march or in battle. Caesarus' troops co-opted the symbols of Roman military and colonial power. At the head of an Iberian army, these symbols spread a message of defiance and resistance. By carrying the Roman standards through contested territory, the Iberians were reasserting their rightful control over the landscape as much as they were mocking their enemy.

Despite his early successes and the clever theatrics of his army, Caesarus' force was eventually defeated by Mummius. In response, the Lusitanians moved south of the Tejo River and attacked Roman possessions and allies—including the city of Conistorgis—in what is now southern Portugal (Appian, *Hisp.* 57).[34] The Lusitanians then, according to a number of different ancient authors, moved across the Straits of Gibraltar and besieged the city of Ocilis in Mauretania. They were defeated there by Mummius (Appian, *Hisp.* 57; Diodorus 31.42; Eutropius 4.9). Roman reprisals into Lusitanian territory followed in 152 BCE. Under the new praetor of *Hispania Ulterior*, M. Atilius Serranus, the Romans destroyed the important indigenous city of Oxthraca, probably located just to the northeast of the Tejo River in Lusitanian territory (Appian, *Hisp* 58).[35]

When Serranus was replaced by the praetor of 151 BCE, Servius Galba, the Lusitanians and other groups in the region were again threatening Roman territory in southern and western Iberia. Galba set out with an army in order to relieve towns

---

[34] See also Vasconcelos 1913: 114. Rather than Lusitanians south of the Tejo River, Appian might have meant the *Celtici*, a related tribal group that Strabo (3.1.6) places between the Tejo and Guadiana rivers. Notably, Strabo refers to Conistorgis as a city belonging to the *Celtici* in his era (3.2.2). Appian's account, given its focus on the Roman involvement in the region, may have ignored the intertribal warfare between the *Lusitanii* and *Celtici* evident in the assault on Conistorgis. Recent archaeological work in this region suggests that it was riven by conflict between indigenous groups long before the arrival of the Roman army. See Mataloto et al. 2007.

[35] Alarcão 1988: 28.

and cities besieged by the *Lusitanii* and their allies. His army was quickly routed, with many dead, and he was forced to retreat to Conistorgis, now controlled by the *Conii* (a member of the greater *Celtici* tribe). Strabo places Conistorgis between the Guadiana and Tejo rivers (3.141), but its exact location is unknown. Nevertheless, the destruction of Oxthraca and the occupation of Conistorgis emphasize the degree to which the Romans had penetrated into the territory of the Lusitanians. As happened in earlier decades, Roman reprisals against indigenous groups served primarily to increase the territory under Roman control.

Following his setback in 151 BCE, Galba coordinated his attack against the Lusitanians with one from the governor of *Hispania Citerior*, L. Licinius Lucullus, as Gracchus and Albinus had done. Galba's forces, bolstered by 20,000 allies, marched from Conistorgis. Lucullus set out with his army from Turdetania. Together they intended to destroy Lusitanian resistance by forcing them to fight a war on two fronts. Additionally, they each set their armies to devastating the landscape (Appian, *Hisp.* 59). The intentional destruction of agricultural lands and produce perhaps heightened the already poor environmental conditions, as discussed above, faced by the Lusitanians. Indeed, it appears that it was this destruction that eventually gave Galba the opportunity for treachery shortly thereafter.

Pressed from both the south and the east and with their year's harvest ruined by the concerted efforts of the invading Roman armies, the *Lusitanii* sought to make a treaty with Galba. He entertained their ambassadors, and promised to settle them on more fertile agricultural land if they would lay down their arms and congregate together in a prearranged location. The Lusitanians agreed, and once all the groups of the disparate *Lusitanii* had gathered, Galba's soldiers massacred as many as 30,000 of them.[36] Galba would go on to sell some of the survivors as slaves in Gaul, although legislation was soon proposed in the Roman Senate to free these individuals (Livy, *Per.* 49.17).[37] Other survivors, including a young Lusitanian warrior by the name of Viriathus, escaped.

From Viriathus to Augustus: The formation of Roman Lusitania

A number of Roman authors voice their opinions about the character of the natives of Iberia and the nature of a landscape filled with these natives. Livy, for instance, wonders how the Greeks at Emporion managed to survive sharing their city with so many "fierce and warlike" Iberians (Livy, 34.9.4). This is not the only characterization of Iberians offered by Livy. In a discussion of the revolt of the

---

[36] This event is recorded by a wide variety of ancient authors, many of whom lament Galba's treachery. These include Livy (45.35–36), Appian (*Hisp.* 58–60), Cicero (*Brut.* 22.86, *De Oratore* 1.227), Suetonius (*Galba* 3), and Valerius Maximus (9.6.2).

[37] Galba would also face trial in Rome for his betrayal of the Lusitanians, but he was able to avoid a conviction by claiming that the Lusitanians had been intending to attack him instead (Livy, *Per.* 49.18–19).

Ilergetians of *Hispania Ulterior*, he claims that the region is populated by "bandits and leaders of bandits, who, although they have enough strength to despoil the territory of their neighbors, to burn their homes, and to steal their cattle, have nothing in a pitched battle" (Livy 28.32.9).[38] Livy's portrayal of the peninsula—and that of many other ancient authors (Appian, *Hisp.* 71; Dio Cassius 37.52.1–4; Florus 1.33.15–17; Plutarch, *Mar.* 6.1, *Sert.* 14.1; Strabo 3.3.8; Valerius Maximus 9.1.5; Varro 1.16.2)—as full of bandits, strife, and disorder reflects an imperial trope. Since the conquered or soon-to-be-conquered region was populated only with bandits, the indigenous Iberians could hold no moral claim to the territory.

The depiction of Iberians, and particularly Lusitanians, as bandits was, of course, a means by which the conquest of a territory can be justified after the fact. Archaeology has revealed a long history of peaceful interactions between Iberians and other Mediterranean peoples. For example, the Ilergetians, like the other peoples of southwestern Iberia, had a long, and often positive, history of contact with the Mediterranean. Phoenician settlements and traders had even penetrated the Pillars of Herakles and reached the Iberians on the northwestern coast.[39] Livy himself contradicts this trope on occasion. As he points out, natives and Greeks had been living peacefully together in Emporion. And, only two chapters after his description of the Ilergetians, Livy describes the armies that they field against Rome (Livy 28.31, 29.1.19–26; see also Polybius 11.33). He even describes the marching formation of the Ilergetian troops as *armati instructique* (Livy 29.2.4). What, then, inspired the portrayals of Iberia's inhabitants as unorganized, cowardly bandits?

The claims of banditry in the peninsula probably reflect the mode of resistance employed by the indigenous peoples of Iberia, and the Lusitanians in particular, against Roman forces. Polybius terms the war that was sparked by Galba's massacre of the Lusitanians the πύρινος πόλεμος, "The War of Fire," for its intensity and ferocity (35.1).[40] Polybius' record of the war portrays it as one of unending, relentless combat. In combination with Livy's description of Iberian banditry, the war that Polybius portrays becomes a smoldering, bloody, guerilla conflict punctuated by larger battles between Lusitanian and Roman armies. Indeed, the description of the "War of Fire" as involving ceaseless conflict perhaps suggests that the Romans felt threatened by irregular fighters who would strike without warning, thus giving the impression of a battle without an end. When not engaged in fighting, the *Lusitanii* could retreat into their native landscape and continue their resistance there. Such resistance is notoriously hard to overcome, even in

---

[38] ...*hic latrones latronumque duces, quibus ut ad populandos finitimorum agros tectaque urenda et rapienda pecora aliqua vis sit, ita in acie ac signis conlatis nullam esse.*

[39] González-Ruibal 2006.

[40] It remains a matter of debate whether Lusitanians fought in organized, regular combat with the Roman army as their primary means of resisting conquest or whether they instead made use of guerilla tactics. They may have made use of both organized infantry combat and guerilla warfare as strategic necessity demanded. See Quesada-Sanz 2011; Schulten 1945.

our own age, and requires both adequate force of arms and sufficient intelligence gathering. Surveillance, whether performed by a sophisticated drone aircraft or by individuals stationed in a watchtower, provides a means through which the invisibility of guerilla fighters may be countered. It is perhaps these guerilla fighters and the extreme difficulty the Romans faced in stamping out their resistance that inspired the characterization of Iberia as a place of endemic brigandage. If we read ancient sources with this interpretation of banditry as guerilla warfare in mind, then their claims of bandits reflect not only a justification for usurping control over the territory but also a slur against any indigenous resistance to Roman imperialism. Resistance, because it took the form of guerilla warfare rather than large field engagements between armies, was mere brigandage in the Roman moral imagination. It was thus made illegitimate.

Viriathus, a survivor of Galba's massacre of the Lusitanians, eventually took control of the forces opposed to the Roman colonization of western Iberia in the 140s BCE. Indeed, Viriathus posed a serious threat to Roman commanders not only because he was often successful in destroying Roman armies (Appian, *Hisp.* 64), but also because his rise from humble beginnings to leadership of the Lusitanians inspired many other guerillas to take up arms (71–73). Additionally, as the Lusitanians under Caesarus had done a few decades before, Viriathus displayed captured Roman standards as a means of both raising morale among his own force and intimidating Roman armies (Florus 1.33.16).

The career of Viriathus has brought both ancient and modern historians to his side. T. Mommsen's description is particularly glowing:

> It seemed as if in that thoroughly prosaic age one of the Homeric heroes had reappeared: the name of Viriathus resounded far and wide through Spain; and the brave nation conceived that in him it had at length found the man who was destined to break the fetters of alien domination.[41]

The Roman historian Florus has a similarly mythologizing take on Viriathus:

> Viriathus, a man of the sharpest cunning, stirred the Lusitanians. From a hunter he had become a bandit, from a bandit he had suddenly become a general, and if fortune had granted it, the Romulus of *Hispania*. Not content to defend the freedom of his people, for fourteen years he devastated everything above and below the Ebro and Tejo rivers with fire and sword, and he assaulted the camps and garrisons of the praetors. He slaughtered the army of Claudius Unimanus almost to the last man and decorated his mountains with conspicuous trophies made from our uniforms and *fasces* that he had captured. In the end the consul [Quintus] Fabius Maximus [Servilianus] overwhelmed him, but the victory was dishonored by his successor, Popilius. As you see, Popilius, desiring to put an end to the matter, attacked the subdued chieftain, who was already considering the last step of surrender, through fraud, plots, and native assassins. He gave this renown to the enemy, that he would

[41] Mommsen 1959: 22.

seem to be invincible by other means [than treachery] (Florus 1.33.15–17).[42]

The summary of Viriathus' career offered above by Florus is, although basic, not altogether negative. Florus allows Viriathus to develop from bandit to *dux* and an equal to the Roman generals that faced him. He also, perhaps surprisingly, likens Viriathus to an Iberian Romulus, and thus a Lusitanian equivalent to the Romans' own ancestor. In doing so, Florus not only adds to the danger overcome by Fabius Maximus, but also suggests that the conquest and colonization of the Lusitanians merely assisted them in the fulfillment of their cultural destiny.

Seventy years after the death of Viriathus, the renegade, disaffected Roman general Quintus Sertorius set about unifying the disparate tribes of western Iberia under his banner (Plutarch, *Sert.* 10–11).[43] His goal was to create, at least to his mind, a new and more just Roman Republic. The civil war that followed would once more plunge Iberia into conflict and set the stage for the final conquest and colonization of western Iberia.[44] Sertorius, representing the remnant *populares* against the ascendant faction of *optimates*, took his cause to the Iberian Peninsula as proconsul in 83 BCE. There, backed by his army, he assumed control of the entire region (Plutarch, *Sert.* 12.2–3). The Lusitanians, after suffering under decades of Roman administration following the defeat of Viriathus, also backed Sertorius (14). He set about building a new republican government, with a Senate made up of Iberian elites and Italian immigrants, all the while assailed by armies sent by the *optimates* in Rome (22.3–4). The followers of Marius who fled Rome following Sulla's victory found a home with Sertorius, and, together with their new Lusitanian allies, formed a Roman Republic-in-exile, even going so far as to appoint new magistrates. Sertorius and his new Iberian republic met with some early successes. In addition, his skill as a diplomat, orator, and leader won over many Lusitanians. On one famous occasion, he convinced the Lusitanians of his authority by claiming that he received advice from the goddess Diana through a tame white fawn (11.3).

Sertorius also won several military victories against the *optimates*. In the end,

---

[42] *Ceterum Lusitanos Viriatus erexit, vir calliditatis acerrimae. Qui ex venatore latro, ex latrone subito dux atque imperator et, si fortuna cessisset, Hispaniae Romulus, non contentus libertatem suorum defendere, per quattuordecim annos omnia citra ultraque Hiberum et Tagum igni ferroque populatus, castra etiam praetorum et praesidia adgressus, Claudium Unimanum paene ad internicionem exercitus cecidit et insignia trabeis et fascibus nostris quae ceperat in montibus suis tropaea fixit. Tandem et eum Fabius Maximus consul oppresserat; sed a successore Popilio violata victoria est. Quippe qui conficiendae rei cupidus, fractum ducem et extrema deditionis agitantem per fraudem et insidias et domesticos percussores adgressus, hanc hosti gloriam dedit, ut videretur aliter vinci non posse.*

[43] Pina Polo and Pérez Casas (1998) suggest that Sertorius' forces were involved in the construction of at least one Roman military camp, the *Castra Aelia*, in western Iberia, but so far little archaeological evidence of this camp has come to light.

[44] Roldán (1980) discusses the expansion of Roman colonial efforts in Iberia in response to the exigencies of the Sertorian War and other Roman civil wars.

however, he too met his end at the hands of an assassin in 72 BCE (Plutarch, *Sert.* 26.4–6). For later authors, Sertorius, it seems, fulfills the role of both dangerous Lusitanian enemy and admirable Roman statesman. Plutarch's biography is especially kind in its portrait of Sertorius as a brilliant exiled general. In creating a new republic in Iberia, Sertorius fulfills the cultural destiny of the Lusitanians hinted at by Florus' discussion of Viriathus. Indeed, if Viriathus was the Lusitanians' Romulus, then Sertorius is their Brutus. Yet, like Viriathus, Sertorius was finally brought down not by Roman military might but by perfidy, corruption, and plotting. Thus the narrative of the nascent Lusitanian republic's destruction becomes an allegory for the destruction of the Roman Republic itself. Invulnerable to foreign enemies, the Roman Republic instead falls victim to conspiracy, coup, and civil war.

The central Alentejo remained ostensibly under Roman control for the next few decades, although there is little historical or material evidence to suggest that Rome took much interest in the region. In 69 BCE, Julius Caesar was assigned the quaestorship of *Hispania Ulterior*, and by 61 BCE he was governor of the province. There he marched an army against the *Lusitanii* and *Callaici*, defeated them, and was awarded a triumph at Rome (Plutarch, *Caesar* 11–12; Suetonius, *Julius* 18.1; Appian, *Hisp.* 102). His attack against the *Lusitanii* and *Callaici* seems to have been unprovoked unless it was in response to some unrecorded, perhaps low-intensity, resistance from the indigenous Iberians.[45] Whatever the case, it is during the middle of the first century BCE that Roman colonial administration, perhaps initiated by Caesar, began to reorganize the central Alentejo. The indigenous city of Évora was raised to the status of *municipium* in the middle decades of the first century BCE by Caesar or Octavian, and the earliest Roman rural settlements, like Castelo da Lousa, were founded at roughly this same colonial moment.

The quote from Appian mentioned above reflects the nature of the colonization that occurred in western Iberia during the end of the first century BCE. When Appian reports that "those Iberians who were doubtful in their allegiance or had not yet submitted to the Romans" were attacked by Caesar (*Hisp.* 102), he is describing an empire built on violence, threats of violence, and taxation. Those Iberians who were spared violence at Caesar's hands were those who paid tribute— established by formal treaty—to the imperial coffers. Pliny the Elder provides a list of forty-five *populi* of Lusitania organized by their tributary status, such as *colonia*, *oppida veteris Latii*, or *oppida stipendiaria* (*HN* 4.117–18). Pliny's list omits *civitates*, but it is likely that settlements such as Ammaia were granted this status.[46] Each indigenous settlement and its territory was obliged to pay *stipendiaria* and,

---

[45] Dio Cassius (37.52.3) suggests that Caesar ordered Lusitanians to move from their mountain strongholds to the plains not to prevent them from raiding the countryside, as Caesar claimed, but because he knew that the Lusitanians would never obey such an order. Their refusal provided Caesar with a convenient *casus belli*.

[46] Alarcão 1990b: 359–60.

it may be assumed, additional taxes were levied on products made or transported through Roman territory as in other parts of the empire. Submission to Rome required material proof of loyalty—the payment of *stipendiaria* and other taxes—and it is likely that the imperial bureaucracy, embodied in large part by the military in this early period, carefully monitored not just the payment of the tax but the region in which the tax was levied. Yet as the quote from Appian suggests, it was still possible in the middle of the first century BCE to comprehend testing Roman power within Lusitania by refusing to pay tribute. The establishment of a system of surveillance within the central Alentejo was perhaps meant to observe this colonized, tribute-paying landscape for any lingering remnant of resistance.

In addition to his subjection of Lusitanian *populi* who failed to pay their tributes, both Caesar and his rivals in Iberia, Sextus and Gnaeus Pompey, enlisted the aid of many natives of western Iberia during the Roman Civil War. The *De Bello Hispaniensi*, a text of uncertain authorship, provides a first-hand account of the war between Caesar and the Pompeians which also includes discussion of many indigenous Iberians involved in the conflict. For example, a native king named Indo and many of his soldiers were killed fighting for Caesar (*B. Hisp.* 10), while the citizens of a town held by Pompeian forces attempted to bargain with Caesar but were rebuffed (*B. Hisp.* 13). In response, the townsfolk attacked Caesar's men from the town's walls, but they themselves were shortly thereafter betrayed and massacred by Cn. Pompey's soldiers (*B. Hisp.* 15). The *De Bello Hispaniensi* often remarks on—frequently unsuccessful—attempts by natives to avoid the violence that Caesar and the sons of Pompey the Great had brought to the Iberian Peninsula. Indeed, if the author of the *De Bello Hispaniensi* is to be believed, the population and the Pompeian legions garrisoning Corduba were so divided in their loyalties that fighting erupted in the streets before Caesar's troops even attacked (*B. Hisp.* 34). Many indigenous Iberians chose to switch allegiances when expedient, to lay down their arms, or to treat with Roman emissaries. The Lusitanians, caught up in this landscape of violence and forced to live between two warring factions of the same colonialist empire, appear often to have sought simply to remain as uninvolved in the conflict as their situations permitted.

Yet, as with Sertorius, it appears that some among the *Lusitanii* chose to fight against Pompey and the *optimates*, although it is unclear whether this was because of any anti-Senatorial sentiment among the Iberians or simply because of the exigencies of survival (*B. Hisp.* 18). Others, like the Lusitanian leaders Philo and Concilius Niger, professed loyalty for Pompey and his cause (*B. Hisp.* 35).[47] The involvement of the *Lusitanii* in both sides of the Roman Civil War reflects the complex disrupted sociopolitical landscape of western Iberia during the first century BCE. In the same region where Caesar had punished those Lusitanian *populi*

---

[47] Their decision to back the Pompeians over Caesar may also reflect residual animosity following Caesar's earlier attacks against Lusitanian settlements unwilling or unable to pay into Rome's coffers.

who had failed to pay the appropriate tribute, other *Lusitanii* had joined his army, and still others favored the Pompeians. We may understand this ongoing violence as a continuance of the almost two centuries of Lusitanian resistance to Roman imperialism. Even during the first century BCE expressions of resistance against Roman power continued. Yet this resistance was now embedded within not only the political conflict between the *optimates* and *populares*, as during the Sertorian War, but also the fractured internecine civil strife that had consumed the Roman Mediterranean.

Following the assassination of Caesar and the tumultuous end of the Roman Republic, it fell to Octavian to complete his reorganization of the Iberian provinces and finally to conquer the most isolated tribes of the peninsula's mountainous northwest. This final struggle, known as the Cantabrian War, occupied Augustus' legions between 25 and 13 BCE. In the end, it appears that the Roman program of colonization, reorganization, and settlement initiated in the central Alentejo during the mid-first century BCE was successful. This landscape, formerly permeated with resistance against Rome, was largely demilitarized. New villas were built, the land was divided amongst new settlers and local favorites, and the landscape was altered both physically and symbolically. Tertullian, writing in the early third century CE, describes the rural spaces of the Roman world thus:

> Everywhere is now accessible, everywhere is known, everywhere is busy. Wildernesses, previously renowned, have now been obliterated by the most pleasant estates. Forests have been conquered by cultivated fields. Wild beasts have been routed by flocks. Sands are being planted, rocks quarried, marshes drained. There are now more cities than there were formerly huts. No longer do islands make us quake with fear nor rocky promontories terrify us. Everywhere there is a household, everywhere a citizen-body, everywhere a community, everywhere life (Tert. *De Anima* 30.7).[48]

The new province of Lusitania—filled with the descendants of Punicus, Caesarus, and Viriathus—persisted in many of its pre-Roman traditions, but also adopted cultural elements brought to the peninsula from Italy by new Roman settlers.[49] The negotiation of power and territory, at least as it was framed in the social and physical landscape of the first century BCE, was settled.

---

[48] *Omnia iam pervia, omnia nota, omnia negotiosa, solitudines famosas retro fundi amoenissimi oblitteraverunt, silvas arva domuerunt, feras pecora fugaverunt, harenae seruntur, saxa panguntur, paludes eliquantur, tantae urbes quantae non casae quondam, iam nec insulae horrent nec scopuli terrent; ubique domus, ubique populus, ubique res publica, ubique vita.*

[49] Stanley (1984), Edmondson (1990, 1992–1993, 1996), Keay (2001) provide a general overview of the impact of Roman imperialism on the rural landscape of Roman Lusitania. Le Roux (1982) explores the role of the Roman military in the Augustan reorganization and administration of the Iberian provinces.

THE ARCHAEOLOGY OF THE EARLY ROMAN ALENTEJO

The previous sections focused on the historical and environmental contexts surrounding the Roman colonization of the central Alentejo. That these contexts, and the region itself, need definition suggests that the pre-Roman and Roman presence in central Alentejo is understudied. This is the result of linguistic barriers as much as institutional ones, and while the central Alentejo has received far less scholarly attention than, for instance, central Latium, a great number of Portuguese, French, and German archaeological projects have been undertaken in the region. Additionally, salvage archaeology preceding the construction of the Alqueva Dam has produced both detailed regional surveys as well as systematic, complete excavations of many different sites over the last two decades. While disparate examples of archaeological research exist, syntheses of the evidence are rare. J. Alarcão's *Roman Portugal* was among the first to attempt a comprehensive treatment of the archaeology of Roman Lusitania.[50] F. Teichner's work on five rural settlements and their economies offered a detailed picture of social and economic life in southern Lusitania.[51] A recent summary of the archaeological remains from Roman Republican Iberia devotes little attention to the conquest of *Hispania Ulterior* and focuses instead on the east, north, and south of the peninsula.[52] C. Fabião's work, which spans numerous regions of Portugal, has often marshaled extant Alentejan archaeological data as part of larger analyses.[53] Thus a synopsis of the relevant sites is essential here and perhaps valuable to others wishing to understand the state of Roman archaeology in the Alentejo and the wider relevance of surveillance to colonial questions.

A review of several of the archaeological sites in the Alentejo region is provided in the remainder of this chapter. Indigenous sites, including hillforts, settlements, and shrines, are discussed first. While data from these sites is sometimes fragmentary or scattered, they nevertheless provide evidence for the organization of both the pre-colonial landscape and the peoples that inhabited it. This section next covers the most recognizable elements of Roman colonialism, *coloniae* and *municipia*, which were established in the Alentejo during the first century BCE. These towns and cities represent clear, tangible examples of the Roman colonization and reorganization of the region. Roman military camps, while exceptionally rare in Lusitania, are considered next, as are the indigenous sites, like Cabeço de Vaiamonte, occupied by Roman soldiers. The last element of the Roman colonial presence in the central Alentejo to be considered here are the villas founded in the

---

[50] Alarcão 1988.
[51] Teichner 2008.
[52] Rodà 2013.
[53] Fabião 2004, 2006.

last years of the first century BCE. Over seven hundred villas have been recorded in Portugal, and many dozens of those lie within the central Alentejo.

Indigenous sites in the central Alentejo

Prior to the middle of the first century BCE the central Alentejo landscape was home to small, scattered farms, shrines, and fortified towns with their origins in the late Bronze Age. Examples of these include the fortification known as Monte de Outeiro just south of the Serra d'Ossa, the rock-cut shrine at Rocha da Mina, and the large indigenous communities at Évoramonte, Serra de Segóvia, Castelo Velho de Veiros, and Castelo Velho de Degebe. Each of these represents a type of settlement present in central Alentejo during the pre-Roman and early Roman periods.

The site of Évoramonte, located adjacent to the thirteenth-century castle of the same name, rests atop a small peak to the west of the Serra d'Ossa. Recent excavations in 2008–2011 have revealed a continuous occupation on the eastern slope beginning in the twelfth century BCE and ending in the second century BCE.[54] When excavated, the site revealed numerous artifacts—including iron tools and complete vessels—in what was identified as three rooms of a large house. There was no evidence of fire or destruction at the site, suggesting that the house, and perhaps the entire settlement, was abandoned suddenly during a period of conflict.[55] Indeed, the inhabitants of this site may have been one of the groups mentioned by Livy (34.17.11–12) and Appian (*Hisp.* 41) who were forcibly removed from their mountain strongholds after Roman military victories.

Given the scale, intensity, and complexity of the colonial encounter in the central Alentejo suggested by literary sources, the forced relocation of indigenous populations from highly defensible settlements such as Évoramonte is unsurprising. At Mesas do Castelinho, a late Iron Age settlement in the lower Alentejo, there is evidence for a different outcome resulting from the Roman presence in the region.[56] Instead of a forced relocation of the population, it appears that the hillfort was integrated into the Roman reorganization of the landscape. Judging from its position and the relative poverty of its surrounding landscape, it has been postulated that Mesas do Castelinho was intended, during the late first century BCE and perhaps earlier, to monitor traffic passing through the Serra do Caldeirão

---

[54] Mataloto et al. 2010.

[55] Mataloto and Alves 2008; Mataloto et al. 2007.

[56] Mesas do Castelinho lies beyond the boundaries of my study area, yet it is included here because the site provides useful insight into the complexity of the colonial relationships between Romans and indigenous settlements. The same colonial negotiation that evoked change in Mesas do Castelinho was undoubtedly at work in the central Alentejo as well, but the paucity of archaeological data currently prevents its clear recognition. The analysis of settlement patterns provided in subsequent chapters will, I hope, help to fill this lacuna in scholarship.

to the Alentejan plain.[57] The town's plan was renovated according to a grid, very probably emulating Roman models, and the defensive walls were removed or incorporated into domestic structures. Excavation under C. Fabião and A. Guerra revealed no evidence for the violent destruction of the indigenous town or its walls.[58] Thus, these changes to the settlement of Mesas do Castelinho appear to have been either imposed on the settlement by a new Roman administration or adopted as part of a negotiated strategy of integration into the new colonial landscape by the indigenous inhabitants.

At Rocha da Mina, collaborating archaeologists from the municipalities of Alandroal and Redondo have uncovered the remains of a first-century BCE indigenous shrine and associated buildings (Fig. 2.5).[59] The structures are built not unlike Caladinho (detailed in Chapter 5) with unmortared walls of the local stone packed together and covered in clay. The site, although not yet entirely excavated, appears to be relatively small. Rocha da Mina's construction is similar in technique to that seen in the *fortins* and *recintos-torre*, yet it does not possess the same regular quadrangular plan seen in those other structures. A set of stairs is cut into an outcrop of bedrock near the first-century BCE structure. The stairs lead to a large platform, suggested by some to be a place for sacrificial offerings. Despite the height of the site, however, it is very difficult to see beyond the surrounding hills, and so Rocha da Mina appears to be well hidden within the landscape.

A fortified settlement south of the Serra d'Ossa was reported in 1997 and measured to be roughly 1 ha in size. This settlement rests on a steep slope surrounded by at least two circuits of walls.[60] This site has been given the name Monte de Outeiro, and little fieldwork has been attempted there since the initial survey.[61] Nevertheless, the limited ceramic evidence from the site suggests it was intermittently occupied from the late Chalcolithic through the late first century BCE.[62] The artifacts are also of a particularly indigenous character, with vessels decorated with both stamps and reeling as well as stone tools.[63] That such a sizeable and defensible indigenous settlement persisted in this region despite the presence of the Romans is testament to the unsettled negotiation over control of this landscape in the first century BCE.

Three large, fortified indigenous centers have been identified in the central Alentejo. They are known to archaeologists as Serra de Segóvia, Castelo Velho de Veiros, and Castelo Velho de Degebe. Serra de Segóvia is a well-fortified settlement situated to the northeast of the Serra d'Ossa. Ample material remains indicate that

---

[57] Fabião and Guerra 2010: 326–27.
[58] Fabião and Guerra 2010: 334–36.
[59] Mataloto et al. 2014: 27–29, 2016: 142–48.
[60] Calado and Mataloto 2001: 60.
[61] Calado and Rocha 1997.
[62] Mataloto 2002: 212.
[63] Calado and Mataloto 2001: 60.

the site was occupied from the late Bronze Age and into the late republican period. It was likely abandoned at the end of the first century BCE as Roman control over the region began to take firmer shape following the Sertorian War.⁶⁴ Nearby, the site of Castelo Velho de Veiros appears to have remained occupied into the first century CE. Like Serra de Segóvia, Castelo Velho de Veiros is a fortified hilltop settlement with multiple dwellings and a significant artifact assemblage recovered during survey and excavation.⁶⁵ A third indigenous fortification, Castelo Velho de Degebe, was also occupied while the *fortins* and *recintos-torre* were constructed in the region. Castelo Velho de Degebe is located on a rocky spur overlooking the Ribeira de Degebe. The site has been largely destroyed in recent decades thanks to the planting of eucalyptus, but the extant remains suggest a robust occupation during the late Iron Age and early Roman periods.⁶⁶

The Roman presence in the Alentejo: the first century BCE to the first century CE

The Roman colonization, reorganization, and settlement of the central Alentejo was initiated in response to the exigencies brought about by war with local indigenous groups as well as Rome's own civil wars. In addition to the reorganization of the countryside, Roman colonization implanted new urban centers and altered those already present in and around the central Alentejo. These include *Pax Iulia* (Beja), *Liberalitas Iulia Ebora* (Évora), and *Civitas Ammaiensis* (Ammaia). These early Roman urban centers represent some of the clearest evidence for the imposition of Roman administration on the central Alentejo and its peoples. Guarding and supervising the territory surrounding these cities, and the natural resources they possessed, was a central concern of Roman colonization, and the surveillance discussed below is one of the means by which this control was organized and maintained. But surveillance did not only serve to protect the cities and their territory, it also helped to claim territory. Since the watchtowers promised reprisal against any banditry, any indigenous resistance was forced into areas where the towers could not effectively observe. The vision of the watchtowers thus not only surveilled territory, it also helped to claim it by encouraging indigenous groups to cede the territory altogether or else to cease resisting.

Both *coloniae* and *municipia* were established in the central Alentejo during the first century BCE, but relatively few villas. *Coloniae* represent new settlements implanted in the landscape by Roman settlers and governed by Roman laws. *Municipia*, in comparison, were indigenous settlements granted some degree of independence and autonomy from Rome, yet still ultimately subject to Roman

---

⁶⁴ Gamito 1981: 32–35. There is some indication that the site was involved in the Sertorian War. See Gamito 1987.
⁶⁵ Arnaud 1970.
⁶⁶ Paço and Gonçalves 1962: 313–16.

taxation and imperial oversight. Distinguishing the two is largely the realm of the epigrapher or numismatist since much of the evidence for each settlement's status is derived from those sources. Nevertheless, it appears that most major colonial settlements in Roman Portugal were originally indigenous centers that allied themselves to the Romans.

In the central Alentejo, Évora and Ammaia were among the largest urban settlements during the first century BCE and afterward. Évora, where coins were minted with the legend *permissu Augusti*, was granted its status as *municipium* late in the first century BCE, yet it was certainly inhabited prior to this date.[67] Ammaia was founded *ex nihilo* in the last years of the first century BCE and served as the administrative and political center of the Ammaienses tribe. While it was considered large enough to be a *civitas* during this period, its status was not raised to that of a *municipium* until the middle of the first century CE.[68] Évora and Ammaia anchor the southwestern and northeastern boundaries of the central Alentejo respectively and their importance as regional centers grew during the first century BCE. During the first decades after their foundations as Roman settlements, their territory was similarly reimagined by colonial forces.

Other Roman settlements include the *colonia Pax Iulia*—the capital of the *Conventus Paciensis* and thus the most important urban center in southern Lusitania—and the capital of Roman Lusitania, *Colonia Augusta Emerita*. *Pax Iulia* represents one of the few *coloniae* founded in the central Alentejo, yet it too was established atop an earlier settlement.[69] The lack of epigraphic and archaeological evidence from *Pax Iulia* has left ample doubt as to the reasons behind the site's location, but its regional importance as an administrative and commercial center following the Augustan-era promotion of the site to *colonia* status is well established.[70] The rich agricultural territory immediately around the settlement appears to have been reorganized along a cadastral plan and, perhaps, distributed to veterans during the late first century BCE.[71] Such a reallocation of the sparse natural resources of the central Alentejo represents the culmination of colonial negotiation over this landscape.

The provincial capital, *Colonia Augusta Emerita*, was established as a veteran colony by Augustus in circa 25 BCE (Dio Cassius 53.26.1; Isid. *Etym.* 15.1.69).[72] While this colonial city rests outside my immediate study area, its importance for the administration and organization of the central Alentejo during the first century BCE cannot be underestimated. All traffic between *Pax Iulia*, Évora, *Colonia*

---

[67] Osland 2006: 30; Faria 1984–1985, 2001: 355
[68] Corsi 2014; Corsi and Vermeulen 2012: 6; Taelman et al. 2010: 59–60; Pereira 2005: 39; Mantas 2000: 397–98; Fernandes 1997: 173.
[69] Faria 1999, 2001: 352–53; Lopes 1996: 65; Mantas 1996b: 47.
[70] Fabião 1998: 255–58
[71] Lopes 1996, 2003; Mantas 1996a, 1996b.
[72] Osland 2006: 45–46; Pérez Vilatela 2000: 82.

Augusta Emerita and other settlements must certainly have passed through the central Alentejo whether it moved overland or via the Guadiana River. Knowledge of the insecurity that had plagued western Iberia during the previous decades may have influenced the Roman administration and reorganization of this region. The many *fortins* and *recintos-torre* established there during the mid- to late first century BCE provided an opportunity to secure this landscape, and thus the colonization of its resources, through surveillance and communication.

The presence of the Roman army in the central Alentejo was once in doubt. Fabião's work on what he terms the "invisible" Roman army—an army quartered amongst the population rather than in their own isolated fortresses—is now central to discussions of the early Roman presence in the region.[73] As yet, no evidence exists for the construction of Roman military camps in the central Alentejo in either the second or first centuries BCE. Yet many rural sites in the region possess examples of *militaria* that confirm the army's presence. Indeed, it appears that the Roman military occupied formerly indigenous fortifications in the central Alentejo rather than building their own *castra*.[74] One such site, Cabeço de Vaiamonte, located in the northern part of the study area, has presented ample evidence for a long-term Roman military occupation. Other sites, particularly colonial settlements such as *Pax Iulia* and Évora, might also have similarly military origins, but these have thus far remained obscured by the dearth of archaeological evidence.

Cabeço de Vaiamonte was investigated in the 1990s by C. Fabião as part of his research into the Romanization of indigenous sites in the Alentejo. The site, excavated at various times between the 1940s and 1960s, has never had its plan properly published, and only the artifacts recovered during those excavations are currently extant.[75] Nevertheless, this artifact assemblage contains a wealth of examples of *militaria* in addition to imported Roman finewares, lamps, and coins. The *militaria* include an iron *pilum* shaft, bronze armor buckles, and a variety of armor decorations and pieces.[76] These artifacts coexist with indigenous artifacts—particularly large, decorated storage jars—that were probably present at Cabeço de Vaiamonte both before and during its Roman military occupation. This assemblage suggests that the Roman military garrisoned existing settlements in the central Alentejo as part of the conquest and colonization of the territory. Thus, while present, the Roman army in the central Alentejo may largely remain archaeologically invisible to us even though it was especially visible to the native inhabitants

---

[73] Fabião 2006: 121–23.

[74] A similar situation may have existed in the *meseta* of central Spain. Archaeologists there have proposed that elements of the Roman army utilized pre-Roman watchtowers associated with the territories of native hillforts. Rather than surveilling the borders of individual settlements, these towers were used by the Romans to control routes of trade and communication through the landscape. See Curchin 2004: 65; Castro López and Gutiérrez Soler 2001: 155.

[75] Fabião 2006: 121.

[76] Fabião 1996: 60.

whose settlements they had garrisoned and whose landscape was being surveilled.

Another site of possible Roman military origin, Monte da Nora, lies only a few kilometers southeast Cabeço de Vaiamonte and the modern city of Estremoz in an area that lacks a great deal of natural defensibility. A salvage excavation there revealed the presence of two deep defensive ditches screening numerous postholes as well as imported Roman finewares and amphorae dating to the middle of the first century BCE.[77] A Roman rural settlement lay above this earliest phase of occupation, and an Islamic cemetery further obscured the remains. Monte da Nora's extant remains, the defensive ditches, the probable existence of a palisade, and the numerous late republican artifacts suggest that it was originally a Roman military camp. As Fabião notes, Monte da Nora's use of defensive ditches, its abundance of imported artifacts, and its indefensible position within the landscape suggests a foreign origin for the inhabitants of Monte da Nora.[78] Whether or not Monte da Nora was a military camp, an "exotic" native settlement, or an indigenous site repurposed by the Roman military remains to be investigated.

The artifact assemblages at Cabeço de Vaiamonte and Monte da Nora are each similar to that of the Republican army camp at Cáceres el Viejo in nearby Extremadura, Spain. The camp, thought to be the *Castra Caecilia* mentioned by Pliny (*HN* 4.117), covers approximately 24 ha and likely housed an entire Roman legion.[79] It was first occupied in circa 78 BCE, during the Sertorian War, by troops loyal to Quintus Caecilius Metellus Pius and destroyed before the conflict's end in 72 BCE.[80] This chronology suggests that Cabeço de Vaiamonte, Monte da Nora, Castelo da Lousa, and many of the *fortins* and *recintos-torre* throughout the central Alentejo were built at roughly the same time or a few years after this camp. Additionally, the material remains of the camp, which includes the expected *militaria* as well as imported Italic amphorae and finewares, resembles the assemblages from Cabeço de Vaiamonte, Castelo da Lousa, and the *fortins* and *recintos-torre*.[81] It also includes a number of indigenous swords, *fibulae*, and belt-plates which probably belonged to members of the Iberian *auxilia*.[82] The defensive wall at Cáceres el Viejo, built of dry slate and extant to a height of 1 m in some areas, also resembles the simple schist construction of many first-century BCE structures in the central Alentejo.[83]

Castelo da Lousa represents an example of an early settlement forced to respond architecturally and symbolically to the insecure, negotiated colonial landscape around it. The site was investigated by archaeologists throughout the last

---

[77] Teichner 2008: 61–91; Teichner and Schierl 2009.
[78] Fabião 2006: 120.
[79] Hanel 2006: 224–27.
[80] Ulbert 1984: 202–205; Pamment Salvatore 1997; Álvarez et al. 2008: 117–18.
[81] Fabião 2006: 121.
[82] Álvarez et al. 2008: 118.
[83] Ulbert 1984: 17–20. See also Jimeno 2005; Dobson 2008: 46; Dobson 2013: 230.

half of the twentieth century but only comprehensively excavated between 1997 and 2002 because of the construction of the Alqueva Dam. The site is situated atop a steep hill overlooking the Guadiana. It boasts a complex plan made up of dry schist construction. The central structure of Castelo da Lousa includes a Roman-style *atrium* with an *impluvium* surrounded by rooms. The structure was built entirely from unmortared local schist that was likely faced with clay and perhaps even plastered. The exterior of the site is walled with several smaller simpler structures (perhaps towers) extant on the slope approaching the river. The architecture of the site, which is both domestic and military in nature, has caused it to be variously identified as a small Roman fortress, a fortified villa, or a trading post.[84]

The artifact assemblage at Castelo da Lousa suggests that the site was built circa 50 BCE and abandoned during the first few decades of the first century CE.[85] A number of Italian imports, including Campanian black gloss, terra sigillata, and thin-walled wares, are prominent in the assemblage, as are Italic amphorae (in addition to those produced in Baetica).[86] The assemblage also contains examples of Roman *militaria*, including lead sling bullets, iron spearheads, and fragments of bronze armor.[87] These finds suggest that Castelo da Lousa, at least during its first phase of occupation, maintained a military function even while its primary purpose was domestic. Indeed, Castelo da Lousa may represent an especially large and well-developed example of the rural surveillance structures considered in later chapters.

Following the reorganization of the landscape in the first century BCE, a new Roman system of settlement, agriculture, and industry was implanted in the central Alentejo. Many of the settlements established in the central Alentejo at the beginning of the first century CE assume a secure landscape and uncontested control over their surrounding natural resources. An important part of this new order

---

[84] Alarcão et al. 2010a: 31–33; Fabião 1998, 2006: 113; Wahl 1985. The most recent rescue excavation of the site concluded that Castelo da Lousa was the home of a Roman wine and pottery merchant whose products were distributed into the central Alentejo region with the help of armed guards (thus explaining the presence of Roman *militaria*). This conclusion does not fit with the relatively few amphorae and finewares recovered from the site, nor do the weapons, armor, and equipment found there suggest the presence of simple caravan guards. Instead, the ceramic assemblage appears to be primary domestic in nature rather than a set of commercial products. Castelo da Lousa likely operated like many of the smaller *fortins* and *recintos-torre* in the region. It housed a group of early settlers or natives willing to work with the new Roman colonial administration in policing the landscape. This explains both the ceramics and the military equipment present in the artifact assemblage as well as the fortified nature of its domestic structure.

[85] Alarcão et al. 2010b: 99–110.

[86] Luís 2010; Carvalho and Morais 2010; Morais 2010a, 2010b. Arruda and Almeida (1999) provide a discussion of the evidence for the importation of Italian wine into western Iberia before and after the Roman conquest of the region.

[87] Ruivo 2010: 498–503.

was the establishment of villas throughout the new territory. Many villas are established in the central Alentejo during this period, among them Torre de Palma and Santa Susana. These villas, which have each been subject to very different amounts of fieldwork, provide insight into the new social organization imposed in this landscape after the first century BCE.

The large agricultural villas at Torre de Palma and Santa Susana were both constructed in the first century CE after the pacification and reorganization of the central Alentejan landscape. Torre de Palma, located near Monforte and Vaiamonte in the northern part of the study area, was excavated over the course of several decades in the latter half of the twentieth century. The site was active for over five centuries. It possesses large domestic and industrial spaces. The domestic space was well appointed with ornate polychrome mosaics, painted frescoes, and a deep *impluvium*. The industrial spaces surrounding the villa's living quarters contained many features, such as large granite grape and olive presses, including *opus signinum* vats containing either wine or olive oil, and evidence for metalworking.

The villa adjacent to the church of Santa Susana in the municipality of Redondo, near to the *fortins* of Monte do Almo and Caladinho, appears quite similar to Torre de Palma. Poorly recorded excavations in the 1930s were undertaken at Santa Susana, and a new survey and excavation project there has only just completed its first season. Nevertheless, ample brick, tile, and pottery on the surface suggest a long occupation beginning in the first century CE, and marble *spolia* from the villa have been incorporated into the structure of the church at the site. The granite weight-stone for a large beam press was recently reused as the base for a sundial outside the church (Fig. 2.6), but its mere presence indicates that the villa was similarly well furnished with industrial equipment. Currently archaeological work at this site will hopefully further illuminate the transition between the unsettled negotiation of the landscape in the first century BCE and the landscape which was invested with villas such as the one at Santa Susana.

The material remains of these two villas exemplify the culmination of the changes wrought on the central Alentejo by Roman colonization. Their archaeological remains suggest an intensification of agricultural production, the establishment of extractive industries, and the reorganization of the landscape to better accommodate new settlers following the first century BCE. Indeed, their chosen architecture, artifact assemblages, and positions within the landscape assume that the landscape will remain free of violence and under the control of these new rural settlements. The colonial processes that reshaped the central Alentejo region were, in part, supported by the use of surveillance in the control and administration of the landscape during the colonial period.

CHAPTER 3

SURVEILLANCE STRUCTURES IN ANCIENT ART, LITERATURE, AND ARCHAEOLOGY

This chapter provides a broad overview of watchtowers and observations posts in Roman art and ancient literature. The depictions of surveillance structures on the Column of Trajan, on African Red Slip pottery, and in wall-paintings from the Bay of Naples suggest aspects of Roman surveillance that are otherwise impossible to glean from archaeological remains alone, and textual sources can provide additional context for both ancient art and archaeology. Roman authors rarely make explicit mention of surveillance structures, and depictions of watchtowers in ancient art are limited to only a handful of extant examples. Nevertheless, these few primary sources provide a useful perspective on both the material remains of surveillance and its place within Roman society. Livy and Appian each provide some context for the use of signaling towers and watchtowers. The *De Bello Hispaniensi*, perhaps attributable to one of Julius Caesar's lieutenants, includes a brief mention of watchtowers in Iberia during the middle of the first century BCE This account gives credence to the potential military purpose of these towers. Seneca the Younger mentions, albeit briefly, the surveillance potential of villas positioned on hills in one of his letters to Lucilius, and Pliny the Younger discusses the tower attached to his country estate. These scattered, ephemeral artistic and literary depictions of surveillance structures are considered below.

SURVEILLANCE STRUCTURES IN ROMAN ART

Ancient depictions of surveillance structures are quite rare. Images of them are most often included as incidental details in larger scenes or as parts of other structures. Three examples most commonly cited by scholars include the watchtowers carved on the Column of Trajan, the so-called "wind towers" present in many paintings of Roman rural villas, and rare images of treehouses molded onto the surface of African Red Slip pottery. These three different media—sculpted relief, wall-painting, and pottery appliqué—likewise represent three different modes of surveillance.

The Column of Trajan dates to the beginning of the second century CE, and its relief, which unrolls around the column as if it were a scroll wrapped around the shaft, portrays the campaigns in Dacia undertaken by the emperor Trajan. The beginning of the scroll, necessarily narrower than the remainder above it, introduces the Dacian Wars with carved images of small fortifications surrounded by palisades and three separate free-standing towers (Fig. 3.1 and Fig. 3.2). The individuals portrayed next to the towers are unrealistically large and are likely heroized depictions of Roman soldiers. The stacks of hay and wood near the first tower have been variously interpreted, but D. J. Woolliscroft has convincingly argued that these materials are merely stacked near the tower in order to dry for the winter.[1] These timber and hay supplies are situated near the tower for their security and for the ready supply of those stationed in the tower and along the *limes*. As such, they contribute to an image of Roman military life along the Danube in the autumn, and suggest that the story told by the Column of Trajan begins late in the year.

The watchtowers depicted on the Column of Trajan appear relatively small, with a square or rectangular plan, and seem no more than two stories tall. Both stories appear to be constructed from stone or brick, and the second story is ringed with a wooden balcony. A torch, for signaling neighboring towers, is attached to each tower's balcony. The towers, assumedly meant to depict towers like those built along the borders of the Roman Empire, formed a signaling network that allowed for swift but limited communication along the border. These fixed permanent military structures observed an established border year round and passed short messages between them regarding the security of the border. Their positions within the landscape form part of a defensive line meant to provide early warning of raids or of the movement of individuals or groups along or through the frontier.[2] Such a system of surveillance relied on the intervisibility of the observation posts as much as on the ability of the watchtowers to see the contested border.

A wall-painting from the villa at Boscotrecase, Italy, depicts so-called "wind towers" attached to other structures. Knauer posits that the structure included in this and other wall-paintings (and the occasional relief) is derived from Egyptian

---

[1] Woolliscroft 2001: 26–30.

[2] Systems of Roman towers along borders have been recorded along the German-Raetian *limes* (*ORL* A 1–5, 7–10, 12–15; Baatz 1976), the Gask Ridge in Scotland (Woolliscroft 1988a, 1988b, 2001; Robertson 1974), Hadrian's Wall in England (Birley 1961: 88–99, 103–10, 116–25; Woolliscroft 2001), the *Limes Arabicus* (Clark and Parker 1987), and the *Limes Tripolitanus* (Goodchild 1950; Trousset 1990). These systems of border surveillance each postdate the *fortins* and *recintos-torre* of the central Alentejo.

ventilation towers which provided cool air to the interior of houses.[3] Instead, like the towers attached to farmhouses throughout the Mediterranean, the structure depicted in this wall-painting may have functioned as a surveillance structure, a secure location to house slaves, or both.[4] Towers of this type are permanent structures, like the towers built along the militarized borders of the empire, yet their surveillance is turned towards the villa's own territory rather than beyond its borders. These towers were meant to observe the work of laborers—likely to have been slaves—in the surrounding agricultural areas. Their use may have been quite regular, even daily, but it is doubtful that they would have been manned by a permanent garrison like the border towers.

The third depiction represents the use of temporary surveillance structures to monitor seasonal labor during harvest time. Such a temporary structure would have operated like the towers attached to villas, where the gaze of surveillance was turned inward, but would not necessarily have been placed near to the villa itself. The best example of such temporary surveillance structures can be seen in the decorations on some African Red Slip fineware and African lamps from the third century CE. These sometimes hold images of a man situated in a treehouse observing a vineyard.[5] His position in the tree is explained by the early Christian treatise *De Duobus Montibus Sina et Sion* by Pseudo-Cyprian. This text describes the use of treehouse-like structures, manned by loyal slaves, to observe and protect vineyards from thieves and to ensure that those involved in the harvest are working to the best of their ability. Seasonal surveillance, which may have utilized temporary structures, remains archaeologically invisible save for its depiction on these sherds of African pottery. Nevertheless, such a program of surveillance of seasonally productive agricultural or viticultural spaces may fit well with many rural settlements which made use of forced or temporary labor.

WATCHTOWERS, OBSERVATION POSTS, AND FORTIFIED VILLAS IN ANCIENT TEXTS

Surveillance structures also feature in some ancient texts, but these references are as rare as depictions of these structures in other media. Like the visual depictions discussed above, however, they provide some useful context for understanding the archaeology of surveillance in the Roman world generally and in ancient Ibe-

---

[3] Knauer (1990: 16) admits that ventilation towers were probably never built in Italy, but suggests that the depiction of these towers in wall-paintings represents the presence of an Egyptianizing motif after the Augustan conquest of Egypt. I posit instead that these wall-paintings, while certainly idealized or even Egyptianized in their depictions, reflect the presence of actual surveillance towers in the territories of Roman villas.

[4] Rossiter (1978: 5) discusses Roman villas with towers inaccessible except by ladder.

[5] Tortorella 2005: 191–94, figs. 15 and 16.

ria in particular. For example, ancient historians sometimes mention isolated, defensive watchtowers and other surveillance structures in Iberia which were related to both indigenous resistance and colonial occupation. Other authors, including Seneca the Younger and Pliny the Younger, discuss towers attached to rural villas, but their characterizations of the houses that utilize these towers are quite different. Suetonius and Horace both discuss, if only in passing, a tower situated within the urban environment of Rome and the potential for surveillance it offered to Maecenas and the emperor Nero.

Livy's account of northeastern Iberia during the Second Punic War makes mention of a number of watchtowers utilized in the defense of the region against banditry. Livy adds a description of the towers' positions within the landscape and their purpose as an explanatory aside during a larger account of the Roman attack on the Punic fleet near the mouth of the Ebro River. It reads:

> Hispania has many towers positioned in high places which they use both for surveillance and as a deterrent against bandits. When the enemy fleet was first spotted from [a tower], a signal was sent to Hasdrubal, and an alarm was raised on land and in the camp before it came to the sea and the ships (Livy 22.19.6–7).[6]

Given the context of the passage, it is clear that these towers, which were used by Carthaginians to spot the approaching Roman fleet, were situated along the coast. The use of these coastal towers as early warning systems was aided by a system of signals and messengers which quickly disseminated the alarm. While this system failed to protect the Punic fleet, Livy's description of the function of these coastal towers may provide some insight into their use farther inland as well.

According to Appian, Scipio's forces constructed a ring of fortification around the city of Numantia during its siege in 133 BCE These fortifications included a number of signaling towers which were used to relay messages by prearranged signals in times of danger (*Hisp.* 90). The description of Scipio's use of signaling towers in the siege of Numantia provides an example, in miniature, of the systems of border surveillance used along the later imperial *limes* in England, Germany, and elsewhere. Indeed, it was Scipio's system of regularly spaced towers each within signaling distance of another that would come to dominate the Roman frontier in England in the form Hadrian's Wall and in Germany as the German-Raetian *limes*.

In addition to the ample archaeological remains for such surveillance systems along the imperial borders, at least eight inscriptions dating to the reign of Commodus in the latter second century CE attest to the use of watch and signaling towers to secure borders of Roman Pannonia Inferior. Each inscription is nearly identical, although most exhibit attempts at erasing the name of Commodus. The

---

[6] *Multas et locis altis positas turres Hispania habet, quibus et speculis et propugnaculis aduersus latrones utuntur, inde primo conspectis hostium navibus datum signum Hasdrubali est, tumultusque prius in terra et castris quam ad mare et ad naves est ortus....*

most complete example of this set of epigraphs reads:

> The emperor Caesar Marcus Aurelius Commodus Antoninus Augustus Pius Sarmaticus Germanicus Britannicus, pontifex maximus, with tribunician power for the sixth time, *imperator* for the fourth time, consul for the fourth time, father of the fatherland, secured the entire river bank with watchtowers constructed from the ground up as well as guardhouses placed throughout areas exposed to covert incursions of raiders through Lucius Cornelius Felix Plotianus legate *pro praetore* (*ILS* 8913).[7]

This inscription suggests that the Danube frontier utilized a system of border surveillance in response to the threat of incursions even during peace time. Additionally, this text explicitly states that these surveillance structures are meant to prevent cross-border raiding into Roman territory. These towers and their garrisons oppose the actions of *latrunculi* rather than *hostes*, and suggest that their purpose was policing the border rather than guarding against any large scale military invasion.

Another inscription indicates that watchtowers, again called *burgi*, could also be found along Roman roads in Numidia. It reads:

> With the emperor Caesar Marcus Aurelius Commodus Antoninus Pius Felix Augustus Germanicus Sarmaticus Britannicus, father of the fatherland, with tribunician power for the twelfth time, as consul for the fifth time. Tiberius Claudius Gordianus, *vir clarissimus*, legate *pro praetore cura agente* of Augustus, ordered that a Commodian surveillance tower be erected between the two roads as a new protection for the safety of travelers… (*CIL* VIII.2495).[8]

These *burgi speculatorii*, best translated as "surveillance towers," were erected in a region where the landscape proved inhospitable to the creation of a defined border. Rather than creating a line of signaling towers, as had been done in Britain, Germany, and elsewhere, the Numidian *burgi* were built along routes of trade and communication in order to provide security to travelers. This brief inscription suggests that the system of internal, borderless surveillance used in the colonization of the central Alentejo remained in use in other less secure regions of the Roman Empire at least into the second century CE.

---

[7] *Imp(erator) Caes(ar) M(arcus) Aur(elius) [[Commodus]] Antoninus / Aug(ustus) Pius Sarm(aticus) Germ(anicus) Brit(annicus) pont(ifex) max(imus) trib(unicia) pot(estate) / VI imp(erator) IIII co(n)sul IIII p(ater) p(atriae) ripam omnem burgis / a solo extructis item praesidiis per lo/ca opportuna ad clandestinos latruncu/lorum transitus oppositis munivit / per L(ucium) Cornelium Felicem / Plotianum leg(atum) pr(o) pr(aetore).*

[8] *Imp(eratore) Caes(are) [M(arco)] Au[relio] / [[[C]ommo[d]o]] Antoni/no Pio Felice Aug(usto) [G]erm(anico) / Sarm(atico) Britannic[o] p(atre) p(atriae) / trib(unicia) p[ot]e(state) XII co(n)s(ule) V / burgum [[Commodi]]/[[anum]] s[p]eculato/rium inter duas vi/as ad salutem comme/antium nova tute/[l]a c[o]nstitui iussit [Ti(berius)] / [Claudi]us [G]ordia[nus] / v(ir) [c(larissimus)] leg(atus) Aug(usti) pr(o) pr(aetore) / [cur]a agen[te ---].*

Returning to Iberia, Julius Caesar also encountered watchtowers during the later stages of the Civil War. Prior to the Battle of Munda, Caesar's forces engaged with troops loyal to Gnaeus Pompey the Younger and Sextus Pompey, the sons of Pompey the Great.[9] The author of the *De Bello Hispaniensi* reports that Pompey the Younger and Caesar fought over possession of a number of tributaries and crossings of the Guadalquivir River as part of the Pompeians' defense of Corduba. During the fighting, both sides occupied high, defensive positions in order better to observe the movements of the other. The account also describes the nature of the landscape as the reason behind the protracted fighting in the area:

> For almost the entirety of the province of *Hispania Ulterior* is difficult and fruitless to assault on account of the fertility of the soil and the none too plentiful springs. Here also, on account of the frequent raids of the natives, every place which is far removed from a town is held by towers and fortifications. Just as in Africa they are covered with loose stone rather than tiles. And likewise they have watchtowers in these places, and on account of their height they surveil far and wide (*B. Hisp.* 8).[10]

Like Hasdrubal's forces during the Second Punic War, both sides in this conflict made use of both the natural and built landscape. Insecurity and violence shaped this landscape into one where surveillance played an important role in determining the locations of settlements and their edifices. Originally this landscape of surveillance was constructed as an indigenous response to persistent violence, but now, as the Civil War spilled into Iberia, Roman imperialism began to repurpose these surveillance structures, both figurative and physical, to more militaristic ends. Yet, according to this same author, local civilians (including children) were tasked with manning some observation posts (*B. Hisp.* 13). The willingness of some individuals to serve in the Roman military or to simply assist it—perhaps in exchange for material reward, elevated status, or protection—speaks to the complex negotiation involved in the encounter between Romans and Iberians even during the republic's death throes.

Fortified rural homes and farms are discussed in letters from Seneca the Younger and Pliny the Younger. Seneca discusses the villas built by Roman military leaders around Baiae in Italy. While his purpose in describing the structures built by Gaius Marius, Pompey the Great, and Julius Caesar is to illuminate stoic virtues that they exhibit, he nevertheless sheds light on a type of rural, elite dwelling. He writes:

[9] Gnaeus Pompey the Younger would be executed in 45 BCE following his defeat at the Battle of Munda. Sextus Pompey escaped and continued his campaign against Caesar and later Augustus for another decade. See Appian, *B. Civ.* 2.103–106.

[10] *Nam fere totius ulterioris Hispaniae regio propter terrae fecundidatem inopem difficilemque habet oppugnationem et non nimis copiosam aquationem. Hic etiam propter barbarorum crebras excursiones omnia loca quae sunt ab oppidis remota, turribus et munitionibus retinentur. Sicut in Africa rudere, non tegulis teguntur. Simulque in his habent speculas et propter altitudinem late longeque prospiciunt.*

Also those men, G. Marius, Cn. Pompey, and Caesar, to whom the prosperity of the Roman people first transferred the wealth of the state, indeed built their villas in the area of Baiae, but they established them on the highest mountain peaks. This seemed more martial in character, to surveil territory spread far and wide from a high place. Consider the position they chose, in which sorts of places they raised up buildings, and what kinds of buildings they were. You will see that they are not country homes but fortresses (Seneca *Ep.* 51.11).[11]

While this description was no doubt originally intended as a didactic tool for teaching stoicism, it still corresponds to archaeological reality.[12] Seneca's description of these elite residences as fortified military structures in rugged places chosen explicitly for their potential to surveil the surrounding territory fits well with our current understanding of fortified villas such as Castelo da Lousa. That these structures may have simply been intended to appear martial in character rather than actually to serve as a fortification remains an open question. Nevertheless, Seneca's passage describes domestic structures whose positions within the landscape were carefully chosen, like the central Alentejan structures considered in subsequent chapters, for their ability to provide surveillance of the surrounding territory.

Another letter, this one written by Pliny the Younger, describes two towers attached to his country home. These towers, he tells us, were used for common domestic activities—sleeping and dining—but offered especially pleasant views of the seashore and neighboring residences (Pliny, *Ep.* 2.17.12–13). The towers at his villa have been transformed from a military or even industrial purpose to structures meant to provide pleasing vistas during dinner parties. This shift likely reflects the nature of Pliny's villa and its surrounding landscape. Pliny does not make direct mention of agricultural production at his country estate, but these towers (or others) may well have provided some surveillance over the surrounding fields. Nevertheless, any defensive function of the towers seems to have been discarded, and their potential to surveil valued for its ability to provide pleasurable views of the landscape. Papyrological evidence also suggests that some rural villas in Roman Egypt were equipped with towers, but it is difficult to ascertain whether these were for enjoying pleasurable views, providing places of refuge, or for monitoring agricultural laborers.[13]

A tower at the house of Maecenas in Rome also, according to Suetonius and

---

[11] ... *Illi quoque ad quos primos fortuna populi Romani publicas opes transtulit, C. Marius et Cn. Pompeius et Caesar, exstruxerunt quidem villas in regione Baiana, sed illas imposuerunt summis iugis montium: videbatur hoc magis militare, ex edito speculari late longeque subiecta. Aspice quam positionem elegerint, quibus aedificia excitaverint locis et qualia: scies non villas esse sed castra.*

[12] Marzano (2007: 37) suggests that the villas built in Italy during the middle of the first century BCE might have had a more military character because of the ongoing political violence of the period.

[13] For papyrological evidence for the presence of towers at Roman-period farms in Egypt, see Rowlandson 1996: 230.

Horace, was meant to offer a vista of the urban landscape. It was from this tower that, according to Suetonius, the emperor Nero observed the Great Fire of Rome in 64 CE (*Nero* 38.2). Horace likewise comments on excellent views of the city offered by this tower, "Forget scornful wealth and the pile [i.e., the tower] reaching up to the lofty clouds, cease to be amazed by the smoke and the riches and the clamor of beautiful Rome (*Carm.* 3.29.10)."[14] This tower, like Pliny the Younger's, was evidently intended to provide a panoramic, pleasurable view of the city of Rome. Thus, despite its position, we may begin to distinguish those towers in both rural and urban contexts that were intended not for surveillance of a territory for the sake of security but for simple amusement.

The unknown author, known as Pseudo-Cyprian, of an obscure third-century CE sermon titled *De Duobus Montibus Sina et Sion* also includes a description of surveillance structures.[15] This sermon suggests that protecting orchards or vineyards from robbers by stationing a young boy, likely a slave, in a treehouse-like structure, called a *speculum quadratum* or "square lookout post," was a common practice. The slave, by observing the vineyard from this high perch, could easily recognize anyone who attempted to steal the harvest, even a single grape:

> At a seasonable time near the days of grape-gathering, they put a boy as guard on a tall timber-beam firmly planted in the middle of the vineyard and on this timber they make a square lookout post from beaten reeds and through each side of the square of the lookout post they make three holes, which add up to twelve holes; the boy as guard keeps watch through this square of holes, inspecting the whole vineyard, singing so that no traveler, entering, disturb the master's vineyard assigned to him and no thieves seek out the vineyard's path. If a troublesome, needy thief wished to enter the vineyard and remove a grape, there the boy, concerned about his vines, cursing and threatening, makes a loud voice from within the lookout post saying: "Walk straight!" so that the traveling thief dare not approach the vineyard. But the thief, fearing the boy's voice threatening him, flees the vineyard. He sees the lookout post, he hears the voice, he does not see the boy within the lookout post threatening him, afraid he hurries on his way.[16]

This excerpt from the sermon illustrates the use of temporary watchtowers (*spec-*

---

[14] *Fastidiosam desere copiam et / molem propinquam nubibus arduis, / omitte mirari beatae / fumum et opes strepitumque Romae.*

[15] For the full text of this sermon, see *CSEL* 3.3 and Burini 1994.

[16] *Uero tempore maturo prope dies uindemiarum ponunt in mediam uineam custodem puerum in alto ligno media uinea confixo et in eo ligno faciunt speculum quadratum de harundinibus quassatis et per singula latera quadraturae speculi faciunt cauerna terna, quae fiunt cauerna duodecim: per quam quadraturam cauernorum custos puer omnem uineam perspiciens custodiat cantans, ne uiator ingrediens uineam dominicam sibi adsignatam uexet uel fures uiam uineae uestigent. Quod si inportunus fur egens in uineam voluerit introire et uuam demere, illic puer sollicitus de uinea sua deintus de speculo dat uocem maledicens et comminans, ne in uineam uiator fur audeat accedere dicens: rectum ambula. Fur autem timens uocem pueri sibi comminantem refugit de uinea, speculum uidet, uocem audit, puerum intus in speculo sibi comminantem non uidet, timens post uiam suam uadit.*

uli) to monitor and protect a vineyard. It was this story that inspired the decoration of African pottery mentioned above.[17] The temporary nature of this surveillance is implied by the slave's position in a treehouse-like structure made of reeds rather than in a permanent structure. It is likely that surveillance of vineyards, orchards, or other agricultural areas was only utilized during harvest time when their agricultural produce was most desirable. Other Biblical texts, including *Isaiah* (5.1–7) and *Matthew* (21.33), understand surveillance structures as routine parts of a working vineyard. In those texts, watchtowers are constructed alongside winepresses when new vineyards are established. We may thus conclude that such structures may have played a role in agricultural production generally. They may have been intended, as in the example of Greek towers, to house and supervise a population of slaves who worked at the vineyard along with their potential use as sentinels against banditry.[18]

Such an arrangement of surveillance structures to observe agricultural areas would not have been uncommon in Lusitania where we are told by multiple ancient sources that banditry was common. Varro, a Roman agricultural author, served as *legatus* in Lusitania under Pompey the Great in the first century BCE. In his *De Re Rustica*, Varro discusses the hinterland of Lusitania as unsuitable for farms because of the presence of thieves:

> For it is not advisable to cultivate the many excellent farms because of the brigandage in the neighborhood, as in Sardinia at certain farms near Oelium, and in Spain near Lusitania (1.16.2).[19]

Varro's description of the territory as full of bandits is especially interesting given that he had served in the region and knew the territory well. The use of surveillance in this region after the establishment of Roman agricultural villas is thus a reasonable response to the threat of brigandage, but the system of towers and "treehouses" that watched over the villas' crops grew out of an earlier system of permanent watchtowers. This earlier system played an important role in the colonization of the region and the expression of Roman imperial authority within the landscape. A catalogue of known watchtowers in the central Alentejo is discussed in the next chapter.

---

[17] Stuiber 1959: 86–89; Tortorella 2005: 191–94; van den Hoek and Herrmann 2013: 67–69.

[18] Morris and Papadopoulos (2005: 188–200) posit the use of rural towers in Greece to house slaves. This is discussed in greater detail in Chapter 5.

[19] ...*multos enim agros egregios colere non expedit propter latrocinia vicinorum, ut in Sardinia quosdam, qui sunt prope Oeliem, et in Hispania prope Lusitaniam....*

CHAPTER 4

A CATALOGUE OF WATCHTOWERS IN EARLY ROMAN CENTRAL PORTUGAL

The southern Alto Alentejo, defined here as the "central Alentejo" and associated with the city of Évora, holds many hundreds of archaeological sites dating to the late Iron Age and early Roman periods in western Iberia (second century BCE to first century CE). Of these many sites, twenty-four *recintos-torre* and *fortins* dating to the first century BCE have thus far been identified (Fig. 1.2). The majority of these structures are located on topographically prominent areas which granted them excellent vantage on their surroundings. The *recintos-torre* of the central Alentejo share many similarities with other small fortified tower-enclosures throughout Iberia. This chapter seeks to establish, concretely, their shared features and more clearly define a typology of these sites. Additionally, it offers a survey of the two dozen small fortified surveillance structures located in the central Alentejo. A brief updated catalogue of these sites serves to place them within their topographic and archaeological contexts.[1] Their individual artifact assemblages, collected sporadically by numerous field survey projects over the last century, are compared whenever possible, and their architectural remains are considered here in as much detail as their exposed features permit.

---

[1] A similar catalogue was published by Mataloto (2002, 2004a). The catalogue presented here is meant to supplement and update his work as well as make these sites better known to an Anglophone audience.

CATALOGUE OF *FORTINS* AND *RECINTOS-TORRE* IN THE CENTRAL ALENTEJO
Defining fortins and recintos-torre

Scholars have used a multitude of terms to discuss the many small fortified structures in western Iberia. This is partly the result of the different languages and archaeological traditions at work in the region, among them Portuguese, Spanish, German, English, and French. In the Alentejo, these structures are called *recintos-torre* or *fortins*, "tower-enclosures" and "small forts" respectively. They are sometimes referred to as *atalayas*, "towers," or *maisons fortes*, "strong houses," in recent Spanish and Portuguese scholarship.[2] Each of these terms puts emphasis on a particular element or interpretation of these sites, and each term is useful as a descriptor for these structures. In the past, scholars have also described these structures as *recintos ciclópicos*, "cyclopean enclosures," or *tours d'Hannibal*, "towers of Hannibal," but this terminology has largely fallen out of favor over the last decade as a better understanding of their chronology has emerged.[3] Only prehistoric or pre-Roman structures are still regularly characterized as *recintos ciclópicos*. Since the structures considered in this chapter are situated only in Portugal, I have chosen here to adopt the Portuguese terminology, *fortins* and *recintos-torre*, for them. These names also emphasize the aspects of these sites that are the most pertinent, namely the presence of towers and defensive architecture.

In the south of Portugal, similar structures called *castella* have been identified. These sites occupy positions in their local landscape similar to those held by *fortins* in the central Alentejo. The dimensions of the *castella* are similar, and their material culture, where it is known, continues to show similarity.[4] Indeed, it seems that the distinction between *castella* and *fortins* is rather specious. Their collective names are merely the result of academic traditions that have grown up around their study, and they may both be called by each other's nomenclature. The difference between the towers studied here and the *castella* of the south lies primarily in their chronology. The southern *castella* have a somewhat earlier date for their occupational period, which began in the early decades of the first century BCE, and recent work by C. Alves has done much to clarify the date of one such structure at Mesas do Castelinho.[5] This slightly earlier chronology for the *castella* should come as no surprise. The use of towers in the central Alentejo to monitor and dissuade resistance is part of a larger program meant inexorably to pacify, reorganize, and settle the Iberian Peninsula. The *castella* of the south provided a ready pattern to follow.

---

[2] Moret 1999, 2010; Moret and Chapa 2004.
[3] García y Bellido 1945: 591–95; Fortea and Bernier 1970; Moret 1990, 2010: 25–27; Calado 1994–1995; Mataloto 2002: 161–62.
[4] Maia 1974b, 1978, 1986; Maia and Maia 1996.
[5] Alves 2010.

Determining the terminology used to discuss these structures is only the first step in their definition. A careful appraisal of their architectural and artifactual remains indicates at least two distinct types of structures, and their differing positions within the landscape may reveal other typological markers. Nevertheless, only one of these small fortifications, Caladinho, has been systematically excavated in the central Alentejo, and thus presents one of the only complete examples of a *fortim* currently available. The rest—save for Rocha de Províncios and Castelinhos do Rosário (excavated illegally) and Castelinho dos Mouros (a *recinto-torre* excavated by a team from the Deutsches Archäologisches Institut between 2008 and 2011)—have not been excavated, and most of their architectural features remain unexposed. A typology of these sites must be built on the best available evidence, drawn from survey data and from comparisons with the excavated structures at Caladinho. Below I follow Mataloto's categorization of these small fortified structures into two types, *fortins* and *recintos-torre*, with some refinements.

Fortins possess thick external walls, but are otherwise relatively small structures with no clearly defined pattern for their internal spaces. They are most often situated in areas with a wide visual field.[6] *Recintos-torre*, on the other hand, are sites which possess a single tower and other smaller buildings nearby meant for habitation. Like *fortins*, these sites also lack homogeneity in the internal organization of the rooms.[7] M. Calado, in a discussion of the so-called "cyclopean" structures around the modern city of Évora, characterizes the *recintos-torre* by their use of large cut stone blocks.[8] Mataloto, however, is critical of this characterization, and of the existence of the category of *recintos-torre*, because of the existence of tower enclosures which do not possess "cyclopean" masonry.[9]

Sites like Caladinho, discussed in the next chapter, throw the distinction between *fortim* and *recinto-torre* into question. Caladinho, originally characterized as a *fortim*, possesses a small tower with thick external walls, a rectangular plan, and visual control over the surrounding territory. After three seasons of excavation, however, an additional structure has been recorded on the hilltop, and evidence for other structures is being investigated. Thus, while the primary difference between these categories is one of size, this distinction may only be the result of a lack of adequate archaeological excavation on *fortins* or formation processes at *recintos-torre* which expose more of the extant remains.[10] Nevertheless, *fortins* are

---

[6] Mataloto 2002: 162. Other, similar sites in neighboring areas of southern Portugal or Extremedura in western Spain have been called both *fortalezas* and *castella* (Rodríguez Díaz and Ortiz Romero 1989: 49; Maia 1974b, 1978, 1986; Maia and Maia 1996: 66).

[7] Mataloto 2002: 196.

[8] Calado 1994–1995.

[9] Mataloto 2002: 196–97. Moret (1995) instead refers to the tower enclosures as *maisons fortes*, "strong houses." While this redefinition is appealing, accepting its usage essentializes the domestic aspects of these structures to the detriment of their other potential purposes within the landscape.

[10] Mataloto (2004a: 32) proposes that *recintos-torre* be understood as a subtype of *fortins* given

considered to be the smaller site, rarely more than the size of a single building. *Recintos-torre* are much larger. The tower and associated structures usually occupy a narrow rectangular area of between 200 and 500 m².[11]

The sites catalogued below present a corpus of material culture that, when understood as a single unit, provides insight into these structures and their inhabitants as well as a useful comparison with the artifact assemblage recovered from Caladinho. Differing methods of survey, collecting, and recording at each of the *fortins* and *recintos-torre*, however, make comparisons between these sites difficult. Furthermore, the vast majority of tower enclosures in the central Alentejo possess a very sparse publication history, meaning that their material remains are largely unknown outside of local archaeological circles.[12] Despite these problems, artifacts from these sites provide some useful insights into aspects of individual sites and of *fortins* and *recintos-torre* as a whole.

As one might expect, ceramics represent the most populous category of artifact collected and recorded among the tower enclosures of the central Alentejo. The sampling strategies employed on most surveys of these sites privileged finewares and transport pottery because of the ease with which they may be recognized and their potential value for chronology. As a result, pottery of these types is overrepresented in the small assemblages recovered from the *fortins* and *recintos-torre*. Differences in the length and intensity of occupation also alter the character of the ceramic assemblages from the *fortins* and *recintos-torre*. Some were occupied for mere decades, while others boast a continual occupation lasting multiple centuries. For the period examined, the assemblage from Caladinho, examined in the next chapter, provides the best representation of a tower enclosure's ceramic assemblage from the first century BCE. The material culture from the *fortins* and *recintos-torre*, although incompletely understood, may yet offer some otherwise imperceptible nuance to our understanding of the inhabitants and sociocultural position of these structures.

Format of the entries

The catalogue of sites is divided into *fortins*, small forts, and *recintos-torre*, tower enclosures. Each site listed below is assigned to one of these categories based on its size, the architectural features visible at the site, and its location within the landscape. As defined above, *fortins* are generally smaller sites, under 200 m², with

---

their similarity in most respects.

[11] Mataloto 2002: 196.

[12] Some exceptions to this include Mataloto 2002, 2004a, 2008, 2010; Mataloto et al. 2014. Chapters in the recent volume edited by Mayoral Herrera and Celestino Pérez (2010) also contain useful information on the central Alentejo and neighboring regions. For some *fortins* and *recintos-torre*, however, the catalogue of *monumentos militares Portugueses* compiled by J. Almeida between 1945 and 1947 presents a significant part of extant data.

one primary, fortified building usually situated so as to have ample vision over its surroundings. *Recintos-torre* are larger sites, between 200 and 500 m², with a well-constructed tower and, sometimes, an enclosure wall. Some sites in the catalogue possess later phases which obscure the first century BCE features.

While many of the central Alentejan *fortins* and *recintos-torre* have been recognized by archaeologists since the first half of the twentieth century, they have only recently garnered significant scholarly attention. The third volume of J. Almeida's early catalogue of monuments lists several of these small sites, but provides little analysis.[13] Over the last twenty years, Portuguese archaeologists began to take a greater interest in these sites, their inhabitants, and their roles within the landscape. A scant few examples were included in J. Alarcão's gazetteer of Roman Portugal, but their descriptions are often simplistic.[14] M. Calado, in 1994–1995, provides the first attempt at cataloguing and characterizing these sites.[15] His work was later incorporated into the official archaeological maps of the central Alentejo.[16] As part of the creation of these maps, many of these small fortified sites were investigated archaeologically for the first time. Simple field walking and surveying revealed enough materials, in most cases, for the archaeologists involved to supply a date for the structures. A complete catalogue of *fortins* and *recintos-torre* in the central Alentejo was presented for the first time in 2002.[17]

Each entry in the catalogue was assigned a designation for ease of correlating the sites to their positions on the visibility analysis maps featured in Chapter 5. The designation is made up of a letter followed by a number. The letter represents the type of site. *Fortins* received an "F" while *recintos-torre* were assigned an "R." The number following each letter matches the numbers assigned to these sites in previous publications (Fig. 1.2).[18] The names of the sites are given next, as are its unique *Código Nacional de Sítio* (CNS). The CNS is each site's unique identifier within the Portuguese national database of archaeological sites, which is maintained by the *Direção-Geral do Património Cultural*.[19] The CNS is followed by each site's CMP Number. This number is assigned to each site by referencing its location in the *Carta Militar de Portugal* (CMP), the standard 1:25,000 scale reference maps for the country's archaeological sites. I have assigned the CMP Numbers by the particular page of the map where they appear. A brief discus-

[13] Almeida 1945.
[14] Alarcão 1988: 158.
[15] Calado 1994–1995.
[16] Calado 1993; Calado and Mataloto 2001.
[17] Mataloto 2002.
[18] These numbers were also used by Mataloto (2002, 2004b), Williams and Mataloto (2011), and Mataloto and Williams (2011, 2012).
[19] The database is freely accessible, and basic information on all the sites presented here can be located by searching for the name of the site or its CNS number. The database can be accessed by visiting http://arqueologia.patrimoniocultural.pt/

sion of each site follows, including a description of the architectural and material remains. Their dates of occupation, established through the analysis of surface collections published over the last decade, are given at the end of each entry in the catalogue. Since the majority of these sites have seen little to no archaeological reconnaissance, only a sparse amount of data exists for each. Together, however, they present a fuller picture of this type of small fortified structure and its place within the early Roman Alentejo.

Fortins

F1. Malhada das Penas 1 and 2
CNS: 11725 and 11733
CMP Number: 370

The first entry in the catalogue is also one of the most complicated. The site at Malhada das Penas includes two separate and architecturally distinct *fortins* situated on a ridge opposite each other, one to the northwest and the other to the southeast. The ridge that they occupy is split between them by the Ribeira da Chaminé. Together, the two *fortins* possess ample visual control over their surrounding landscape thanks to their positions at the highest (and steepest) part of the ridge. They are referred to here as Malhada das Penas 1 and 2 and in subsequent chapters as F1.

Malhada das Penas 1 is located above the southeastern bank of the Ribeira da Chaminé. The site occupies roughly 60 m by 20 m at the top of the ridge. A large "tumulus" of stone debris marks the far western side of the ridge.[20] This debris is likely the remains of a tower like the one excavated at Caladinho (discussed in the following chapter). The 1 m-wide stone wall visible on the south of the debris pile supports this characterization. In combination with the site's steep and difficult terrain to the north, east, and west, such a substantial fortification wall on the southern side would have provided ample protection for this *fortim*. Malhada das Penas 2 is located on the ridge directly opposite Malhada das Penas 1. A quadrangular building is implanted on the top of this northwestern part of the ridge. It measures roughly 14 m by 12 m according to previous examinations of the visible architectural features at the site.[21] The walls of this structure are built from the local schist stone in a manner similar to what was observed at Caladinho (discussed in the next chapter).

Neither excavation nor intensive systematic survey have been attempted at either Malhada das Penas 1 or 2. As a result no artifacts have been recovered from this site. A handful of pre-Roman ceramics have been identified in the immediate

---

[20] Mataloto 2002: 163–64.
[21] Mataloto 2002: 164.

area of the ridge, but no definitive date for these structures has been assigned.[22] Since prehistoric ceramics also appear at Caladinho, a similar situation may exist at Malhada das Penas. The prehistoric ceramics may simply be the residual artifacts of a lengthy prehistoric occupation of the ridge.

Given their proximity, it is likely that these structures were meant to act in concert, and their different architectural features complement each other. As surveillance structures, Malhada das Penas 1 and 2 are well situated to observe and control the route down the banks of Ribeira da Chaminé as well as the surrounding area. Malhada das Penas 2 is particularly suited to this role given its somewhat higher position. Malhada das Penas 1 may have instead served as a domestic or defensive structure for those operating the observation post. The two *fortins* may have originally been linked by, perhaps, a simple wooden bridge, but no evidence of such a construction survives.

F2. Beiçudos
CNS: 11730
CMP Number: 384

The site of Beiçudos is named after the ridge on which it is built. It has not been assigned a geodesic marker, but one has been placed along the same ridge to the northwest. Beiçudos is located to the northwest of Malhada das Penas, and is similarly positioned over a river. Here, the Ribeira Grande winds through the landscape just to the south and east of Beiçudos. The site itself, identified as a *fortim* by Mataloto, is situated on a narrow rocky spur above the river's course.[23] It is not located at the highest point of the ridge (where the geodesic marker is placed), but instead is again placed in a defensive position that overlooks a route of movement through the landscape. The position of this site is fundamentally the same as many others presented in this catalogue, and its potential for surveillance seems essential for interpreting the site and its place in the larger cultural landscape.

The *fortim* at Beiçudos has received no attention from archaeologists save for the brief informal survey performed by Mataloto in 2002. The site appears as a heap of debris with some visible architectural features (Fig. 4.1). The debris is primarily schist, much like the debris cleared from Caladinho. A substantial amount of burned clay is also present at the site, suggesting that the upper story may have been constructed from mud brick or the walls lined with clay. A number of retaining walls, made from local schist, divide the ridge into terraces. The ceramics present at the site do not lend themselves to a precise dating, although Mataloto identified a small number of late Iron Age sherds.[24]

---

[22] Mataloto 2002: 164.
[23] Mataloto 2002: 165.
[24] Mataloto 2002: 165.

F3. Penedo do Ferro
CNS: 19648
CMP Number: 413

The *fortim* at Penedo do Ferro was observed by the author during the summer of 2006. This informal survey, which did not involve the collection of artifacts, supplements the survey performed by Mataloto in 2002. The site is constructed on a low rise in the landscape that does not stand out from its surroundings by more than a few meters of elevation. Nevertheless, few other locations in the immediate area offer a higher or substantively more defensible position. The site is positioned to observe a traversable path through the landscape that runs from east to west along the banks of the Ribeira da Colónia. Its position grants it visual command of this route. Owing to the local geology, the site is built from granite rather than unworked schist. Although unexcavated, the site is believed to occupy roughly 70 m by 40 m of this hilltop with a variety of structures.

Three structures are visible on the hilltop of Penedo do Ferro. The largest is a tower built on the western side of the hill. The tower appears in much the same condition as Caladinho before its excavation (discussed in Chapter 5). Two other smaller structures are placed between granite outcrops on the southeast of the hilltop. The functions of these smaller structures remain unclear because of the lack of archaeological investigation at Penedo do Ferro. Some artifacts were collected from Penedo do Ferro by Mataloto in 2002. These included both prehistoric pottery and ceramics imported from Baetica. The most recognizable of the Baetican imports identified was the rim of a Haltern 70 amphora.[25] Since amphorae of this type are commonly dated to the late first century BCE and first century CE, it is likely that Penedo do Ferro, like other *fortins*, was occupied during this relatively brief window. Additional fieldwork at the site may serve to narrow this chronology further.

F4. Soeiros
CNS: 19649
CMP Number: 410

Thanks to the Soeiros Dam, the *fortim* at Soeiros is now situated on an island. Its current location, however, emphasizes its position high in the landscape since it remains above the water unlike its local surroundings. The site was investigated prior to the dam's construction, and the oscillations of the water level have caused a great deal of erosion at the site. While the remains have been damaged and the overall picture of the site made unclear, the erosion has exposed a great deal of ce-

---

[25] Mataloto 2002: 167.

ramics and faunal remains. These materials have been collected as part of a small number of studies after the dam's construction.[26]

The ceramic assemblage from Soeiros includes examples of imported amphorae, thin-walled ware, Campanian black gloss ware, and common wares imported from Baetica.[27] The amphorae are primarily of the Haltern 70 and Dressel 7–11 types. In conjunction with a single Campanian black gloss sherd of form Lamboglia 3, these artifacts suggest that the site was occupied in the last half of the first century BCE and into the early to mid-first century CE.[28] It is likely that this site—along with many of the other *fortins* and *recintos-torre*—is among the first to be occupied during the Roman colonization and resettlement of the central Alentejo.[29] The thin-walled wares have proven too fragmentary to provide a classification, but elements of the fabric suggest that they were produced in Baetica.[30] It is also certainly plausible that they were imported from Italy much like the Campanian black gloss vessel. The common wares have similar implications for the connections between Soeiros and other parts of the Iberian Peninsula. Two main groups of imported common wares were identified among the assemblage from Soeiros. They are characterized as a cream or beige-colored fabric, likely from Baetica, and a much grittier fabric with an orange surface and gray core, perhaps from the area of Lisbon.[31] These forms are primarily drinking cups, and it is assumed that they were imported alongside the amphorae.[32]

F5. Cortes
CNS: 19650
CMP Number: 439

The *fortim* known as Cortes was originally included in the list of *recintos ciclópicos* compiled by Calado.[33] It was reclassified by Mataloto as a *fortim* since it is located atop a steep slope, is small in size, and possesses little of the material culture that

[26] For example, see Calado and Rocha 1997; Calado et al. 2000; Mataloto 2002.
[27] Calado et al. 2000, fig. 5.
[28] Calado et al. 2000: 764–65.
[29] Calado and Rocha 1997: 102; Mataloto 2002: 168.
[30] Calado et al. 2000: 765.
[31] Calado et al. 2000: 766. I disagree here with the characterization of the orange and gray fabric by Calado et al., although I have never personally seen the sherds from Soeiros under discussion. They assert that the origin of this fabric was likely Baetica. All the first-century BCE ceramics from Baetica encountered during the excavation of Caladinho were in a chalky, cream, or beige fabric. The more orange, gritty fabric appears to have originated in the area of Lisbon. The ceramic fabrics from Caladinho are discussed in greater detail in Chapter 5. Mataloto (2008: 132–33) characterizes the amphorae from Soeiros as Lusitanian. See Dias et al. (2012) and Morais and Fabião (2007) for recent discussions of this fabric and the amphorae produced in it.
[32] Fabião 1998: 415.
[33] Calado 1994–1995.

usually defines the *recintos ciclópicos*.³⁴ The site sits atop a narrow spur as many of the other central Alentejan *fortins* do when the local topography permits. This spur is part of a ridge on the northern slope of the Serra d'Ossa, and it overlooks one of the most easily traversable routes through the range (Fig. 4.2). This site's position in the landscape is one of the primary distinguishing features of a *fortim*. Together with its architectural features, there is no doubt that this site belongs to the category of *fortins* rather than *recintos ciclópicos*. Nevertheless, while there are significant differences between these two structural types, the *fortins* are, perhaps, a development of *recintos ciclópicos* adapted to the new circumstances of colonialism.

A significant portion of the extant structure is exposed. A 12 m-long building constructed from blocks of schist stretches across the top of the ridge. Some of the extant walls are exposed to a height of 1 m, and each is almost 1 m in width.³⁵ The area around the extant structure appears to have been intentionally leveled, and perhaps other structures remain to be discovered on the hilltop. Survey on the site produced a small number of ceramics, including an amphora fragment that may be an amphora of the Haltern 70 type.³⁶ The ceramics from Cortes are primarily local pottery of the type described by I. Vaz Pinto and A. Schmitt in the catalogue of ceramics from the excavations at Castelo da Lousa.³⁷ These vessels possess an inscribed decoration of a wavy line usually set between two inscribed bands. They were formerly dated to the pre-Roman period, but recent analysis places their production and usage in the latter half of the first century BCE and first century CE.³⁸

F6. Outeiro Pintado
CNS: 19651
CMP Number: 427

The *fortim* at Outeiro Pintado is located atop a steep hill overlooking the Ribeira de Mures. The extant remains give the hill the appearance almost of a plateau. It is constructed from unworked or roughly worked rectangular blocks of schist. Interestingly, a number of roof tiles, *imbrices*, were identified at the site during survey.³⁹ Tile roofs are a particularly Roman innovation introduced to the region during the first century BCE (and only incorporated into many structures in the first century CE). The presence of tiles at Outeiro Pintado suggests that this site

---

³⁴ Mataloto 2002: 172. The tower at Caladinho, discussed in the next chapter, was built in roughly the same dimensions.
³⁵ Mataloto 2002: 173.
³⁶ Mataloto 2002: 173.
³⁷ Vaz Pinto and Schmitt 2010: 322–24.
³⁸ Vaz Pinto 2003: 567.
³⁹ Mataloto 2002: 174.

was occupied during the first century BCE and probably either housed or was otherwise closely connected to Roman colonists. Another particularly Roman architectural feature was recorded near the base of the north side of the hill. A hydraulic feature of unknown purpose was installed there (Fig. 4.3). It is constructed from schist and mortar and feeds a small artificial pond. The hydraulic feature was probably connected with the Ribeira de Mures, although their linkage is no longer extant. The relationship between the *fortim* and this hydraulic feature requires further investigation.

F7. Três Moinhos (S. Rafael)
CNS: 19652
CMP Number: 441-A

The *fortim* of Três Moinhos (S. Rafael) remains poorly understood. It is located at the top of a hill next to the Guadiana River. The hill rises over 30 m above the banks of the river and provides ample surveillance over the river's course. A single artifact from the site, a pottery wheel, has garnered some limited attention from scholars of ceramic production and technology.[40] The structure itself is approximately 12 m in length. It was constructed, with some care, from large cut blocks of schist (Fig. 4.4). The extant walls rise to a maximum of 1 m in some areas.[41] Traces of other structures exist on the hilltop, but without further archaeological investigation our best way of understanding the *fortim* at Três Moinhos is by comparing it to other sites of the same type, such as those listed in this catalogue or the excavated example, Caladinho, discussed in the next chapter.

F8. Monte do Almo
CNS: 19663
CMP Number: 450

The *fortim* at Monte do Almo is located on a hilltop to the northwest of Caladinho near the modern town of Redondo. On account of the surrounding topography, Monte do Almo is readily able to surveil the territory to the southwest of the Serra d'Ossa. It observes both the route which links Évora and the Guadiana River and the western pass across the Serra d'Ossa (Fig. 4.5). This pass is the same one that the *fortim* known as Cortes is situated above.[42] Access to this site is not as difficult as to some of the others included in this catalogue. The hill possesses relatively gentle slopes on all sides save the northern one.

A large pile of rubble obscures the precise dimensions of the extant structure

---

[40] EDIA 1999: 146; Silva 1999: 416; Mataloto 2002: 176.
[41] Mataloto 2004a: 35.
[42] Mataloto 2002: 177.

at the northern, highest end of the hill, but it appears to be 10 m by 8 m, roughly the same size as the tower at Caladinho. The visible walls are roughly 1 m wide and situated next to a schist promontory that overlooks the north and east. A second structure is visible on a large flat platform on the southern side of the hilltop. This structure appears substantially larger than the first at 15 m by 8 m. Both structures are built from blocks of schist in different sizes.[43] Other construction material is also present at the site, including ceramic bricks, *tegulae*, and *imbrices*, suggesting the presence of a hitherto unrecognized Roman villa at the site in addition to the *fortim*.[44]

Storage pottery, including fragments of Roman-style *dolia*, greatly outweighs the other artifacts observed at Monte do Almo during survey. One storage vessel sherd appears to have been inscribed with the Latin character *A* (and perhaps other characters) prior to firing.[45] Imported ceramics, either from the Iberian Peninsula or farther abroad, are rare at the site, but survey did reveal the presence of Haltern 70 amphorae from the first century CE.[46] The site also possesses examples of Campanian black gloss ware and imported cups and bowls from Baetica. Future excavations are planned for this site, but as of the time of this writing only limited surface collection of artifacts has been conducted. Together, however, this assemblage provides a relatively concrete period of occupation for Monte do Almo from the mid-first century BCE and into the first century CE. The site requires additional fieldwork in order to ascertain a more precise chronology.

F9. Caladinho (Castelo da Defesinha)
CNS: 19662
CMP Number: 451

The *fortim* known as Caladinho possesses one of the most visually commanding positions within the central Alentejo (Fig. 4.6). Caladinho's inhabitants, architecture, and position in the landscape, in both a physical as well as social sense, are explored in detail in the next chapter. This site has been the subject of four seasons of excavation directed by the author and R. Mataloto in an effort to better understand the *fortins* and *recintos-torre* of the central Alentejo region. Surface survey near the site has revealed the presence of a Roman villa, named Azinhalinho, immediately north of Caladinho.[47] The close proximity of this villa and its preliminary dating by surface materials suggest that it, like many of the other villas discussed in relation to the *fortins* and *recintos-torre*, was built in the same

[43] Mataloto 2002: 178.
[44] Calado and Mataloto 2001: 73; Mataloto 2002: 178.
[45] Mataloto 2002: 178.
[46] Calado and Mataloto 2001: 73; Mataloto 2004a: 37.
[47] Saavedra Machado 1964: 169; Alarcão 1988: 158; Calado and Mataloto 2001: 101. Previous excavation at the base of the hill has also revealed a Neolithic tomb, the Tholos of Caladinho (CNS: 19040).

years when the tower was abandoned. Azinhalinho may have become the home of Caladinho's inhabitants after the tower fell into disuse. The archaeological data presented in Chapter 5 provide comparanda for the architectural and artifactual remains surveyed among the sites catalogued in this chapter.

F10. Castelinho
CNS: 19661
CMP Number: 451

The site at Castelinho was constructed in a locale unlike any of the other *fortins* and *recintos-torre*. It is situated in a relatively inaccessible part of the municipality of Alandroal between Caladinho and Castelinhos do Rosário.[48] The *fortim* was built on an imposing, steep outcrop that rises above the winding course of the Ribeira de Lucefécit. A sheer cliff face rises to the north, east, and south, opposite the outcrop on the other bank of the river. This cliff face obscures the view from the tower in almost ever direction, save for the river below it (Fig. 4.7). This *fortim* may not have been intended to observe the landscape inasmuch as it was meant to observe the course of the river, one of the few traversable paths through this rugged landscape.

Much of the outcrop is too narrow or uneven to permit the building of a structure. Thus, the *fortim* at Castelinho is relatively small. Like many of the other *fortins* in this catalogue, Castelinho is recognizable today as a pile of debris with some visible schist walls, including one that blocks access to the site from its eastern side. The site appears to have been situated and constructed with defensibility in mind, yet also with the aim of observing an otherwise invisible part of the river. This river, too shallow to be navigable, nevertheless provided an important pedestrian route of transit through the region, and served to link the area to the larger networks accessible via the Guadiana River to the east. Thus Castelinho was positioned to monitor this otherwise hidden route.

The material remains of Castelinho must be assembled from the notes and publications of three different Portuguese archaeologists. Vasconcelos, the first investigator of Castelinho, notes that a bronze *fibula* of an unknown type was found at the site as well as a spindle whorl.[49] Calado and Mataloto report the presence of imported Baetican amphorae, likely of the Haltern 70 type from the first century CE but recognizable only in nondiagnostic body sherds, from around the top of the outcrop.[50] Informal walking survey by the author and a team of field

---

[48] This catalogue entry relies primarily on personal observations made by the author during a visit to Castelinho in 2010. It is supplemented by information from Vasconcelos (1895: 212–13), Calado (1993: 61), Fernandes and Neto (1997), and Mataloto (2002: 181, 2004a: 39).

[49] Vasconcelos 1895: 212–13. See also the discussion of this *fibula* by Calado (1993: 61). For spindle whorls from the region, see Vaz Pinto and Schmitt 2010: 324–27.

[50] Calado 1993: 61; Mataloto 2002: 181, 2004a: 39.

school students in 2010 revealed the presence of both wheel-made and hand-built common wares as well as a significant amount of slag. No artifacts were collected during this visit to the site.

F11. Províncios
CNS: 19660
CMP Number: 452

The *fortim* at Províncios is situated on a bedrock outcrop above the Ribeira de Províncios. In addition to its excellent defensive position, the site is positioned to observe both the course of the river and the broad, open plains to the east between the *fortim* and the Guadiana River. In other directions, the site's visibility is limited to its immediate region by the presence of the Olivença Mountains.[51]

At some point in the recent past, Províncios was the victim of illegal amateur excavation. Although the looting of the site has disrupted its stratigraphy and stripped it of an unknown fraction of its artifact assemblage, it also revealed that the *fortim* at Províncios was a relatively small tower, 6 m by 7 m, internally divided into at least three small rooms. The visible walls stand at a height of roughly 1 m and are 1.1 m wide.[52] They are constructed, like many ancient and modern walls in the central Alentejo, from carefully stacked unmortared slabs of schist which were then covered with mud, plaster, or both. Other parts of the outcrop have not been excavated either professionally or illegally, and these areas may hold other related structures.

Perhaps because of the looting mentioned above, there are few material remains from Províncios on the surface of the outcrop. Survey at the site recorded the presence of only hand-built pottery of a likely prehistoric date.[53] Calado, drawing on evidence from nearby sites, proposed that the *fortim* at Províncios was occupied during the late Iron Age, prior to the Roman occupation of the territory, but no artifacts from Rocha de Províncios support this or any other dating of the site.[54] Judging from the architectural features and the site's location in the landscape, Províncios appears similar enough to other *fortins* in the central Alentejo to date it to the latter half of the first century BCE. This new date of the *fortim* is no more or less certain than the earlier date assigned to it by Calado, and further fieldwork at Rocha de Províncios is needed to clarify the site's phasing.

---

[51] Fernandes and Neto 1997; Mataloto 2002: 182.
[52] Mataloto 2002: 182.
[53] Mataloto 2002: 183.
[54] Calado 1993: 96. See also EDIA 1999: 155.

F12. Castelinhos do Rosário (Outeiro do Castelinho)
CNS: 19659
CMP Number: 452

Castelinhos do Rosário, like Províncios above, was excavated by amateurs during the modern era.[55] Unlike Províncios and the majority of the other *fortins* and *recintos-torre*, however, Castelinhos do Rosário appears to have been occupied throughout the Roman period rather than only in the first century BCE and first century CE. The lengthy occupation of the structure is obvious when the scale of its final, most visible, villa-like phase is examined. The structure is implanted atop a steep hill located between a fork in the Ribeira do Lucefécit, downstream from Castelinho. The area around Castelinhos do Rosário is dotted with small mines (Fig. 2.4), and the land is considered to be both fertile and well watered.[56]

The site was fully exposed by amateurs in the 1970s. They revealed—without properly recording features, contexts, or artifacts—a ca. 2500 m² structure featuring multiple rooms organized around a central *atrium* and flanked by other wings (Fig. 4.8). The walls of this structure are impressively built and quite thick, roughly 1 to 1.5 m, especially at the northern corner that overlooks the Ribeira do Lucefécit (Fig. 4.9). All the visible walls appear to be mortared. The clandestine excavation also included a great deal of earth-moving. A large cistern, made of four chambers each almost 2.5 m deep, was fully exposed, revealing *opus signinum* in remarkably good condition (Fig. 4.10). Floors made of *opus signinum* are also visible in parts of the main structure. Based solely upon the appearance of its visible architecture, Castelinhos do Rosário might be characterized simply as a fortified Roman villa were it not for the similarity of its topographic location to the *fortins* and *recintos-torre* of the region.[57]

It appears that this site was, perhaps, a *fortim* in its original configuration, albeit one that has undergone significant expansion after it was first occupied. The identification of this site as a fortified hilltop villa is not contradicted by characterizing its earliest phase as a structure similar to the *fortins* of the first century BCE.[58] This transformation of a fortified surveillance tower into a villa also occurs with many of the *recintos-torre* discussed in the next section below. Lack of sys-

---

[55] Castelinhos do Rosário was visited by the author during the 2011 field season. This catalogue entry is derived from this investigation of the site as well as from accounts from other authors, including Calado (1993: 102), EDIA (1999: 153), Gomes et al. (2002: 134–38), and Mataloto (2002: 184–86, 2004a: 39). Systematic survey at Castelinhos do Rosário is planned for future field seasons.

[56] Mataloto 2002: 184.

[57] Calado (1993: 102) does indeed categorize Castelinhos do Rosário as a fortified Roman villa of the first century BCE Mataloto (2002: 186, 2004a: 39) argues for its characterization as a *fortim* based on its location near the river and its proximity to mining concerns.

[58] Castelo da Lousa, a fortified villa on the Guadiana to the south of Castelinhos do Rosário, may provide an excellent comparison. See Alarcão (1988: 63–65) and Wahl (1985) for additional *comparanda* and Alarcão et al. (2010c) for a full report on the salvage excavation at Castelo da Lousa.

tematic archaeological recording at Castelinhos do Rosário has made it thus far impossible to identify different phases of construction on the hilltop. Indeed, the chronology of this site also lacks good definition. Calado records the existence of Italian terra sigillata of the late first century BCE and other later sigillatas imported from both Gaul and Spain. Both local common wares and imported amphorae were also recognized at Castelinhos do Rosário, but no provenience or typology is given for either class of ceramic.[59] Given the ceramic evidence available, it is likely that Castelinhos do Rosário, in some form, was occupied during the latter half of first century BCE, and it is certainly plausible that it was originally a *fortim* like the many other sites of this date in similar topographic situations. Its transformation into a hilltop Roman villa similarly follows an established pattern for surveillance sites in this region. Further systematic recording of the site is necessary.

F13. Castelo da Pena de Alfange (Outeiro do Pombo)
CNS: 12398
CMP Number: 463

Castelo da Pena de Alfange is the name given to a *fortim* located on the western bank of the Guadiana River to the southeast of Castelinhos do Rosário. The site is set atop a tall steep hill at a height of over three dozen meters above the riverbank. This choice of location was likely a strategic choice since there are two narrow, shallow, and calm parts of the river where it is eminently possible to ford the Guadiana to the south of the *fortim*. The slopes of this hill fall especially precipitously on the eastern side, making Castelo da Pena de Alfange unapproachable from this direction.[60] The hill's other sides are only marginally less sheer, making it clear that this location was chosen for its defensive potential as much as its ability to surveil the course and crossings of the Guadiana.

A quadrangular structure is visible on the highest point on the hill. Some segments of this structure's walls are visible on the surface. While Calado assigns this site to the late Iron Age based on the appearance of indigenous ceramics, Mataloto's subsequent survey noted the presence of sherds of Baetican amphorae of the Haltern 70 type. This suggests that occupation of this site occurred somewhere between the middle of the first century BCE to the second century CE.[61] The size, quadrangular plan, and topographic location of this site suggest it is among the other *fortins* of the late first century BCE, although this early Roman occupation does not eliminate the possibility that Castelo da Pena de Alfange was also occupied prior to the Roman conquest. Still, given the numerous examples of *fortins*

[59] Calado 1993: 102, 158. See also Mataloto 2002: 218 n. 3.
[60] Fernandes and Neto 1997; Fernandes and Neto 1998; Mataloto 2002: 187.
[61] For the evidence supporting the late Iron Age chronology, see Calado 1993: 141 and EDIA 1996: 169. Mataloto (2002: 188) provides data supporting the first-century BCE occupation of Castelo da Pena de Alfange.

with similar assemblages of both indigenous and Roman material culture, it seems likely that the inhabitants of this isolated site simply made use of what pottery they could get, whether it was indigenous common wares or imported Roman products.

F14. Monte do Gato 2
CNS: 16442
CMP Number: 474

The *fortim* at Monte do Gato 2 is situated, like many of the sites in this catalogue, on a spur of bedrock above the course of the Ribeira do Azevel, which feeds into the Guadiana River. It is typologized narrowly within the national database as an *atalaia* or "watchtower," although the site possesses the dimensions and features found in the larger *fortins*. The site is difficult to approach because of the presence of large outcrops on the only side of the spur that does not possess a steep slope. The *fortim* possesses ample visibility over the course of the Ribeira do Azevel and the Guadiana itself and approaches to it from the south. In other directions, however, the site's location does not offer any advantage for surveillance.[62]

The surface area available at this site is limited, but it is possible to discern the walls of a structure, roughly 7 m by 6 m in size, at the top of the spur. Surrounding that structure, a few artifacts of several different types have been recorded. Present at Monte do Gato 2 are wheel-made common wares, Baetican amphorae fragments, decorated spindle whorls, and a great deal of metal production waste, including hardened droplets of molten lead that may be waste from the making of lead sling bullets.[63] These finds fit well with the materials surveyed at a number of other sites in this catalogue and with the assemblage excavated from Caladinho (discussed in Chapter 5).

A dam and set of hydraulic features, similar to the feature recorded at Rocha de Províncios, were recorded during survey of Monte do Gato 2 in 1999. These hydraulic features were discovered at the base of the hill next to the Ribeira do Azevel. They were dated to the first century BCE based on the presence of a great deal of late republican materials.[64] Mataloto suggests that the dam and hydraulic features were likely not related to the *fortim* situated above them, but his conclusion is based on the difficulty of traversing the rugged terrain between the hydraulic features and the *fortim*.[65] It may be that Monte de Gato 2 was intended to provide surveillance over the hydraulic features in order to protect them from vandalism or destruction. If these features and the site at the top of Monte de Gato 2 were

[62] Mataloto 2002: 189.
[63] Mataloto 2002: 189.
[64] EDIA 1999: 202.
[65] Mataloto 2002: 189.

related beyond the *fortim*'s oversight, the precise nature of that relationship is unclear largely because the purpose of the hydraulic features remains unknown. Since this site was inundated as a result of the completion of the Alqueva Dam, it is highly unlikely that this question will ever be answered.

F15. Defesinha 1 – Núcleo 2
CNS: 13567
CMP Number: 482

Defesinha is located on a small gently sloping hill next to the Ribeira da Defesinha, a small tributary of the Guadiana River. Unlike the majority of sites in this catalogue, Defensinha, despite its name, is not located in an especially defensible location. It is easy to approach this site from all sides, and this is likely why it is typologized as a *habitat* in the national database rather than as a *fortim*. The structure itself is quadrangular in size, but difficult to distinguish at the surface. Mataloto argues that this *fortim* was built in a location chosen for its control over the Ribeira da Defesinha, the course of which provides easy access to both the Guadiana and Castelo da Lousa downstream.[66] Given the position of Defesinha, the defensibility of this *fortim* does not appear to have been the highest priority in the determination of its place in the landscape. Instead, the builders chose a position that would permit the greatest degree of vision over the Ribeira da Defesinha and its crossing. The surveillance potential of the structure thus outweighed its ability to provide a greater degree of safety to its inhabitants.

The site was investigated in the 1990s as part of the plan to mitigate the impact of the Alqueva Dam project on the cultural resources of the Alentejo region. Salvage excavation around the hilltop revealed the presence of Italian terra sigillata as well as a bronze fibula, among other materials. The fibula was analyzed by C. Fabião who identified it as belonging to the Schüle 4h type, a style of fibula used immediately prior to the Roman conquest and during the first decades of Roman occupation.[67] Together, the ceramic evidence and the fibula indicate that this *fortim*, like the majority of the others, was occupied during the late first century BCE.

F16. Moinho do Tojal 1
CNS: 14569
CMP Number: 481

The *fortim* at Moinho do Tojal, the last such structure to be included in this catalogue, is situated atop a rocky outcrop that towers above the valley of the Rio Degebe, another tributary of the Guadiana. Its position, like that of many of the

---

[66] Mataloto 2002: 190, 2004a: 40.
[67] Fabião 1998: 109.

other *fortins*, allows it to observe the most easily traversable route through its immediate landscape. A quadrangular structure, made entirely from unmortared schist slabs and measuring 7.60 m by 6.20 m, is perched atop the highest point of the outcrop. The external walls of the *fortim* are a roughly uniform width of 0.9 m, and the visible walls survive to a height of 1 m in many parts of the structure.[68]

A number of surface surveys undertaken at Moinho do Tojal in 1998 and 1999 recorded numerous fragments of both local and imported pottery.[69] Foremost among the assemblage are examples of Campanian black gloss ware of the Campana B production. Additionally, local imitations of Campanian black gloss were identified by Mataloto at Moinho do Tojal. While in local pastes, these vessels attempt to imitate Campanian forms.[70] Similar examples of imitation Roman fineware were recovered during excavation of Castelo da Lousa and Caladinho.[71] These fineware imitations, which appear to have a widespread distribution among the *fortins*, represent a growing desire for Roman-style goods in the central Alentejo.

Recintos-torre

R17. Castelo / Monte do Mariano
CNS: 19658
CMP Number: 398

The *recinto-torre* at Mariano rests on a small, rough, rock-strewn outcrop near the Ribeira de Ana Loura. It is surrounded on all but the western side by hills which truncate the site's potential to surveil in any direction but the course of the river. The structure is built from the local stone, gabbro, which also forms the outcrop. Several walls are visible on the surface, four of which complete the outline of a single room. This room measures 17.5 m by 12.5 m and possesses walls that rise to a height of over 2 m in some areas. Mataloto characterizes the construction of these walls as *tosca*, "clumsy," and indeed they do not appear as well built as the schist walls of some other *recintos-torre* and *fortins* (Fig. 4.11).[72] Despite the lack of skill or care in their organization, the stones used in this wall are quite large and certainly required immense effort to move into place.

Around the site, Mataloto recorded the presence of several classes of ceramics on the surface. Two sherds of Campanian black gloss of the Morel 2654 series and 2562 series in the Campana B fabric were recognized at the site, and have been

---

[68] Mataloto 2002: 191.
[69] EDIA 1999: 374.
[70] Mataloto 2002: 191, 2004a: 40.
[71] Vaz Pinto and Schmitt 2010: 252–57. Mataloto and Williams 2015: 23. The imitation finewares from Caladinho are discussed in detail in Chapter 5.
[72] Mataloto 2002: 197.

used to date the *recinto-torre* at Mariano to the late second or first century BCE (Fig. 4.12).[73] Other ceramics recorded from Mariano include the rim of a globular pot, likely used for cooking, and the base of a thin-walled vessel. Numerous body sherds, including sherds of Baetican amphorae, were recognized but not collected.[74]

R18. Outeiro da Mina
CNS: 19657
CMP Number: 398

The tower-enclosure at Outeiro da Mina is located on a relatively low and easily accessible ridge near the Ribeira do Almuro. The site's position does not permit it to observe much of the landscape, save for a river crossing to the southwest, nor does it offer a particularly defensible position. Instead, this site is only visible when approached from the western bank of the river, and it was this approach that Outeiro da Mina was likely meant to surveil. Little else about the site's location suggests an alternative reason for its presence. There is little arable land in its immediate vicinity, no major colonial cities to protect, and no indigenous settlements to watch. Instead, Outeiro da Mina seems to have been positioned to observe only this river crossing. Doing so would have allowed the inhabitants to keep watch over traffic entering the region.

Like the *recinto-torre* at Castelo / Monte do Mariano, the structure here appears rather poor in its construction, although extant walls are made from very large granite blocks stacked to a height of 1.5 m in some parts of the site. The site is quite large when compared to the *fortins* discussed above. An enclosure wall stretches north to west at a length of 55 m. The northern end of the wall is much narrower at 13 m than the 40 m-wide south end. Within the enclosure wall, the 12 m-long wall of a large structure is visible.[75] The wall is built atop part of the outcrop that forms the ridge.

Few artifacts were recorded at Outeiro da Mina during field survey. One, an amphora sherd, is potentially interesting (Fig. 4.13). Mataloto identifies this sherd as a Lusitanian fabric originating from the western coast near Lisbon.[76] Its stamp reads *Silvi(i)* and is likely a maker's mark. The dearth of dateable stratified materials from this site makes it difficult to date Outeiro da Mina and this stamp, but comparison with other *fortins* and *recintos-torre* suggests a first-century BCE date.[77] Lusitanian amphorae were also recovered during the excavation of Caladinho (discussed in the next chapter).

[73] Mataloto 2002: 198.
[74] Mataloto 2002: 197–99.
[75] Mataloto 2002: 199.
[76] Mataloto 2002: 200.
[77] Boaventura and Banha 2006: 391.

R19. Terrugem
CNS: 19655
CMP Number: 413

The site at Terrugem is positioned in a depression between outcrops of schist. The Riberio do Ordem runs to the east of Terrugem, and the region is considered to be particularly fertile.[78] The site holds little prominence beyond its local landscape, although it does enjoy visual control over the southern course of the nearby river. Very little of the *recinto-torre* at Terrugem is exposed, but nevertheless it is possible to gauge the size of the structure. Judging from the exposed corners, it measures roughly 19.5 m by 17.5 m. The visible walls, constructed of blocks of granite each cut to roughly 1 m in length, rise to a height of a little over 0.5 m, although it is likely that substantially more of this structure may lie beneath the surface.

Hydraulic structures, which make use of Roman *opus signinum*, are located near Terrugem, but their nature and function have only received cursory examination. A single sherd of Hispanic terra sigillata provides the date for this site, but this sherd is likely a contamination brought to the *recinto-torre* during the use of the hydraulic feature.[79] Alternatively, Terrugem may possess a longer occupational period than the majority of the *fortins* and *recintos-torre*. This is true of Castelinhos do Rosário (discussed above), so it is certainly plausible for Terrugem as well. Indeed, Terrugem, like Castelinhos do Rosário, may have been expanded, transformed, or incorporated into a rural Roman villa complex. Only additional fieldwork at this site will provide concrete answers to these questions.

R20. Castelo do Mau Vizinho
CNS: 3946
CMP Number: 438

The *recinto-torre* known as Castelo do Mau Vizinho is situated on a flat-topped, gently sloping hill amid fertile, rolling plains. The hill is topped by an artificial platform measuring roughly 40 m^2 (Fig. 4.14). This platform provides ample visibility over the surrounding countryside.[80] The site was first recognized by M. Heleno in the 1960s, but little fieldwork has been attempted beyond a few informal surveys.[81] Two walls on the north and west sides of the site are visible. The structure's remaining walls are only partially exposed, but appear to follow the course and size of the northern and western walls. The structure was originally

---

[78] Mataloto 2002: 201.
[79] Mataloto 2002: 201.
[80] Mataloto 2002: 202.
[81] Saavedra Machado 1964: 138.

measured to be 16.5 m by 14 m, but Mataloto's investigation of the site revealed that the exposed walls have suffered some degradation over the last few decades.[82]

The walls of Castelo do Mau Vizinho are constructed from worked blocks of granite, unlike the majority of the other *fortins* and *recintos-torre* in the central Alentejo. Each block is a roughly uniform size, and the exposed walls measure 1.5 m thick, unusually sturdy even for a *fortim* or *recinto-torre*. The extant walls rise to a height of a little more than 1 m in some parts.[83] The size of the extant walls strongly suggests the presence of a second floor. As is the case at many of the *fortins* and *recintos-torre*, the area surrounding Castelo do Mau Vizinho is occupied by the remains of a Roman villa, indicated by the presence of column bases, and material from this later structure has obscured the chronology of the *recinto-torre*.[84] Additional fieldwork is needed to confirm whether the villa was constructed immediately following the abandonment of this tower enclosure, but this seems to be a likely scenario given the established settlement pattern.

R21. Santa Justa
CNS: 19665
CMP Number: 438

Like Castelo do Mau Vizinho above and Sempre-Noiva below, Santa Justa is situated very near the later ruins of a Roman villa.[85] This villa site is greatly disturbed by a eucalyptus plantation, and it is impossible to determine the origin of materials on the surface. Unlike the villa, the *recinto-torre* remains largely undisturbed by the eucalyptus. It possesses walls, approximately 1.5 m thick, made from uniform granite blocks. The walls are visible at the surface to a height of 1 m. They form a roughly square structure of around 13.5 m². The site is positioned on a slight elevation.[86] Were it not for the eucalyptus grove, the site's position would give it ample vision of the surrounding plains. Santa Justa's proximity to the nearby villa suggests that the villa was in some way associated with the tower enclosure and perhaps occupied subsequently to the enclosure's abandonment. The disruption of the villa precludes any certainty in this analysis, and additional fieldwork is necessary to confirm the dating of the *recinto-torre* itself.

---

[82] Saavedra Machado 1964: 138; Mataloto 2002: 202.

[83] Mataloto 2002: 202.

[84] Alarcão 1988: 158; Mataloto 2002: 203.

[85] The architectural and artifactual remains of the villa at Santa Justa include column drums, bases, and capitals made of granite, a great deal of brick and tile, and numerous sherds of South Gaulish and Hispanic terra sigillata among other ceramics visible on the surface. See Calado (1994–1995) and Mataloto (2002: 203) for brief discussions of the site.

[86] Mataloto 2002: 203.

R22. Sempre-Noiva (Vale de Sobrados)
CNS: 10185
CMP Number: 437

The spur of bedrock near Sempre-Noiva on the Ribeira de Vale de Sobrados holds a *recinto-torre* at its highest point. Like other *recintos-torre*, this site is located near the remains of a Roman villa that was founded around the same moment that Sempre-Noiva was abandoned.[87] It is therefore not out of the question that the villa was the inheritor of Sempre-Noiva's inhabitants, as appears to be the case at many of the other *fortins* and *recintos-torre*. The tower-enclosure is constructed from large blocks of worked granite, many of which are fitted together with some care. The walls of this structure are particularly large and sturdy because of the size of the granite blocks used in its construction. The size of these blocks was originally used as justification for the classification of this site as a prehistoric "cyclopean" enclosure.[88] The walls are exposed to a height of 1.5 m in many parts of the structure, and are a consistent width of around 1.5 m. The structure itself measures approximately 14 m by 13.5 m. While no artifacts have been recorded at this site, it is comparable to the other *recintos-torre* and *fortins* of the region.

R23. Castelo dos Mouros
CNS: 19653
CMP Number: 448

The tower-enclosure known as Castelo dos Mouros is located on a gently rising hill amid undulating plains. The Ribeira do Divor winds through the landscape to the southeast. The northern and eastern walls of the structure have been lost, but the southern and western walls remain extant (Fig. 4.15). These walls suggest that Castelo dos Mouros was among the larger enclosures in the central Alentejo. The south wall extends 21.5 m while the west wall measures approximately 25 m. Both walls are exposed to a height of over 2 m. The walls are almost 2 m wide in some parts. The extreme thickness of these walls is made possible by the use of exceptionally large—even "cyclopean"—blocks of granite in their construction (Fig. 4.16).[89]

Recent fieldwork at Castelo dos Mouros has provided a fuller picture of its occupation and chronology. Ceramics, including body sherds of Campanian black gloss, several diagnostic pieces of Baetican and Lusitanian amphorae (Fig. 4.17), and local common wares (Fig. 4.18), were present primarily on the southeastern

---

[87] Mataloto (2002: 204) reports the presence of abundant construction materials covering an area of approximately 2 ha around the *recinto-torre*.

[88] Calado 1994–1995; Silva and Perdigão 1998: 138.

[89] Mataloto 2008: 123–28; Mataloto 2002: 205. See Calado (1994–1995) for discussion of other so-called "cyclopean" enclosures of the central Alentejo.

slope near the *recinto-torre*. These finds suggest a first-century BCE foundation for the structure. The surface of the southern slope was found to be littered with materials from the first century CE, including body sherds of Gaulish and Hispanic terra sigillata.[90] Mataloto proposes that this *recintos-torre*, as with the others in the region north of Évora, was built as part of a program of pacification, reorganization, and settlement in the new colony's territory.[91]

R24. Vale d'El-Rei de Cima
CNS: 7086
CMP Number: 448

The site of Val d'El-Rei de Cima, also known as Cabeço do Diabo, is the last of the central Alentejan *fortins* and *recintos-torre* included in this catalogue. It is located atop a small but steep hill that rises over the surrounding plains (Fig. 4.19). The hilltop is 22.5 m by 21 m in size. Walls from the structure are visible at the northern end, and a corner is preserved on the northeastern side of the site. The walls are carefully constructed from worked blocks of granite, each of a uniform size and shape. They are stacked, unmortared, to form the extant wall which is roughly 1.25 m thick at its widest point. The wall rises to a height of just under 1 meter, but it is not fully exposed at the surface.[92]

Val d'El-Rei de Cima is among the best studied of all the *recintos-torre*. Fieldwork undertaken in the 1980s by an English team under the direction of C. Burgess suggests a long period of occupation that likely culminated in the transformation or incorporation of this structure into a larger villa complex. Their survey and cleaning of the site revealed the presence of ceramics dating from the late Iron Age through the early Imperial period, including both South Gaulish terra sigillata and fragments of a Dressel 20 amphora.[93] Subsequent analysis of the materials suggests that the site was primarily occupied during the first century BCE.[94] A great deal of Roman construction material is deposited approximately one hundred meters from the *recintos-torre*, suggesting the presence of a villa.

SURVEILLANCE STRUCTURES AFTER THE FIRST CENTURY BCE

The majority of *fortins* and *recintos-torre*, those which possessed a high degree of topographic prominence, appear to have been abandoned after the first century

---

[90] Mataloto 2008: 128–30.
[91] Mataloto 2008: 130.
[92] Mataloto 2002: 206.
[93] Burgess 1987: 55.
[94] Gibson et al. 1998: 244.

BCE. The disappearance or transformation of the structures involved in surveillance signals the end of the territorial negotiation begun in the mid-first century BCE. Control of the newly organized province of Lusitania and within it the newly reorganized landscape of the central Alentejo was not in question. New settlements and cities occupied this landscape. Italian immigrants, drawn by the prospect of valuable natural resources, began to exploit the territory. And, we should assume, locals who had collaborated or benefited the Roman colonial effort found themselves in a better position than they had before.

Occupation of the areas near some of the *fortins* and *recintos-torre*, however, appears to continue despite the abandonment of those structures. A few even seem to have transformed into villas. For instance, evidence exists for the foundation of first-century CE villas immediately adjacent to the earlier *recintos-torre* north of Évora.[95] Other sites, like Castelinhos do Rosário and perhaps Castelo da Lousa, appear to have developed into fortified, *villa*-like structures from their first phases as simple *fortins*. These structures maintained their surveillance over their surrounding territory, but the nature of the surveillance was altered. Rather than watching a region in order to monitor or control movement through it, these structures instead sought to oversee activities within their own claimed territory. At Castelinhos do Rosário, for example, visibility was maintained over small mines—perhaps worked by slaves—well within the site's viewshed.

As discussed in Chapter 2, proper Roman rural villas were not established in the central Alentejo until the first century CE. Many of these early villas appear to have been built immediately adjacent to abandoned *fortins* and *recintos-torre* or else very near to them.[96] For example, the area south of the Serra d'Ossa—the location of three *fortins* and the indigenous stronghold of Monte do Outeiro—becomes home to eight villas (Fig. 4.20). These structures appear to be situated along the road established between Évora and the provincial capital, *Augusta Emerita*, thus linking them closely with the Roman occupation of the region and its resources.

While none of these sites have yet received significant archaeological investigation, other Alentejan villas do possess some evidence for the presence of surveillance structures, including structures that have sometimes been identified towers.[97] The villa at Torre de Palma, just north of the Serra d'Ossa, may have possessed a tower meant to observe agricultural workers. J. Lancha et al. suggest that a substantial quadrangular foundation near the *pars urbana* represents the remains of a watertower meant to feed the nearby bath.[98] The watertower, according to their reconstruction of the site, was fed by a large, above-ground aqueduct.

---

[95] Mataloto 2002: 203, but see the catalogue above for additional examples.

[96] For an example, the villa of Azinhalinho, known primarily from surface survey, was constructed immediately adjacent to the *fortim* Caladinho (F9). Fig. 4.2 displays their relative positions.

[97] See the discussion of other potential uses for towers at villas in Chapter 3.

[98] Lancha et al. 2000.

No evidence of an aqueduct, either above or below ground, has yet been recovered from the site in over fifty years of archaeological investigation.[99] While this structure may have had some hydraulic purpose (a large cistern is located nearby), it was both well built and well positioned to function as a watchtower which would monitor the adjacent road, groves, pastures, and fields. It is plausible that its primary purpose was the observation of an enslaved (or otherwise subjugated) workforce laboring in the surrounding countryside. Such a purpose would not be unknown among rural farmhouses of the ancient Mediterranean.[100] Nearby, the seventeenth-century farm of Herdade de Palma possesses a large tower of its own, and it was used even in living memory to observe peasants working in the surrounding countryside.

While the evidence for surveillance structures at both Torre de Palma is far from certain, there is good evidence for the use of surveillance in the administration of Roman villas and ancient farmhouses generally. African Red Slip pottery, among the most widely distributed wares in the ancient Mediterranean, sometimes includes depictions of treehouses, manned by slaves, set up to observe olive groves and vineyards.[101] Such ephemeral structures, common enough to be included as decoration on pottery, would leave no archaeological traces. Thus, even villas which do not possess evidence for permanent towers may have operated temporary surveillance systems when slaves were engaged in agricultural work or unharvested crops were vulnerable to banditry.

---

[99] A survey conducted at Torre de Palma in 2005, in which the author participated, set out to search for such an aqueduct. It was determined that no such structure could have existed at the site. If such an aqueduct had existed, it would have been necessary to construct a very large and expensive above-ground span in order to link the villa with the nearest source of groundwater. Instead, the inhabitants of the site likely made use of the multiple cisterns and wells that were installed around the villa. The results of this survey remain unpublished, but see Maloney and Hale 1996; Fugate 2000; Maloney and Hoffstot 2002; Langley 2006; Boaventura and Banha 2006 for further information about Torre de Palma.

[100] For example, Morris and Papadopoulos (2005: 155–57, 188–200) provide an ample discussion of towers associated with farms, vineyards, mines, and quarries in Greece. Moret (1995, 1999, 2010: 18–25) suggests that the *fortins* and *recintos-torre* of the central Alentejo might also be the remains of farmhouses following the same model. Carter (2003: 120–27) discusses the development of Greek and Roman farmhouses with attached towers in the *chora* of Chersonesos.

[101] Stuiber 1959: 86–89; Tortorella 2005: 191–94; van den Hoek and Herrmann 2013: 67–69. These depictions are also discussed in Chapter 3.

CHAPTER 5

THE FIRST CENTURY BCE WATCHTOWER AT CALADINHO

The excavation at Caladinho, near Redondo, Portugal, represents the first systematic archaeological investigation of a *fortim* in the central Alentejo.[1] Caladinho, also known as Castelo da Defensinha or locally as the Casinha do Alfaiate (the "little house of the tailor"), was first identified by J. Almeida in his 1945 catalogue, and the municipal archaeological maps of the late twentieth century also make mention of the structure.[2] The site is located atop a steep-sloped ridge that, while relatively small, represents one of the highest points in the surrounding landscape. The ridge, with the tower set atop it, would have permitted the surveillance of the territory to the north and east between Caladinho, the Serra d'Ossa, and the quarries of the Estremoz Anticline (Fig. 1.2). The land to the west is provided with excellent natural drainage in the form of the Ribeira do Calado, and there is especially good agricultural land near the slope of the ridge.[3] The land to the south and southwest of Caladinho is hilly, rocky, and rugged. It is primarily used for pasture. The ridge itself is dotted with outcrops of schist, and the structure, like many ancient and modern buildings in the Alentejo, is made primarily from this stone.

Caladinho was first investigated in 2002 as part of R. Mataloto's survey of *fortins* and *recintos-torre* in the central Alentejo.[4] Mataloto, the station archaeologist for the municipality of Redondo, reported the presence of artifacts dating to the Chalcolithic and late Iron Age/early Roman period, including lithics, handmade ceramics, Italian terra sigillata and amphorae, glass, metal production waste, and

---

[1] Castelinho dos Mouros, a *recintos-torre* near Alcoutim in the Algarve region, was excavated by a Luso-Austrian team between 2008 and 2012. See Teichner et al. 2010 and Teichner and Schierl 2010. Other similar structures have been excavated in many parts of Iberia. See Maia 1974a, 1974b, 1978, 1986; Maia and Maia 1996; Rodríguez Díaz and Ortiz Romero 2003; Ortiz Romero 1991, 1995, among others.

[2] Almeida 1945; Calado 1993: 55; Calado and Mataloto 2001: 103–104.

[3] Mataloto and Williams 2012: 1.

[4] Mataloto 2002: 179–80.

loom weights of various sizes (Fig. 5.1).[5] Little evidence for a post-Roman occupation of Caladinho appeared during survey, and the site was judged to have seen relatively little disturbance after its abandonment. The project was planned in 2009, and Caladinho was excavated during the summers of 2010 through 2013. The excavation was undertaken with the assistance of numerous Portuguese students and professionals as well as field school students from North America and Europe.[6]

The four seasons of excavation at Caladinho have revealed a substantial, if briefly occupied, set of structures implanted on a hilltop outside of the modern town of Redondo, Portugal. The excavation focused on the top of the ridge, with the primary goal of completely exposing and recording the remains of a small fortified tower and the area surrounding it. The tower itself was named Sector 1, and continues to garner the lion's share of attention (Fig. 5.2). A second structure immediately to the north of the tower was identified at the end of the 2010 season and excavated in 2011 and 2012. This second structure is known as Sector 3 (Fig. 5.3). In all, over 100 m^2 of the hilltop have been systematically excavated to a depth of almost three meters in some areas. A single 2.5 m by 1 m test pit, named Sector 2, was dug on the northeast slope of the hill in 2010, but the ceramic assemblage was contaminated by modern ceramics even at the strata immediately above bedrock (Fig. 5.4).

Caladinho was excavated using the open area methodology described by P. Barker and E. Harris.[7] Each stratigraphic unit (SU) was assigned as changes in context were identified on the basis of differences between deposits. Sectors 1, 2, and 3 contain their own set of SUs. Each SU is given a unique identifying number, most often assigned in ascending order as each unit is revealed and recorded. Sector 1's SUs are expressed as CAL[0], CAL[1], CAL[2], and so on, with CAL[0] representing the opening surface stratum. Sector 2 and Sector 3's SUs are organized in a similar way with the sector number preceding the specific unit number. For instance, Sector 3's SUs are numbered CAL[300], CAL[301], CAL[302], and upward. When initially planned, it was not anticipated that the Caladinho excavation would require more than a single field season. As a result, once Sector 3 was opened, some of the initial, opening-layer SUs from Sector 1 and Sector 3 were

---

[5] Calado and Mataloto 2001: 103–104; Mataloto 2002: 180; Williams and Mataloto 2011: 24; Mataloto et al. 2014: 30–38; Mataloto and Williams 2015; Mataloto et al. 2016: 146–48.

[6] I would like to thank my co-director, R. Mataloto, for his assistance, support, and enthusiasm for the excavation at Caladinho. The staff of the Caladinho Archaeological Project—including B. Bethke, R. Clemente, I. Conde, A. Donnelly, E. Ljung, M. Pawlowski, K. Sheldon, and R. Vennarucci—were each indispensable to this research. Many dozens of field school students and volunteers helped to make this research possible. All work conducted at Caladinho was performed under the auspices of the *Instituto de Gestão do Património Arquitectónico e Arqueológico*, the *Direção-Geral do Património Cultural*, the PortAnta Archaeological Cooperative, and the Municipality of Redondo, Portugal.

[7] Barker 2005; Harris 1989.

shared. For instance, while Sector 1's surface unit is CAL[0], the same surface layer covering Sector 3 is CAL[300]. The precise relationships between Sector 1's SUs are properly expressed by the site's Harris Matrix (Fig. 5.5). Sector 3's SUs, however, only overlap Sector 1's at the uppermost surface layers and so are not included on the above Harris Matrix.

Both diagnostic and non-diagnostic artifacts were recorded in the site catalogue. For ease of recording, each diagnostic artifact—defined as a rim, base, handle, decorated or otherwise uniquely interesting pottery sherd, or an artifact of a material other than ceramic—was assigned an artifact number. Examples of fineware, such as Italian terra sigillata (ITS), received an artifact number regardless of whether it was properly diagnostic. Each SU possesses its own set of artifact numbers, usually assigned in ascending order. For example, CAL[100] possesses over twenty artifacts, among them the rim of a Lusitanian pot numbered CAL[100]21. Another rim sherd from the same unit is numbered CAL[100]22. When discussed here, the "CAL" designation will be omitted. Non-diagnostic artifacts, most often body sherds, were assigned the number of their SU but not a unique artifact number. These body sherds were each carefully sorted by ware or, when possible, by their fabric. Once sorted, they were counted and weighed, and they are included in the discussion below.

A significant amount of prehistoric pottery dating to the Chalcolithic period was recovered from Caladinho in addition to the materials dating to the early Roman period. These prehistoric ceramics suggest that the hilltop was occupied long before the period in question here, but there is no evidence for the occupation of the site in the intervening millennia. The prehistoric pottery and other artifacts—including lithics, cylindrical loom weights, and an exceptionally well preserved bronze point—were used as fill for the tower and associated structures (Fig. 5.6).[8] While they are suggestive of a substantial and long-lived inhabitation of Caladinho during the Chalcolithic period, by the first century BCE they are more properly considered to be construction material. Identifying and separating the prehistoric ceramics from the rest of the assemblage resulted in the creation of the fabric typology discussed below.

THE ARCHAEOLOGICAL REMAINS

Much of the structure at Caladinho is remarkably well preserved. Some of the walls of the main structure, the tower, survive to a height of over 2 m (Fig. 5.7).

---

[8] A fuller analysis of the Chalcolithic artifacts from Caladinho and a brief discussion of the prehistoric occupation of the site are presented in other publications, including Mataloto and Williams 2011, 2012, and Williams and Mataloto 2011. Mataloto et al. (2007) provides useful contextualization for the prehistoric materials at Caladinho through a discussion of a major Chalcolithic fortification called São Pedro.

The exterior walls of the tower are each roughly a meter thick, and a significant amount of building material—including rough schist, prehistoric ceramics, and a few unfired bricks—was recovered from the interior of the tower (Fig. 5.8). The interior walls of the structure, although braced during excavation, lean precariously, indicating that the tower collapsed inward and onto itself (Fig. 5.9). Together, these suggest that the tower at Caladinho was originally quite tall, with a first story between 2.5 m and 3 m, and a second story of roughly the same height constructed from lighter materials like mud brick.[9]

While the structure appears to have been constructed without the use of mortar, some of the excavated deposits indicate that the walls were surfaced with clay, and perhaps even plastered. Similar construction techniques continue to be used in the Alentejo (Fig. 5.10). The plastered (and sometimes painted) surface protects the interior of the wall from the elements. Weathering can remove the plaster covering and, within only a few years, the walls may become unstable and collapse. At Caladinho the walls appear to have collapsed inward, filling the interior of the first floor with rubble and materials from the second floor. Judging from the multitude of SUs, particularly near the walls of Sector 1, the deterioration of the tower was at first a slow gradual process that progressed to a final catastrophic collapse.

Sector 1 comprises the tower that once dominated the hilltop. The structure is relatively small, 9 m by 5 m, and possesses a single ground-floor entrance on the eastern side of the northern corner (Fig. 5.3). The southern corner of the structure does not survive, probably because of erosive processes, but the majority of the walls are in good condition. The external walls of the tower are a relatively uniform size of 1 m, while the two supporting internal walls are roughly half that width. Some parts of the wall have been disturbed by the growth of tree roots, and evidence of similar bioturbulation extends into the deeper SUs of the sector.

Sector 1 may be divided into four rooms: the entrance, storeroom, hallway, and large room. Each room has been excavated down to bedrock, and the internal faces of every wall have been exposed. A simple stone paving is placed immediately inside the entrance and provides a platform for stepping down into the hallway or the storeroom (Fig. 5.11). The storeroom, originally a narrow area beneath the stairs to the second floor, was carved on its northeastern side into an outcropping of bedrock. The other sides, and the extant upper part of the northeastern wall, were built in the same manner as the rest of the structure. The inward collapse of the structure deposited the stairs ([93])—formed from large flat slabs of schist—inside the storeroom (Fig. 5.12). The result was that the contents of the storeroom were trapped beneath the stairs and, while all were crushed to a greater of lesser degree, much of the storeroom's contents are preserved. They are discussed in greater detail below. The staircase itself was accessed from the exterior of the tow-

---

[9] Friedman (2008: 205), in her study of observation towers around Roman imperial mines in Jordan, estimates the height of these towers to be 6 m, roughly the same as at Caladinho.

er through a second door. The pivot point for this door is visible on the exterior of the tower, and a bronze handle, [96]3, recovered from the SU immediately below the fallen stairs, may belong to this door (Fig. 5.13).

Passing by the storeroom, the entrance turns left into a hallway roughly the same length as the storeroom. This hallway ends at its southwestern end with a door to the large room. The southwestern wall of the hallway divides the tower into two roughly equivalent halves. There was, however, no apparent need for this hallway. The southwestern wall could have been omitted, leaving a larger area open inside the tower, or access to the large room could have been provided by an opening immediately in line with the entrance (thereby creating a second narrow storeroom). Instead, the builders positioned the two entrances to the hallway on opposite ends, complicating access to the large room and creating a space, the hallway, which could not be used for storage. This was probably done for reasons of structural stability. The second internal wall provided additional support for the upper floor(s). The floor of the second story, probably made of wood, needed to span only half of the structure without support at most. The placement of the two entrances at opposite ends of the hallway may also reflect a desire to control access to the large room of the tower.

The large room itself, which makes up the southern half of the tower's ground floor, has remained stratigraphically complex throughout its excavation. Numerous layers of debris, including very many large schist stones, filled the room to a depth of over 2 m. Their removal revealed that the western corner of the tower was, like the eastern corner, built atop an outcrop of bedrock. This outcrop, however, is much larger, and rises to a height of over 3 m above the current ground level and over 5 m above the ground floor of the tower (Fig. 5.14). The tower must have been at least 5 m in order for its inhabitants to see over the outcrop which today dominates the hilltop.

While the southern corner of the large room is not preserved *in situ*, the walls are otherwise in good condition (Fig. 5.15). The excavation also revealed that the room was originally floored with packed earth at a level lower than the hallway. The entrance to the large room from the hallway was marked with a stone threshold, but no evidence of a door survives. The packed earth floor was raised from the uneven bedrock by means of a fill made from debris, including both residual Chalcolithic artifacts and large fragments of a late Iron Age/early Roman period storage vessel, recorded primarily as feature [133]. The majority of the fragments of this vessel were recovered against the northwestern wall of the large room, which suggests that it might have been a whole vessel set into the floor at the time of the structure's collapse. Yet all the fragments were recovered with their exterior sides facing the wall indicating that they had been consciously placed in that position individually.

Sector 3 is located to the north of Sector 1 (Fig. 5.3). Excavation of the area has revealed the presence of a second structure on the hilltop, one roughly equivalent to the tower in size. Two entrances provide access to the Sector 3 structure. The first is on the easternmost corner of the northeastern wall, while the second is directly opposite on the southeastern corner. Both entrances are in line with the entrance to the ground floor of the tower. The walls of Sector 3 are roughly 0.5 m thick, the same size as the internal walls of Sector 1. These thinner external walls indicate that this structure was comprised of only a single story. It too has been successfully excavated to bedrock. The amount of debris in this structure was less substantial than that excavated from Sector 1 and included a great deal more burned clay. It is likely that the walls of this secondary structure were constructed primarily from mud brick atop the dry schist foundations. As in Sector 1, the floor of this structure was leveled, with some areas of bedrock cut flat and other deeper areas filled in. A large hearth was constructed against the southeastern wall of the structure (Fig. 5.16). Thus this room undoubtedly served a domestic purpose, although domestic artifacts also appear in the tower itself.

Additional connected structures to the northeast of Sector 3 have yet to be completely excavated as of 2016. Surface finds and visible features indicate that at least one building in roughly the same dimensions as the tower and the structure in Sector 3 remain to be uncovered. Given the secure brief chronology presented in Sector 1 and Sector 3 and the apparent single phase of construction and occupation during the late first century BCE, excavation of the remainder of the hilltop is not necessary for our understanding of the site.

Dating the structure

The stratigraphic sequence at Caladinho appears complicated at first glance, but several sherds from different SUs possess joins (Fig. 5.5). Among these is the base of an ITS platter recovered in three different stratigraphic contexts, recorded as artifacts [2]1, [23]2, and [129]1 (Fig. 5.17). Once joined together, the entire ring foot of the base is preserved. Another example consists of two fragments, [42]7 and [81]4, of a Baetican imitation fineware cup. These finds, although scattered both horizontally and vertically on the site, indicate either that the collapse of the upper floors was sudden and violent or that the site was thoroughly disturbed—perhaps scavenged—in antiquity. If the latter were true, we would expect to find materials that postdate the late first-century BCE to early first-century CE chronology of the remainder of the assemblage. No mid- to late first-century CE materials have been recovered from stratified contexts or from the surface. Indeed, the material remains from the surface of the site suggest that the hilltop was entirely abandoned between the early first century CE and the modern period.

Despite the paucity of later ceramics contaminating the site, there are some indications of scavenging or a secondary occupation at Caladinho. The bronze door handle excavated near the bottom of the storeroom in Sector 1 is the only extant example of an architectural decoration to be recovered (Fig. 5.13). This single bronze fixture was discovered during the second season of excavation at a depth of almost 2 m from the original surface. It stands to reason that other valuable fixtures were originally part of Caladinho, but were perhaps more easily accessible to looters. Nevertheless, this evidence is largely circumstantial, and the individual artifacts that are preserved may be the result of other formation processes.

Apart from residual Chalcolithic artifacts incorporated into the structure, the assemblage suggests that Caladinho was occupied circa 50 BCE to 20 CE. Four stamped ITS fragments provide the primary evidence for this dating, and they are supported by a number of other dateable finds. The first, recorded as [19]1, is a stamped base of a small Italian terra sigillata bowl of uncertain typology (Fig. 5.18). The stamp is very hard to read, since the text contains several ligatures. I read this stamp as *Camur(ius) f(ecit)*, a name attested in ITS productions found in Lusitania.[10] This vessel was probably produced during the first decades of the first century CE, and is probably an example of the last ceramics used at Caladinho or else it may be an intrusive artifact from the years soon after its abandonment.

The next stamped vessel, [8]1, was among the first artifacts used to establish the Caladinho's chronology (Fig. 5.19). It is the base of a small bowl of form *Consp.* B1.2 with a radial internal stamp that reads *Dar/eus* (Fig. 5.20). Examples from Dareus' workshop are not well known, but the stamp dates to 30–20 BCE and is thought to originate from Lyon, intended for the legions stationed on the German *limes*.[11] Its presence here at Caladinho, far from the German *limes*, represents tenuous evidence for a connection between these towers and central Portugal's legionary garrison.

Another ITS stamp, this time on the interior of a small cup of form *Consp.* 14.1, was excavated from Sector 1 during the first season. The vessel was broken into several pieces when discovered, and is catalogued as [17]1, [17]2, [17]3, [17]4, and [58]6. This last fragment was uncovered during the second season of excavation in a substantially deeper SU. The stamp, not recorded in the *Corpus Vasorum Arretinorum*, reads *Avil(i) / fig(uli)* (Fig. 5.21). H. Dressel records this stamp among other *instrumenta domestica* in his addition to the *CIL*, but there is no other published example of it readily available.[12] Stamps of Avilius are relatively common, and many different examples are known, but none exhibit the title *figulus* ("potter"). The other examples of Avilius' stamps date to between 20 BCE and 40 CE, which suggests that this example dates to this period also.[13] Further narrowing the potential dates of production, stamps from other potteries that include the title *figulus* were produced only briefly between 30 and 15 BCE.[14]

[10] OCK 514–16; Jérez Linde 2005: 65, fig. 20 no. 31.
[11] OCK 724.
[12] *CIL* XV.5047.
[13] OCK 371.
[14] OCK 2168, 2398.

The third stamp is the least legible. It is placed on a small sherd, [23]3, probably the bottom of a small cup or bowl, but no trace of the foot survives to provide a typological identification. The stamp is divided into two registers separated by a laurel branch. The top line is badly damaged, and the bottom line is also missing at least part of one letter. It reads, perhaps, *Dio(medes) / Ṣcro(fula)* (Fig. 5.22). Stamps from the workshop of A. Vibius Scrofula are well known, although a potter by the name of Diomedes is not recorded on any other stamp from Scrofula. This workshop is thought to have produced terra sigillata between the years 20 and 5 BCE.[15]

Excavation also recovered three sherds of Campanian black gloss ware, but only two of these were diagnostic. Both appear to have originated at the end of the black gloss industry, although, as is discussed below, this fineware continued to influence the pottery traditions of the central Alentejo during the late first century BCE, given that many imitations were produced in the same forms. The first black gloss sherd, [70]1, is a rim from a large platter, form Lamboglia 7, produced in a buff, clean, cream-colored fabric with a very fine matte black slip (Fig. 5.23). Considering the above dates, this is most likely an example of the last Campana B productions of the latter half of the first century BCE.[16]

The second sherd, [314]1, is a ring-footed base with a large stamp on the interior center of the vessel (Fig. 5.24). The stamp is a diamond with four radial arms terminating in the shape of petals. This stamp appears on other black gloss *paterae* from the latter half of the first century BCE.[17] The fabric of this sherd is a uniform grey with few inclusions and sharp, concave, glass-like breaks. The slip is brown and not well preserved. It is probable that this sherd, like *comparanda* from Castelo da Lousa and Mesas do Castelinho, was produced in southern Baetica, rather than in Campania, at the end of the first century BCE.[18] Other examples of this black gloss production appear in great numbers in central and southern Iberia. This Iberian black gloss production likely grew out of a desire for Italian-type finewares among Roman settlers, soldiers, and their local allies in the peninsula. Indeed, given the similarity of this vessel's stamp and that found on Campanian black gloss ware, it is possible that some Italian potters, perhaps attached to the army, began producing these finewares in their new homes in Baetica during the end of the first century BCE.

Other chronologically significant artifacts support the above dates. Among these are two ITS rim sherds. While these vessels are not stamped, they are of a form, *Consp.* 7.1, commonly thought to have been produced during the middle to

---

[15] OCK 2411.

[16] I thank J. Principal for his assistance with the identification of this form and fabric.

[17] Pedroni 2000: 197.

[18] For Castelo da Lousa, see Luís 2010: 112–14; Wahl 1985: fig. 6. For Mesas do Castelinho, see Alves 2010: 78.

late Augustan period.[19] Both, catalogued as [90]1 and [94]1, are small fragments of plain-rimmed bowls or cups with slightly sloping walls (Fig. 5.25). Late republican amphorae of the Haltern 70 type were also recovered from Caladinho during both the preliminary survey and the excavation. Among the best preserved is an amphora mouth catalogued as [100]7 (Fig. 5.26). In a recent review of this form, C. Carreras Monfort suggested that Haltern 70 amphorae were produced in Baetica along the Guadalquivir from 80 BCE to the second century CE.[20] A fragment of an amphora in a cream-colored fabric, probably from a Haltern 70 amphora, was incorporated into the northeastern wall of the large room in Sector 1. While no positive identification of the sherd can be made while it is embedded in the wall, it strongly suggests that the tower at Caladinho was built during the first century BCE, especially when considered alongside ceramics like the ones discussed above.

Taken together, these artifacts suggest that Caladinho was built during the latter half of the first century BCE and occupied perhaps as late as the first decade of the first century CE. Such a brief, secure chronology, despite the presence of residual Chalcolithic materials, positions Caladinho squarely amid the tumultuous early years of the Roman presence in the central Alentejo. Given the nature of the rest of the artifact assemblage and the architectural remains, it seems likely that the primary occupation of Caladinho lasted at most only half a century. The short-lived use of Caladinho and other sites like it in the area indicates that their role in the landscape was limited to the negotiation of colonial power in central Portugal under the Romans.

Ceramic classes

The artifact assemblage recovered from Caladinho during the 2002 survey and the 2010 through 2013 excavations includes 7570 pottery sherds. When analyzed, these sherds were divided by class (a largely functional category), by form and typology, and by their fabric. Identifying the different ceramic fabrics present at Caladinho was especially beneficial since it permitted us to excise the prehistoric ceramics from the remainder of the assemblage.[21] Additionally, the different fabrics at Caladinho point to the material, economic, and social connections between this site, its most local neighbors, and the larger Mediterranean region. Analysis of vessel forms, with typological identification made whenever possible, allows for

---

[19] *Consp.*: 64.

[20] Carreras Monfort 2003.

[21] The residual Chalcolithic and few intrusive modern surface materials were separated out from the total assemblage since they were not relevant to the interpretation of the tower beyond their use as fill and construction material. These ceramics will be presented in the final report of the excavation at Caladinho where they will be crucial to the interpretation of the prehistoric occupation of the hilltop. The sherds from the test pit, Sector 2, were likewise not included when quantifying the total ceramic assemblage since that sector was contaminated by modern materials. Once done, a catalogue of 4,849 sherds from Sectors 1, 3, and 4 was organized and analyzed.

a discussion not only of daily life at the site but also a discussion of the cultural identity of Caladinho's inhabitants.

The ceramic assemblage is organized below into six different classes: finewares, imitation finewares, common wares, cookwares, transport pottery, and storage pottery. Each sherd was assigned to one of these categories based upon its apparent function. The finewares represent those especially well-made tablewares, usually imported from Italy, that are often understood as markers of Roman identity or at least dining habits. At Caladinho they include Italian terra sigillata (ITS), thin-walled wares from Italy and southern Iberia, and a few rare pieces of Campanian black gloss ware. They are especially useful for dating, as discussed above, because of their well-understood typologies and chronologies of production. Additionally, they are easily recognized because fineware sherds often possess noticeably cleaner fabrics, slips, or especially delicate forms.

Imitation finewares, like true finewares, serve as tablewares, but they are locally made, and often possess inferior fabrics and crude attempts at mimicking the forms of true finewares. At Caladinho, this class of ceramic is easily recognizable in the assemblage, and as will be discussed below, was largely produced locally. The imitation finewares from Caladinho recall the forms of both Campanian black gloss and ITS vessels.[22] While their fabrics lack the purity of true finewares, they have undergone a more thorough process of levigation than other local productions. Even more interesting, the imitation finewares from Caladinho appear to be highly burnished, perhaps an attempt at matching the slip present on black gloss and terra sigillata vessels. Some imitation finewares were formed in the local reddish clay, making them appear outwardly similar to terra sigillata vessels in both form and color. Others, however, appear to have been intentionally overfired, or fired in a reducing atmosphere, leaving them blackened not only on the surface but also throughout the fabric of these sherds. This may have been an attempt at matching the color of black gloss wares. Given the temperatures necessary to achieve this degree of overfiring, the breakage rate during the production of this local imitation of Campanian black gloss must have been quite high. Attempting such a costly mode of production may reflect the growing desire for Roman style tableware in this isolated colonial landscape in the first century BCE.

Roman transport pottery, primarily amphorae, is also easily recognized in an artifact assemblage. The amphorae from Caladinho represent a small but important part of the assemblage. The diagnostic sherds, while few in comparison to the number of non-diagnostic body pieces, suggest linkages between Caladinho and its wider economic region. Amphorae are best typologized by their handles, rims,

---

[22] Vaz Pinto and Schmitt (2010: 252–57) include forty-three examples of imitation black gloss and Italian terra sigillata in their catalogue of ceramics from Castelo da Lousa. Interestingly, at Castelo da Lousa examples of imitation Campanian black gloss greatly outnumber examples of imitation terra sigillata. The imitation finewares from both Caladinho and Castelo da Lousa are compared below.

or toes, but the relative uniformity and purity of most amphora fabrics makes body sherds from each class relatively easy to recognize in an assemblage. At Caladinho they are present in only three general fabric types: 1) those produced in southern Spain around the bay of Cadiz or north along the Guadalquivir River, 2) those produced on the western coast of the peninsula along the Tejo or lower Sado rivers, and 3) those produced in a local fabric, "Fab. 2a," which is discussed further below.

Cookwares, like finewares, are especially interesting for what they suggest about ancient dining practices and, by extension, identity. Pompeiian Red Ware baking pans and covers, for example, have long been considered a marker of a Roman presence.[23] Roman cuisine included casseroles, stews, and baked breads, none of which appear in the central Alentejo prior to the Roman conquest. Numerous baking pans and covers (all in local clay) were recovered from Caladinho in addition to other examples of cookware, especially globular cooking pots.[24] While all examples of cookware from Caladinho appear to have been locally produced, their forms are often very similar to cookwares produced during the same period in Italy. This comparison is discussed in greater detail below. Cookwares are best characterized as having a fabric tempered by medium to large inclusions. These inclusions help the vessel to withstand the thermal shock concomitant with repeated applications of fire. Additionally, as would be expected from their usage, cookwares are very often blackened by soot and fire on one side.

Storage pottery, because of the size of the vessels involved, often dominates the total weight of an assemblage. Storage vessels are large, often installed into the floors of sites, and used to hold grain, water, or other products. They are recognizable by the thickness and size of the sherds, as well as the presence of medium to large inclusions in the fabric meant to help the vessel weather the strains of shrinkage and firing during production. Roman storage vessels, known as *dolia*, were oval-shaped vessels with wide, open mouths. Very few storage vessels which are recognizable as *dolia* have been recovered from Caladinho. Instead, the storage vessels appear to be primarily in the local indigenous tradition. These local storage vessels are easily recognizable by the incised (by a finger or tool) and undulating wave decoration on the shoulder.[25] This decorative motif appears to have been relatively common during the latter half of the first century BCE and may be an adaptation of a stamped decoration common in the region during the late Iron Age.[26]

Common ware, as a class of ceramics, represents a very large and sometimes

[23] Hayes 2008: 119–20.

[24] Olcese (2003: 26–28) reports very similar cooking ware forms from Rome and sites around it during the first century BCE and first century CE.

[25] Vaz Pinto and Schmitt 2010: figs. 95–113.

[26] Vaz Pinto and Schmitt 2010: 322–23; Vaz Pinto 2003: 567; Mataloto 2002: 179–80; Fabião 1996: 49, 1998: 90; Fabião and Guerra 1987: 291.

indistinct category. Common ware includes those vessels whose form, fabric, or function precludes them from being a part of other classes. They may be used for serving, mixing, storage, or any number of other purposes. Roman common wares from the Alentejo were first typologized thanks to the efforts of J. U. Smit Nolen.[27] Her typology of common wares from the Alto Alentejo, derived from whole vessels excavated from a number of *necropoleis* around Vila Viçosa, remains essential to the archaeology of the region.[28] Nevertheless, our understanding of the forms and fabrics of late republican common wares from the Alentejo lacks much definition.[29] In addition to the expected bowls, plates, and pots, Roman-period common wares also appear in a number of lidded jugs and pitchers. Lidded forms were unknown in the Alentejo prior to contact with the Romans and so these forms represent an important part of the ceramic assemblage from Caladinho.

These classes should be understood as descriptive rather than prescriptive. That is, the attempt at separating the assemblage into classes based on the supposed function must take into account that while function might usually be derived from form, there always remains the possibility that any given ceramic vessel was used for purposes other than what was originally intended. A transport amphora, for example, could be repurposed as a storage vessel, particularly at a site where an amphora does not necessarily represent the most convenient mode of packaging and shipping. With this interpretive hurdle in mind, the ceramic evidence is presented according to this classification below.

Ceramic fabrics

Analysis of the ceramic assemblage revealed eight recognizable fabrics among the diagnostic sherds, not including the fabrics of finewares already established. These were named Fab. 1, Fab. 1a, Fabs. 2a, 2b, and 2c, Fab. 3, Lusitanian, and Baetican.[30] The latter two fabrics are imported from the coastal areas of the peninsula. Lusitanian pottery was produced on the western coast near Lisbon, along the Tejo and lower Sado rivers. Baetican pottery comes primarily from the bay of Cadiz or north of Cadiz along the Guadalquivir River. Fab. 1, made up of 2,407 total sherds, represents the residual Chalcolithic pottery at Caladinho. It is a very poor fabric

---

[27] Smit Nolen 1985.

[28] Problematically, Smit Nolen's analysis of fabric colors appears to have been made on the exterior surface of sherds rather than on fresh breaks. Given the many pre- and post-depositional processes that can affect the color of a vessel's surface, it is advisable to ignore her record of the color of Alentejan common wares. Later work, particularly the fabric catalogue developed by Vaz Pinto and Schmitt (2010: 223–41), has done much to correct this deficiency in Smit Nolen's analysis.

[29] Vaz Pinto and Schmitt 2010: 222–23. The publication of the common wares from Castelo da Lousa represents a great leap forward in our understanding of Alentejan common wares of the first century BCE

[30] A. Donnelly and R. Mataloto assisted in the creation of this fabric catalogue.

with many small, medium, and large inclusions, reddish-orange to grey colored fabric, and a rough surface texture. It is best characterized as rocks held together by clay. Vessels in this fabric were hand-built as wheel-throwing technology did not exist in western Iberia during the Chalcolithic period. Complicating matters, however, is Fab. 1a. It is in all respects identical to Fab. 1 save for the appearance of marks on the surface of the sherds which indicate that the vessels have been turned on a wheel. Fab. 1a may represent a surviving production of the earlier Chalcolithic ware adapted to the technology of the potter's wheel. Whatever the case, it is rare in the assemblage, represented by only 19 diagnostic sherds.

The second series of fabrics, Fabs. 2a, 2b, and 2c, represents local productions. They are each produced from the same or similar clay sources and include several hues of red (2.5 YR 4/6), reddish brown (5 YR 4/4), dark red (2.5 YR 3/6), and reddish black (2.5 YR 2.5/1).[31] Pottery in this fabric continues to be produced in the region around Caladinho, and examples can be purchased from the potters in the nearby town of Redondo. Fab. 2a is widely distributed among several different classes of ceramic, predominantly common wares, but also appears in cookwares, storage wares, and even locally produced amphorae. It possesses a rough-textured fabric with small to medium white and dark grey inclusions. Fab. 2b is similar in its composition, but possesses many more of the same inclusions with some additional quartzite inclusions. It appears primarily in cookware, but examples of Fab. 2b also appear in Caladinho's common ware, storage pottery, and local amphorae. Fab. 2c is a cleaner, well-levigated version of the previous local fabrics. While produced from the same clay sources as Fab. 2a and Fab. 2b, it possesses fewer inclusions. Those present are the same white and dark grey inclusions, but of an even more reduced size. Examples of Fab. 2c are all imitation finewares with some few exceptions done in relatively fine common ware. When freshly broken, examples of Fab. 2 possess relatively smooth textures. Some examples of Fab. 2c seem to have been intentionally exposed to unusually high temperatures and perhaps a reducing atmosphere during production in order to give them the appearance of Campanian black gloss ware. Individual examples from these fabrics are discussed below.

Fab. 3, like the locally produced Fab. 2c, appears almost exclusively in imitation finewares. One rare exception is a fragment of a small hand-built lamp, [106]8, recovered from the occupational layers of the tower's ground floor. Fab. 3 appears in colors that range from yellowish-red (5 YR 4/6) to black (2.5 Y 2.5/1), with the majority of examples tending toward the latter hue. Fab. 3 appears well levigated and so possesses far fewer and far smaller inclusions than the Fab. 2 series. Those inclusions that are present are easy to distinguish from other fabrics in the assemblage. They are primarily very small black inclusions with additional flecks of mica present in some Fab. 3 sherds. Additionally, the surfaces of Fab. 3 sherds are

---

[31] Colors were derived from the *Munsell Soil Color Chart*.

almost always very well burnished. Unlike the more local fabrics, Fab. 3 appears almost sandy in texture. Fab. 3 appears very similar in its inclusions, texture, and color to examples originating from the Tejo and lower Sado river valleys near Lisbon, a fabric here referred to as Lusitanian.

Lusitanian fabrics are similar to Fab. 3 in most respects.[32] They exist in only two classes of ceramic from Caladinho, amphorae and common ware, indicating that Fab. 3 may be an imitation fineware originating from these same clay beds and production sites near Lisbon on the western coast. Lusitanian fabrics are best characterized by their orange to orange-red clays (primarily 2.5 YR 5/6 red), the presence of small white, black, and mica inclusions, and sandy or gritty breaks. Some differences between Lusitanian amphorae and common ware fabrics (and between those fabrics and Fab. 3) are apparent, but are likely the result of the different clay compositions necessary for forming these functionally different ceramic classes. In the first century CE and later, Lusitanian amphorae became very common among the assemblages of coastal sites in Portugal, Spain, and the Mediterranean.[33]

Like the Lusitanian fabrics, Baetican fabrics display some compositional differences across the different ceramic classes produced in it. Pottery in Baetican fabric originates along the southern Guadalquivir River, primarily around the bay of Cadiz, although numerous other workshops exist in the region.[34] The pottery, particularly amphorae and imitation fineware, produced along the bay of Cadiz are in an especially clean, well-levigated version of the fabric. Other production centers located along the Guadalquivir north of Cadiz exported examples of the same vessels in poorer versions of the fabric, although distinguishing between different regional products is sometimes impossible without chemical analysis. Despite these differences of quality, as a whole vessels in Baetican fabrics are relatively easy to recognize in an assemblage. The fabric is a creamy white color, and often chalky in texture, especially in the cleanest examples of fineware. Examples produced outside of the bay of Cadiz are sometimes more yellow or orange in color and possess far more inclusions. Baetican amphorae (discussed above as well as in the next section) represent the largest portion of the transport pottery from Caladinho.

Some other fabrics are also recognizable in Caladinho's assemblage.[35] While each is only a very small (even singular) part of the total assemblage, they repre-

---

[32] For fuller descriptions of this fabric and the amphorae produced in it, see Dias et al. 2012; Morais and Fabião 2007; Arruda et al. 2006; Pimenta et al. 2006; Diogo 1987.

[33] Morais 2010b, 2003; Pimenta et al. 2006.

[34] Almeida (2008) provides an overview of Baetican amphorae, their forms and fabrics, and the place of this industry in both Iberia and the wider Mediterranean.

[35] In comparison to the ceramic assemblage at Caladinho, Vaz Pinto and Schmitt (2010: 223–42) distinguish eighteen different local fabrics present at Castelo da Lousa. Castelo da Lousa's greater size and longer occupational period no doubt contribute to its larger number of identified fabrics.

sent some material connection with other regions. The most notable of these is the grey fabric which probably originated from the area of Granada in the southeastern part of Spain. This fabric is quite clean and uniformly grey in color with only a few small white and black inclusions in the larger vessels. Only seven diagnostic examples of this fabric have been excavated from Caladinho, with the majority being particularly fine examples of local common ware or true imitations of Roman fineware forms. A single example of a thin-walled ware in this fabric was also recovered from the site. While this grey fabric and its production and distribution in Central Portugal are not yet well understood, its presence at Caladinho suggests further peninsular connections for the site's inhabitants.

Analysis of the ceramic assemblage

This section is not intended as a comprehensive catalogue of every ceramic fragment recovered from Caladinho. Instead, it provides a description of the most important examples from each class of ceramic and a discussion of their relevance to the interpretation of this surveillance structure within the larger context of a colonized landscape. Additionally, this section provides quantification of the artifact assemblage, first beginning with the whole and then quantifying each ceramic class in turn. This qualitative and quantitative evidence is discussed here in order to support the final section of this chapter's analysis of occupational period at Caladinho.

The total ceramic assemblage from Caladinho numbers 7,570 individual sherds. Chalcolithic pottery in Fab. 1, intrusive modern ceramics, and materials from Sector 2 were excluded from any additional sorting or analysis (although the Chalcolithic pottery will be examined independent of the first century BCE material at a later date). The non-diagnostic sherds were sorted by their basic ceramic class, as defined above, and quantified according to the total count of sherds and total weight of sherds from each class. Diagnostic sherds were analyzed in additional detail. Out of the assemblage of 4,849 sherds thus analyzed, the majority are, unsurprisingly, common ware (Fig. 5.27). When measured, the total assemblage weighs almost 230 kg. Minus the Chalcolithic pottery and the contaminated material from the Sector 2 test pit, the assemblage weighs in at 181.83 kg. The total weight of the assemblage is dominated by the much larger and heavier sherds of storage pottery that comprise only 21 percent of the total number of sherds (Fig. 5.28).

Despite common ware and storage vessels dominating the total count and total weight of the assemblage respectively, some interesting patterns emerge. Tablewares, including finewares and imitation/regional finewares, make up 11 percent of the total number of sherds, roughly equivalent to the number of cookware sherds present on the site. The paucity of cookware at Caladinho may be the result of the relatively short occupational period. Since the site was only occupied for a relatively brief period, there was little opportunity for the normally high breakage rate of cookware to necessitate much replacement. The desire for Roman-style finewares—be they imported from Italy, produced in a nearby region, or produced in the central Alentejo itself—is evident. The inhabitants of Caladinho desired to eat from characteristically Roman tablewares. Indeed, as discussed above, they were so desirous for Roman black gloss and terra sigillata that they turned to locally produced imitations when the number of imported vessels failed to meet the demand. The relative dearth of amphorae similarly emphasizes the isolated nature of Caladinho. Making up only 3 percent of the total number of sherds and 6 percent of the total weight of the assemblage, transport pottery remains a rare find at the site. The forms that have been recognized at Caladinho are important for dating the site, as discussed above, but also point to the inhabitant's limited connection to other parts of the Mediterranean—or even to other parts of the Iberian Peninsula.

The proportion of local versus imported pottery also emphasizes the isolated nature of Caladinho. Locally produced ceramics dominate the assemblage, representing 86 percent of the total sherd count (Fig. 5.29) and 89 percent of the total sherd weight (Fig. 5.30). The remaining fraction of the total sherd count is divided between Iberian and Italian imports. The two major centers of ceramic production in first century BCE Iberia—the bay of Cadiz/Guadalquivir and western Tejo/lower Sado river valleys—contribute 11 percent of the total count of the assemblage. Pottery in the easily recognizable Baetican fabric, produced primarily around the bay of Cadiz, makes up 6 percent of this fraction, while ceramics in the Lusitanian fabric, produced near the mouth of the Tejo and Sado rivers around Lisbon, make up the other 5 percent. The ceramics at Caladinho that were produced outside of western Iberia include sherds of Italian terra sigillata, Campanian black gloss ware, and thin-walled ware. These sherds represent only 2 percent of the total count and less than 1 percent of the total weight (this last number is in large part thanks to the small, fine nature of most sherds of these types). The last fraction of the assemblage is made up of sherds whose provenance is unknown or uncertain.

Altogether, the ITS sherds from Caladinho represent a miniscule part of the total assemblage in comparison to the other larger classes of pottery. The artifact assemblage includes only fifty-eight individual ITS vessels (including the pottery important to the chronology of the site discussed above). Thirty-two of these are represented by non-diagnostic body sherds. The remaining twenty-six ITS vessels fall into two categories: small cups and bowls and larger serving platters. The specific forms include cups or bowls of forms *Consp.* 7.1, 8.1, 14.1, 24.1, and 26 (Fig. 5.31) and larger plates and platters of *Consp.* 10, 12.1, and 12.2 (Fig. 5.32).

These forms are commonly found together within the so-called Haltern I service of the mid- to late first century BCE, although some forms, like the *Consp.* 24 and 26 examples, appear in the first-century CE Haltern II service. Other slightly different forms that are part of the Haltern II service are not found at Caladinho, although they are present at nearby sites which date to the mid- to late first century CE.[36] The majority of the ITS (and other finewares) were recovered from the tower of Caladinho, suggesting that this structure was used for domestic purposes in addition to its utility in surveilling the surrounding landscape. The large hearth uncovered in Sector 3, however, implies that meals were prepared in that space even if they were served in the ITS platters, plates, and bowls found in the tower.

The *Consp.* 7.1 vessels, defined as cups or bowls with a sloping wall and plain rim, include [90]1 and [94]1.[37] Vessels [52]1, [92]1, [96]1, [104]5, and [400]1 represent the small *Consp.* 14.1 bowls. With five extant examples, these bowls are ITS form most commonly identified at Caladinho. Each of these possesses a high foot with a base that rises higher than the bottom of the vessel's wall. Their narrow hanging lips are also distinctive. Both *Consp.* 7 and 14 forms are thought to have been produced during the middle Augustan period, during the last decades of the first century BCE and first decade of the first century CE.[38] Functionally, these tablewares would have been useful both in serving discrete, individual portions as well as serving small foods that are meant to be shared during communal meals.

The larger plates and platters are represented by a number of individual vessels (Fig. 5.32). Four examples of *Consp.* 12 (of subforms 12.1 and 12.2) were recovered from Caladinho. Each of these sherds represents a plate or medium-sized platter with a variously articulated overhanging lip. *Consp.* 10.3, a larger broad-rimmed platter, is represented by one sherd, [52]1, recovered during the second season of excavation.[39] While extant as only a small rim sherd, it would have originally been quite large and probably used for serving large portions. Three sherds from three different stratigraphic units represent what is most probably an example of another a large plate or platter although only its foot and base are extant.[40] The first sherd, [2]1, was found near the surface during the first season of excavation. The second, [23]2, was recovered during that same season but at a lower stratigraphic unit (Fig. 5.17). The last piece, [129]1, was only recovered in the third season, and it provided the link between the other sherds. Together, they form the ring foot of a very large platter with rouletting on the interior base. As the diagnostic lip of this vessel does not survive, the foot may be classified instead as *Consp.* B1. This large flat platter was, like the example of *Consp.* 10.3, probably used for serving larger portions that were then further divided onto individual elements of the ITS service during the meal.

The ITS from Caladinho shares some similarities with the assemblage ex-

---

[36] Viegas 2003: 101; Jérez Linde 2005: 41.
[37] *Consp.*: 64.
[38] *Consp.*: 76.
[39] *Consp.*: 68.
[40] *Consp.*: 70.

cavated from Castelo da Lousa.[41] At Castelo da Lousa, the assemblage contains plates and bowls with a single example of a decorated cup. Additionally, the ITS from Castelo da Lousa represents a very small amount of the site's total ceramic assemblage. Only 72 identifiable sherds of ITS (and 120 sherds of Campanian black gloss) were recovered in six years of fieldwork.[42] In conjunction with the much fuller assortment of Campanian black gloss ware from Castelo da Lousa, the finewares suggest that this site, although positioned on the Guadiana, only maintained a tenuous, infrequent connection with Italy. The Roman character of most architectural elements and of the remainder of the material culture, however, indicates a much stronger cultural connection between Castelo da Lousa and Roman identity than the finewares alone would suggest. For example, this site was built along the lines of a classical atrium-style house, albeit using locally available materials and methods. Indeed, it appears that Castelo da Lousa's construction during the beginning of the first century BCE positioned it within a landscape that was even more isolated from imported products than Caladinho. Thus the inhabitants' attempt to live in a Roman manner was expressed architecturally while it could not be expressed through the regular use of imported ceramics.

The remainder of the finewares from Caladinho include three sherds of Campanian black gloss, discussed briefly above for their relevance to dating, and many small pieces of thin-walled wares. The vast majority of the thin-walled wares from Caladinho are very fragmentary body sherds that defy any attempt at typology. Their fabrics, however, are somewhat easier to analyze. Of the fifty sherds of thin-walled ware collected, twelve appear in the buff cream-colored fabric common to ceramics from Baetica. Thirty-seven either possess Italian fabrics or else bear decoration similar to published examples of Italian thin-walled wares. A single sherd in a very clean grey fabric may have originated in the area of Granada, but this identification remains tenuous.[43]

Imitation and regionally produced finewares represent a portion of the total assemblage nearly five times larger than all of Caladinho's imported finewares combined (Fig. 5.27).[44] The imitations, while quite rare, attempt to mimic Campanian black gloss and Italian terra sigillata in color, size, and form. Indeed, several of the imitation fineware sherds collected during the Caladinho excavation are so similar to the forms of Italian finewares that they may be characterized according to the same typologies as the imported finewares. Such an attention to detail among the imitation finewares suggests that both producers and consumers

[41] Carvalho and Morais 2010.

[42] Carvalho and Morais 2010: 140; Luís 2010: 124.

[43] I am grateful to A. M. A. Auroux for his assistance with the tentative identification of this fabric and its place of origin.

[44] The identification of imitation finewares within the assemblage was intentionally conservative. Only those forms that imitated three or more characteristics of true finewares or else possessed a form indistinguishable from a black gloss or terra sigillata vessel were counted as imitations.

of these wares were desirous of accurate replicas of forms that they could not otherwise obtain. The other locally produced finewares, which make up a more significant part of the assemblage, do not attempt to imitate directly the forms of black gloss or sigillata. Nevertheless, they possess the clean fabrics, smoothed (sometimes burnished) exteriors, and light delicate forms that would have made them appropriate as tablewares.

The far greater proportion of imitation finewares and regional tablewares to those finewares imported from outside Iberia suggests that the inhabitants of Caladinho sought Roman-style pottery from within a region where such products could not easily be found. The isolated position of Caladinho prevented the importation of large enough quantities of Italian pottery, and so the inhabitants turned to local reproductions, imitations, and equivalents. The presence of such a significant percentage of imitation/regional finewares in the assemblage speaks to the cultural identity of Caladinho's inhabitants. The inhabitants of Caladinho sought out material culture that would allow them to dine in a Roman style. Whether the inhabitants of Caladinho were culturally Roman or merely emulating Romans, the imitation/regional fineware is indicative of the growing Roman cultural presence in the central Alentejo during the first century BCE.

While more common ware sherds were recovered from Caladinho than any other class of ceramic, only a few pieces are especially important for characterizing the site. This is partly the result of the lack of scholarly attention paid to common ware, but also because of the "catch-all" nature of the category itself. Nevertheless, a number of common ware vessels, particularly those with lids, are indicative of the Roman colonization of the region during the mid- to late first century BCE. These forms are characterized here according to the typology developed by Smit Nolen. Some forms, however, have *comparanda* with examples from Castelo da Lousa.

Like common wares, cookwares are an understudied class of ceramics in the central Alentejo region. Many sherds of the cookware recovered from Caladinho, however, possess recognizable forms. Several *orlo bifido* baking trays were discovered at the site (Fig. 5.33). These baking trays are considered particularly important markers for contact with Italy and the adoption of Roman meals.[45] S. Rotroff argues that they are common during the first century BCE through the first century CE.[46] At Caladinho, these distinctively Roman baking pans appear in a local fabric, indicating that they were produced because of a local demand that was not met by imports.

As discussed above, Caladinho's amphorae represent a much smaller fraction of the total ceramic assemblage than was anticipated after the initial survey of the site. In fact, a substantial fraction of the total number of transport pottery sherds

---

[45] Berlin 1997: 105–106; Rotroff 2006: 193; Olcese 2003: 26–28.
[46] Rotroff 2006: 193.

recovered from Caladinho was recorded either during survey or in the surface stratum. The majority of transport pottery may have been stored in an as yet undiscovered part of the site, and so this ceramic class may currently be underrepresented in the artifact assemblage. Regardless, the transport pottery is present at the site in only three fabrics and a similarly small number of forms, primarily Haltern 70 and Dressel 7–11 (Fig. 5.34).

Amphorae only appear in local, Lusitanian, and Baetican fabrics at Caladinho. Baetican amphorae significantly overshadow Lusitanian and local productions in terms of both total sherd count (Fig. 5.35) and total sherd weight (Fig. 5.36). Despite the presence of Italian finewares and the indications that the inhabitants of Caladinho desired Italian products and cooked in Roman-style pottery, no Italian amphorae have yet been recovered from the site. This may simply be the result of the site's position within the landscape. Caladinho is far from any navigable waterway, and thus amphorae were not the most convenient shipping container. In a similar vein, the paucity of amphorae may reflect the isolated nature of the central Alentejo. Few amphorae (and no extra-peninsular amphorae) exist at Caladinho because relatively few imports penetrated into the interior of Iberia during the first century BCE regardless of what products the population desired.

While Caladinho was too marginal to the wider Mediterranean or even regional economy to receive regular shipments of amphorae from the Guadalquivir or Tejo river valleys, its inhabitants still desired those products and their containers. In response to the lack of supply, they appear to have turned to locally produced imitation amphorae just as they had resorted to using local imitation finewares. These Alentejan amphorae are not yet well understood by scholars. Two diagnostic examples have been identified in the assemblage from Caladinho. The first is a large, almost bulbous base, [100]6, with a manually added toe (Fig. 5.34).[47] Rather than create the amphora's toe while it was turned on the wheel, the potter chose to add the toe after forming the body of the vessel. The fabric is a local brown clay with numerous small to medium white inclusions. It does not appear to be well fired. The result is an amphora that seems amateurish in both form and fabric in comparison to the well-developed forms of larger coastal producers.

The desire for these imitation amphorae betrays a desire among the inhabitants of Caladinho for imported Roman-style foods. Without a traversable waterway in the central Alentejo, the locally produced Alentejan amphorae would have served very little practical purpose in the export of local goods. Simply put, these shipping containers could not have been conveniently shipped in the region where they were produced. Instead, these local amphorae are perhaps reflective of a desire for properly Roman-style containers to hold various prestigious, culturally significant foods such as wine or *garum*. These Alentejan amphorae, made in strange forms and limited in their function, held a cultural significance for the

---

[47] For additional examples of Alentejan imitation amphorae, see Mataloto et al. 2016: 142–48.

inhabitants of this early colonial site. Nevertheless, they are few in number, and a significant amount of work remains to be done before they are fully understood.

Finally, seven *mortaria* have been identified among Caladinho's assemblage. The best preserved examples of these vessels possess a Baetican fabric, although two have been produced in local clay. The Baetican *mortaria* are similar to the first production of these vessels in southern Iberia.[48] One example, [34]5, possesses a form very similar to early Roman-period *mortaria* recorded at Emporion in northeastern Spain (Fig. 5.37).[49] Closer to western Iberia, this vessel appears similar to the first series of *mortaria* identified by Pinto and Morais.[50]

Other materials from Caladinho

Loom weights are the most common "special find" at Caladinho. Forty-two have been found scattered throughout the site, in both stratified and unstratified contexts. The loom weights were produced in a variety of sizes and shapes, ranging from 42 g ([3]2) to 1.24 kg ([104]3). The smallest of these loom weights were probably meant to add additional weight where necessary. The average weight for the complete normal-sized loom weights in the assemblage is 545 g. In addition to the very small examples, the complete loom weights are, on average, 8.9 cm in length, 5.9 cm in width at the bottom, and 4.3 cm in thickness at the bottom. They each narrow somewhat near their top. The loom weights are divided into four types: rectangular, pyramidal, rectangular-pyramidal, and pyramidal-rectangular.

While a handful of the loom weights from Caladinho are badly damaged, the majority are in relatively good condition. The loom weights recovered often possess evidence of extensive usage. Their corners are chipped from use on a loom and their bottoms and sides are often well worn. The loom weight numbered [94]3 is an excellent example of the use-wear on the weight's bottom corners (Fig. 5.38). The loom weights also often possess inscribed *graffiti* in the form of a "T," a simple line on [93]3, or in the case of [71]1, a trident (Fig. 5.39). This set of loom weights suggests some limited familiarity with Latin letters among the inhabitants. Indeed, since the inscribed "T" may represent an abbreviated name, we may be able to speculate that the owner of the loom weights possessed a Latin *praenomen*.

Several quotidian metal objects make up the majority of Caladinho's assemblage of iron and bronze artifacts. Among these are a few tools, decorative fixtures, and items of personal adornment. A long, thin, squared shaft of iron, [301]4, has been tentatively identified as an agricultural tool based on *comparanda* in the collection of the Castelo de Vila Viçosa (Fig. 5.40). A bronze door handle, [96]3, mentioned above, was excavated from the stratum between two of the fallen stairs (Fig. 5.13). The handle is well made and well preserved, hollow, and apparently

---

[48] Quaresma 2006: 151.
[49] Quaresma 2006: 150.
[50] Vaz Pinto and Morais 2007: 238.

whole. Among the few items of personal adornment, two bronze *fibulae* and an iron ring were also recovered. The *fibula*, [66]1, was excavated from the hallway during the second season (Fig. 5.41). It is badly damaged, however, and a proper identification has thus far proven impossible. The second *fibula* is similarly damaged and has not been typologized.

A single coin represents perhaps one of the most important finds from Caladinho. It was excavated from near the bottom of the large room. The coin is bronze with an even flan which indicates that it was cut rather than mold-made. It measures 2.85 cm by 2.85 cm and weighs 15 g, placing it firmly within the size of the late republican and early imperial *aes*.[51] The obverse is illegible, but the reverse holds an image of a laurel wreath perhaps surrounding some illegible text. This matches the iconography present on coins minted in Évora under Augustus circa 16/15 BCE.[52] Despite being the only coin discovered during the excavation of Caladinho, this single example suggests a tentative connection between this site and the Roman military. Very few coins of any type appear in indigenous contexts even after the Roman colonization of the region. For one to appear at Caladinho, the occupants of the site must have had some connection with Rome, likely through its legionary garrison.

Finally, two relatively well-preserved mud bricks were recognized during the excavation of the collapsed portion of the tower. The survival of these unfired bricks is a testament to the dry climate and the undisturbed nature of the deepest stratigraphic layers above the occupational floor of the tower. They measure 29 by 22 by 5.5 cm, the standard size of many fired Roman bricks.[53] While the lower course of the walls was constructed using indigenous methods, the upper floors appear to have been built from mud brick. The use of a standardized Roman size and shape in the construction of the tower at Caladinho is another indicator of a Roman or Romanized presence at the site.

TOWARDS AN UNDERSTANDING OF *FORTINS* AND *RECINTOS-TORRE*

Caladinho's archaeological remains present some of the best extant evidence for understanding the role of *fortins* and *recintos-torre* in the central Alentejan cultural landscape. The artifacts, architecture, and spatial analysis of the site permit a number of important conclusions to be drawn concerning the identity of the inhabitants and the sociopolitical role played by these isolated tower enclosures. The comparison of these structures and this landscape with similarly colonized areas of the Roman world—such as the watchtowers around the quarries at Mons

---

[51] I am grateful to E. Ljung for the lending of her numismatic expertise with this coin.
[52] *RPC* 51.
[53] For a discussion of common Roman brick sizes in Lusitania, see Teichner 2008: 638–40.

Claudianus in Egypt—also provides useful insight.

The identity of Caladinho's inhabitants

The material remains from Caladinho permit several conclusions to be drawn about the place of these sites in the social and physical landscape of the central Alentejo, but the identity of the inhabitants of the site remains difficult to establish thanks to the complexity of the data. While Caladinho possesses few imports, those that are extant at the site reveal ties with both Roman Iberia and Roman Italy. Locally produced pottery overwhelmingly outweighs the imported finds, yet even the local ceramics appear in Roman forms. Because of the desire for Roman-style finewares their number outstrips that of imported black gloss and terra sigillata vessels, and locally produced imitations make up almost five times the number of sherds of true imported finewares of all types. The cookwares are particularly interesting here since they reveal the introduction of Roman foods and methods of cooking.[54] These patterns point to inhabitants that either brought their expectations for food and dining with them from Italy, or else adopted Roman culinary practices from the new masters of the region.

Among the most telling artifacts recovered from Caladinho are the two fragments of imitation ovoid amphorae made in the local rough brown Alentejan clay.[55] Given the nature of the local landscape, these amphorae are impractical shipping containers. Instead, they were perhaps produced with a different purpose in mind. Rather than shipping, these were meant for display. Ownership of amphorae marked one as linked not only to wider Mediterranean markets, but also to the tastes, expectations, and sophistication of the Roman administrators and settlers. These amphorae, like the imitation finewares recovered from Caladinho, represent either the settlers' nostalgia for Roman things in a decidedly non-Roman land, or else a growing desire for Roman products on the part of the local indigenous peoples. Whatever the case, the presence of imitation Alentejan amphorae at Caladinho suggests that the inhabitants had either Roman or Romanized expectations about their diet.

Ceramic evidence from the site of Monte da Nora suggests a similarly entangled set of identities there. Monte da Nora was a well-fortified indigenous site that lies to the north of the present study area, but still in Alto Alentejo. Its finds indicate a continuous occupation from the late Iron Age into the Roman imperial period. The indigenous character of the material culture and architecture persists, but by the first century BCE significant evidence for the advent of Roman settlers can be seen in the form of imported Campanian ware, Italian terra sigillata, and amphorae, although a significant amount of the pottery used at the site was pro-

---

[54] Rotroff 2006: 192–93. Examples of the very similar *orlo bifido* pans, which originated in Italy, exist in the Roman *circumvallatio* at Numantia in Spain. See Koenen 1929: 292.

[55] Mataloto et al. 2016: 144–48.

duced locally.⁵⁶

In addition to the pottery, other artifacts from Caladinho hint at further connections with Roman culture. The *graffiti* on loom weights at the site point to at least some facility with written language and perhaps the Latin alphabet. The metal decorations and adornments from the site also suggest a level of wealth that, while certainly not the equal of even the poorest villa of the first century CE, elevated Caladinho beyond the other indigenous inhabitants of the region. And a bronze coin found at the site, although too corroded to be legible, connects Caladinho to the monetary culture of Rome and even, perhaps, to the Roman military. This connection with the military does not, as is discussed below, preclude Roman civilians, or even indigenous collaborators, from inhabiting the site and reaping the rewards of a close relationship to the new provincial administration.

The architecture of Caladinho appears similarly entangled in both the indigenous and the Roman. Caladinho's walls, relatively well built from unmortared and unworked slabs of schist, were lined with clay on their interior surface. This method of construction is common among the region's architectural vernacular. Parts of the structure were built atop cut sections of bedrock. Very similar building techniques can be seen at the indigenous shrine at Rocha da Mina and the late Iron Age farmhouse at Herdade de Sapatoa, and dry schist construction of this type is still used in the region today. The upper story was constructed from mud bricks, some of which have survived after the structure's collapse. These unfired mud bricks, as mentioned above, follow the standard size of Roman fired brick. This blending of Roman standards with indigenous construction methods offers one of the best examples of the entanglements common in colonial situations.

This type of construction even persisted for the brief period between the abandonment of the towers and the establishment of elaborate elite rural residences in the region. The earliest phases of many new villas in the region (such as Quinta do Freixo and Santa Susana) are constructed from dry schist in the same manner as Caladinho. Indeed, it appears that the only time when this vernacular dry-schist construction method was not used to build structures in Alentejo was during the few centuries when Romans were building there with concrete, brick, and mortar. The abandonment and transformation of the towers may thus suggest the identity of those that occupied them, at least in the first century CE. At Caladinho and other tower sites, a villa was established at the bottom of the hillslope just as the tower itself appears to have been abandoned.⁵⁷ At others, the *fortins* and *recintos-torre* were incorporated into characteristically Roman villas. Thus it seems that the towers were perhaps occupied by the those that sided with the new colonial adminis-

⁵⁶ Teichner 2008: 61–91. For comparable indigenous, imitation, and imported ceramics from Monta da Nora, see Teichner 2008: figs. 112–25.

⁵⁷ This villa, known as Azinhalinho, remains largely unexplored, but other rural Roman villas near the territory of Caladinho, such as Quinta do Freixo and Santa Susana, are now being excavated. Results from these projects are forthcoming.

tration or were otherwise entangled within it.

Caladinho appears to be an indigenous construction, yet its material culture indicates a clear connection with Roman cookery, economy, and culture. Thus it seems reasonable that the inhabitants of Caladinho, and perhaps the other *fortins* and *recintos-torre* in the central Alentejo, were indigenous Iberians who possessed close ties to the new Roman administration, members of a local *auxilia*, or first generation colonists. While their architecture remained in the local vernacular, the inhabitants adopted certain foreign products and, given the surveillance potential of many *fortins* and *recintos-torre*, collaborated with the Roman military in surveilling and policing this colonized landscape. Thus, the close cultural and economic connections between the inhabitants of Caladinho and the Roman occupation suggested by the site's material culture point to a system of surveillance that relied on complicit local actors to monitor the landscape.

Manning observation posts like Caladinho with local civilians rather than Roman soldiers is not unheard of, and the civilians involved in such a system enjoyed the official sanction, and thus protection, of the local Roman administration. For example, during Caesar's siege of Ategua (near Corduba), the Pompeian forces stationed a boy, probably a native of the town, inside a defensive tower in order to observe the siege engines arrayed outside the city (*B. Hisp.* 13). Farther removed from Iberia, *ostraka* from Mons Claudianus in Egypt indicate that *skopelarioi* (watchmen) occupied isolated *skopeloi* (lookouts) along the roads in order to monitor the access to the quarries as well as the quarries themselves.[58] Based on the evidence of several *ostraka*, D. Peacock and V. Maxfield suggest that the inhabitants of these outposts were civilians, and H. Friedman has argued for a similar civilian-run system for the monitoring of Roman mines in Jordan.[59] In the example from Mons Claudianus, civilians were rewarded by the Roman military for their service.[60] The inhabitants of many of the *fortins* and *recintos-torre* in the central Alentejo seem also to fit with the idea of civilians, whether locals or early colonists, who aid Roman military forces in policing the landscape.

One *ostrakon*, recorded by R. S. Bagnall, displays a letter sent by a Roman decurion, Herennius Antoninus, to another Roman official, Amatius, regarding the personnel manning the *skopeloi*. It reads, "Since the son of Balaneus who is in the

---

[58] Bagnall 1977: 69–71. See in particular the ostraka discussed by Bingen et al. 1992: 175–76. For a discussion of the towers themselves, see Sidebotham et al. 1991: 595–600; Peacock and Maxfield 1997: 254–55; Jackson 2002: 56.

[59] Bagnall 1977: 69–71; Bingen et al. 1992: 175–76; Peacock and Maxfield 1997: 254–55; Friedman 2008: 183–89. The example of Mons Claudianus is discussed further below in Chapter 7.

[60] Interestingly, some inscriptions from Iberia mention *speculatores* attached to the Roman army, individuals with, perhaps, occupations similar to the *skopelarioi*. Most scholars, however, identify *speculatores* as scouts or spies, and in later periods as merely a rank or honorific within the legions, so this evidence is far from certain. Instead, *stationarii*, the local officials who manned the stations along the imperial *cursus publicus*, may be the inheritors of this early colonial surveillance system.

watchtower is a boy, speak to the *dekanos* [a civilian commander] so that he may place a young man in his stead; for I also have sent orders to him [the *dekanos*] about him [the boy]."[61] Thus it appears that the *skopelarioi* manning the lookouts were managed by a *dekanos*, another civilian, who in turn was under the command of a Roman army officer. A similar system may have been in place at Caladinho and the other *fortins* and *recintos-torre* of the central Alentejo.

Another *ostrakon* suggests that the inhabitants of the *skopeloi* were universally Egyptian.[62] The text discusses the *skopelarioi Isideou*, the "watchmen of Isideion," who were probably involved in monitoring the landscape around a particular quarry near Mons Claudianus. Each of the names mentioned is Egyptian in origin, thus clearly setting the *skopelarioi* apart from the Roman military administration. It is unclear whether each individual listed on the tablet (which also includes the name of their *dekanos*) manned a *skopelos* or if this text is the schedule of individuals who each manned the same watchtower at different times.[63] The identification of the *skopelarioi* and *dekanoi* as almost certainly local in origin suggests that Caladinho and the other *fortins* and *recintos-torre* may have likewise been occupied by locals contracted by the Roman army. This connection to the military occupation may explain the presence of Roman material culture among the *fortins* and *recintos-torre*.

The *skopeloi* along the road from Mons Claudianus to the Nile are similar in the materials and methods used to build them, but are far smaller than the *fortins* and *recintos-torre* of the central Alentejo. Survey of the primary road linking the quarries with the Nile revealed over a hundred lookout posts, each approximately 2m wide. Their walls stand only 1.5m, but were probably originally taller.[64] These lookouts served as signaling platforms as well as observation posts since each possesses a great deal of intervisibility with others along the route and its *hydreumata* (watering-stations).[65] These watering-stations are essential to any desert crossing, and the *skopeloi* ensure that access to them is controlled. Pottery recovered from the *skopeloi* during survey suggests that the watchmen were regularly supplied with amphorae of water. Such a supply system might also explain the relatively small number of amphorae at Caladinho. Indeed, given the lack of a cistern, the inhabitants of Caladinho were almost certainly forced to transport water to the tower in amphorae and perhaps store it in either amphorae or the larger locally made storage vessels found in and around the site as well.

Around Mons Claudianus, it appears that the unpleasant and uncomfortable

---

[61] Bagnall 1977: 69. For the text of the *ostrakon*, see *O. Florida* 2.

[62] Bagnall 1977: 70–71. For the text, see *O. Florida* 24. *O. Amst.* 10 lists another eight Egyptian *skopelarioi*.

[63] Another text discussed by Bagnall (1977: 70), *O. Amst.* 8, discusses the schedule of *skopelarioi* assigned to various *skopeloi* and on what days.

[64] Sidebotham et al. 1991: 595–600.

[65] Peacock and Maxfield 1997: 254.

job of manning the small outposts was assigned to Egyptian civilians on a rotating basis.[66] Unlike the *skopelarioi*, the inhabitants of Caladinho appear to have been posted at the site at least semi-permanently. The spartan remains of the various *skopeloi* include little in the way of dining wares, and it would have been quite impossible for the *skopelarioi* to have farmed in the desert. At Caladinho, on the other hand, the inhabitants enjoyed some small comforts, such as fine tablewares, and were equipped with adequate domestic artifacts, such as a loom, implying, perhaps, the presence of women.[67] Caladinho was likely occupied year round by a single group, perhaps a family composed of first generation settlers or indigenous collaborators, whose primary occupation was agricultural but who were also expected to report on the comings and goings in the landscape when necessary to local officials.

In Greece, towers were associated with isolated rural farms and used to house slaves.[68] The possibility that the *fortins* like Caladinho were used to house and monitor slaves in the manner of the Greek towers was one of the first interpretations of Caladinho prior to its excavation. This no longer seems the most plausible explanation for the towers nor the most likely identity for the site's inhabitants. First, the material culture recovered from the tower included numerous imported finewares, oil, wine, and garum amphorae, a bronze coin, and some few pieces of personal adornment (two *fibulae* and a finger ring). While these artifacts are not especially rich, they do not appear consistent with a population of slaves living in the tower. Many of these artifacts were from the bottom floor of the tower itself, beneath the collapsed layer, and so represent the occupational surface. Additionally, while the presence of loom weights at Caladinho suggests some domestic and agriculturally productive activity, no farming implements have been recovered from the site. Other *fortins*, such as Castelinho, are remarkably isolated from any adequate farmland, making their use as housing for slaves engaged in farming appear unlikely.

Caladinho's architecture also appears devoid of the features we would expect in a tower meant to house slaves, such as a secure domestic space on the bottom floor and lockable doors. The bottom, most secure floor of the tower was also lined with large fragments of pottery, suggesting that it was a waterproof working floor rather than a space to house slaves. Additionally, the door thresholds at the site do not possess any indication of a locking mechanism (although this might have been achieved in a different way). Thus, while it is entirely possible that slaves lived and

---

[66] Bingen et al. (1992: 176) presents an official request (recorded on an *ostrakon* known as *O. Claud. I* 175) for a man to occupy a *skopelos*.

[67] Numerous loom weights were also recovered from buildings VI and XI in the nearby Roman camp at Cáceres el Viejo (Hanel 2006: 227), which suggests that either women travelled with the Roman military in Iberia or soldiers were responsible for the production of textiles. It is unclear who was responsible for the weaving evident at Caladinho.

[68] Morris and Papadopoulos 2005.

worked at Caladinho, it seems unlikely that they would have been locked inside the tower for safekeeping as happened at Greek farms and their towers.

The apparent purpose of the towers like Caladinho, discussed in detail in the next chapter, also indicates that these were not structures meant to house and control slaves. While the towers do not appear to have been engaged in a larger regional network of surveillance, many of them do appear to work in concert to observe routes of passage or especially defensible positions. The lack of intervisibility would have hindered communication between the towers, but each appears to have been positioned to provide visual control over a specific feature of the landscape rather than positioned to allow signaling between a network of towers.

Ultimately, we may never know the identity of the inhabitants of the *fortins* and *recintos-torre*. They may have been local collaborators, or they may have been the first-generation Italian immigrants. Or as C. Fabião has suggested, they may have been soldiers of the local *auxilia*. Indeed, the cultural identity of the inhabitants is unclear because the nature of the colonial encounter between natives and Romans resulted in unclear, entangled identities. Their material culture, construction, and successive replacement by villas suggest that their inhabitants were invested in the Roman colonization of the region.

The position of the sites within the landscape allows us to draw conclusions regarding their purpose and thus their connection to the new colonial administration. The surveillance they provided was a tool used by the Romans to impose a new physical, social, economic, and ideological order on the landscape. The *fortins* and *recintos-torre* often occupied especially prominent locations in order better to surveil the landscape, and were each constructed in strategically valuable locations. The position of the undoubtedly indigenous site of Rocha da Mina, discussed in Chapter 2, suggests an attempt at avoiding conflict by a strategy of security through obscurity. Rocha da Mina is positioned in a location that is difficult to see from the wider landscape. The choices involved in these different placements indicate different allegiances, identities, and agendas among the builders. Visibility analysis of the landscape, detailed in the next chapter, provides an excellent tool for the detection of varying topographic prominence among these structures and for examining the surveillance system imposed on the colonial Alentejo.

CHAPTER 6

VISIBILITY ANALYSIS OF A ROMAN COLONIAL LANDSCAPE

This chapter deploys GIS-based visibility analysis of *fortins*, *recintos-torre*, and other sites in the central Alentejo dating between 100 BCE and 100 CE. Analysis of this kind reveals the total areas under surveillance in this landscape as well as the structures that were strategically placed to avoid detection. Sixteen *fortins* and eight *recintos-torre* (described in Chapter 4) were analyzed for their relative topographic prominence. While the majority of these sites appear to possess some observational potential over their surrounding landscape or particularly important routes through it, a number of them lack the topographic prominence necessary to be considered surveillance structures. Through a clear depiction of the specific, quantifiable areas subjected to surveillance, this chapter is intended to bolster the evidence for the use of surveillance in the negotiation of control over a colonial landscape presented in previous chapters. By also demonstrating that the builders of some *fortins* and *recintos-torre* sought to avoid this surveillance, the chapter argues as well for a more nuanced understanding of surveillance in contexts where power is contested, control is negotiated, and cultures are materially and symbolically entangled.

GEOGRAPHIC INFORMATION SYSTEMS AND VISIBILITY ANALYSIS: BUILDING A DATABASE
Methodology and sources of information

The visibility analysis of the central Alentejo provided below is drawn from a number of surveys, reports, and government-supplied, freely available datasets. The high-resolution digital elevation maps (DEMs) which make visibility analysis possible were accessed online from the Advanced Spaceborne Thermal Emission and Reflection Radiometer Global Digital Elevation Model Version 2 dataset (AS-

TER GDEM2).[1] These DEMs provide excellent topographic data from the entire planet in a resolution of 1 arc second. The resulting maps are presented as a set of tiles called a raster where every tile is assigned altimetric information. A recent assessment of the ASTER GDEM2 data indicates that it is vertically accurate to within 10 meters with even better accuracy rates for undeveloped or lightly forested areas.[2]

The various archaeological maps of the Alentejan administrative regions are foremost among the sources of information for the locations of sites. These publications were excellent guides to the locations of sites on the *Carta Militar de Portugal* (CMP). The CMP, a 1:25,000 scale topographic map of the country, was therefore also an essential resource for the identification of sites in the present study area.[3] Sites without published coordinates were located in the CMP. These pages were then georeferenced and ortho-rectified. All maps were projected in the ASTER GDEM2's native WGS84 datum and Universal Transverse Mercator (UTM) coordinate system. Some data made available by the municipality of Redondo, Portugal, were originally in the Lisbon Haverford-Gauss projection, but these were also reprojected in the ASTER GDEM2's native system and rectified against the CMP.[4]

ArcGIS 10, made available thanks to the University at Buffalo, provided the computational tools necessary to perform a comprehensive viewshed analysis. Each site was first located, a georeferenced point assigned, and finally viewshed analysis performed against the ASTER GDEM2. The resulting viewsheds were compared for the extent of their surveillance potential. Those that lacked a significant degree of intervisibility with their landscape were judged to lack topographic prominence, while those that possessed a high degree of intervisibility were noted for their greater surveillance potential. Not all sites with low topographic prominence should be removed from the category of surveillance structures, however, as they may have been intended to observe only very specific, isolated parts of their local landscape.

Defining the entries

Each site entered into the ArcGIS database was defined according to one of seven categories. These include *fortins* and *recintos-torre*, urban centers, indigenous

---

[1] The ASTER GDEM2 data were obtained through the online Data Pool at the NASA Land Processes Distributed Active Archive Center (LP DAAC), USGS/Earth Resources Observation and Science (EROS) Center, Sioux Falls, South Dakota (https://lpdaac.usgs.gov/dataset_discovery). ASTER GDEM2 is a product of NASA and METI.
[2] Tachikawa et al. 2011.
[3] The CMP is made freely available online by the *Instituto Geografico de Portugal*.
[4] Data from the *Sistema de Informação Geográfica do Município de Redondo*, SIGRED, were obtained through the municipality's website (http://www.cm-redondo.pt/pt/).

settlements, and villas. *Fortins* and *recintos-torre* are closely related categories of sites. They are defined, and the examples used here identified, in Chapter 4. Urban centers founded during the early Roman period, including both *coloniae* and *municipia*, are also included as their own category. Those included are Évora and Ammaia. Although *Pax Iulia* is mentioned in the text, it remains peripheral to this study and lies at too great a distance to include on the provided maps at a scale that would remain legible. Urban centers are relatively few and distant from each other in the ancient central Alentejo and so Évora and Ammaia are also used to define the limits of the rural setting of this study.

Indigenous settlements, including small farms and towns, are also discussed below in relation to the *fortins* and *recintos-torre* and their viewsheds. These include the pre-Roman shrine at Rocha da Mina, the fortified indigenous settlements of Monte do Outeiro, Serra de Segóvia, Castelo Velho de Veiros, and Castelo Velho de Degebe. Each of these appears to have been occupied during the first century BCE and most continued to be inhabited, although often diminished, in the first century CE. While this is not a comprehensive catalogue of indigenous settlements in the region, the four discussed here possess good evidence for their occupational histories and significant extant fortifications. Other smaller indigenous sites, like Herdade de Sapatoa, did exist beyond these four fortified settlements, but they are either very small isolated farms or else do not possess adequate extant material to establish their nature and chronology.

Sites identified as belonging to the Roman military are quite rare, and those that have been so identified—particularly Cabeço de Vaiamonte—also present evidence of an indigenous population. The archaeological remains from these sites leave little doubt that Roman soldiers were quartered among the local population rather than within their own camps. This is C. Fabião's "invisible" Roman army at work. Fabião posits that the Roman army's presence in the Alentejo remains archaeologically "invisible" or "hidden" because the armies were used as small garrisons for captured indigenous communities rather than being quartered all together in a single camp.[5] The dispersal of military units throughout the landscape in this way gives further credence to the idea that the *fortins* and *recintos-torre* themselves had a connection to the military.

Understanding the role that the Roman military played in the surveilled landscape presents an important part of this analysis. While the identities of the towers' inhabitants remains obscured by the nature of archaeological evidence, comparison with the system used around the Roman quarries in Egypt suggests that they were civilians in the employ of the military. The material culture found at the towers, exemplified by the assemblage at Caladinho, indicates that their inhabitants were closely connected to the new administration of the province and were either Romans themselves or else had adopted many facets of Roman culture. The

---

[5] Fabião 2006: 121–23.

construction of the towers themselves is more ambiguous. The presence of unfired mud brick at Caladinho in the dimensions of a Roman brick does suggest that some Roman expectations played a role in the building of the tower. Comparable nearby structures, like Castelo da Lousa, Cabeço de Vaiamonte, and Monte de Nora, all possess examples of Roman *militaria*. While Roman soldiers may not have occupied the towers, a connection between the occupants of the towers and the Roman military and the new colonial administration seems likely.

Similarly, the villas established in the central Alentejo region following the first century BCE present ample opportunity for the study of the changing role of surveillance post-conquest. Villas are defined here as large, rural, productive habitations with material and cultural connections to both their region and to the greater Roman Empire. They represent the introduction of a new and particularly Roman method of agricultural production. The dozen villas around the modern town of Redondo provide a case study here. Additionally, they are excellent markers of the imposition of a new colonial order on the landscape. Mines and quarries, the final category included in this analysis, are also excellent indicators of the success of Roman imperial policy in the Luso-Roman colonial encounter. As resistance waned in the early years of the first century CE, the extraction of the region's valuable mineral wealth began in earnest.

While the sites in this region surely occupied more than the narrowly defined roles presented here, only sites that fit the above types were included in this analysis both because of the relative completeness of the archaeological record for these sites and the brevity of occupation required by a project of this nature. Thus, this analysis is best understood as a case study of one aspect of the landscape, surveillance, rather than a comprehensive examination of the archaeology of the central Alentejo.

Estimating height of observers

The relative height of each point on the ArcGIS map is an essential part of visibility analysis. While the height of locations within the landscape is known and recorded on each tile of the ASTER GDEM2 raster, the additional height added by individual structures is not included on this data. In order to take this additional data into account during the visibility analysis, it is important to estimate a standard height for each category of structures, such as the *fortins* and *recintos-torre*, and of the observers themselves. I estimated the height of a human observer in all visibility analyses at 1.75 m, a standard measurement used in visibility studies.[6] This estimate of human height is not meant to represent any single individual, nor does it take into account non-observers such as children or the elderly. It is merely intended as a standard, close-to-the-norm height for humans.

---

[6] Gillings and Wheatley 2001: 33; Friedman 2008: 201.

The height of the *fortins* and *recintos-torre* is estimated to have been 6 m. This measurement is based on the archaeological remains of Caladinho, discussed in the previous chapter, and on the height of other ancient towers. The tower walls at Caladinho are preserved to a height in excess of 2 m. A large outcropping of bedrock juts from the hill where Caladinho is situated and rises to a height of roughly 6 m from the surface. In order to see beyond this outcrop, the tower at Caladinho, the walls of which incorporate the outcrop, must have risen above it. In Jordan, H. Friedman identified a watchtower of similar dimensions to the *fortins* of the central Alentejo.[7] Her conservative estimate of the height of that tower and other freestanding towers in Roman Jordan was 6 m, although she estimates the height of towers attached to buildings to be 10 m. Given the substantial, well-built walls at many *fortins* and *recintos-torre* and the large amount of debris present at collapsed *fortins*, the estimate of 6 m may appear conservative.

Combining these estimates, 7.75 m was added to the height of every freestanding *fortim* and *recinto-torre* included in the visibility analysis below. Urban centers and indigenous settlements, which possessed walls, were assigned an additional 10 m of height. 7.75 m was added to villas where towers were identified, or only 1.75 m where no extant surveillance structure was found.[8] Additional height was added to each point through the use of the "offseta" field on the attribute table for each entry in the database. The offset was taken into account when the viewshed was calculated for each point. The maximum visible distance from each observer was estimated at 6.2 km. This estimation of visual acuity is the accepted physical norm for the ability of unaided human eyesight to discern clearly activity, objects, or individuals within a given landscape.[9] It may be possible to discern movement, especially the movement of a large group, beyond this distance. Thus this estimate, like the estimate of observer height, should be understood only as a working average rather than the absolute limit to the power of surveillance.

VISIBILITY ANALYSIS OF THE CENTRAL ALENTEJO IN THE FIRST CENTURY BCE

The twenty-four *fortins* and *recintos-torre* of the central Alentejo provide ample evidence for the use and avoidance of surveillance during the first century BCE. These two closely related site types, defined and discussed in Chapters 4 and 5, present the means by which the peoples of the first century BCE manipulated vis-

---

[7] Friedman 2008: 204.

[8] Note that this does not take into consideration the presence of temporary surveillance structures in use at villas, such as the treehouses and similar structures depicted on some African Red Slip appliques and described by Pseudo-Cyprian in his *De Duobus Montibus Sina et Sion*. Both of these examples are discussed in Chapter 3.

[9] Higuchi 1988; Wheatley and Gillings 2000: 15–20; Friedman 2008: 200.

ibility in the negotiation over control of the central Alentejo region. The inherent viewsheds offered here represent estimations of the areas under surveillance from each of these structures. When a group of sites appear very near each other or when they are situated on or around the same geographical feature, a cumulative viewshed of all the sites is presented. Cumulative viewsheds present the area under surveillance from multiple points, including areas where vision overlaps. Both inherent viewsheds and cumulative viewsheds are discussed below, and each form of analysis contributes new information to the discussion of vision, visibility, and the use of surveillance in the control over this colonized landscape.

Detailed analysis begins with the northernmost structures, including the *fortins* F1 (Malhada das Penas), F2 (Beiçudos), and F3 (Penedo do Ferro), and the *recintos-torre* R17 (Mariano), R18 (Outeiro da Mina), and R19 (Terrugem) (Fig. 1.2). These sites and the others included in Chapter 4's catalogue are referred to exclusively by their designating numbers throughout the remainder of this chapter. Additionally, other sites in the local landscape are considered, namely the site of Cabeço de Vaiamonte, an indigenous site occupied by the Roman military in the early first century BCE, Torre de Palma, a small pre-Roman settlement eventually enlarged into one of the largest villas in Iberia, and three indigenous fortifications that were inhabited contemporaneously to the *fortins* and *recintos-torre*.[10]

The F1 site, made up of two *fortins* set opposite each other over a pass in a steep ridge, observes a significant part of its local territory (Fig. 6.1). Together the two *fortins* provide surveillance over the pass and the territory to the northeast and southwest. The F1 viewshed is an excellent example of the use of surveillance to control particular features in the landscape. The passage between these two *fortins*, and the approach to the passage, are under careful observation. These sites were likewise visible from the surrounding landscape, and their surveillance capability was certainly apparent. Any person or group approaching the passage through the ridge, the only readily accessible point in the immediate landscape, would immediately know that they were being watched. In contrast, the inhabitants of this site were empowered by their position both in the landscape and within the new colonial system that placed them there.

The F2 viewshed demonstrates that this site also enjoyed ample surveillance over its landscape (Fig. 6.2), and was positioned just outside of the effective vision of F1, R17, and R18. F2 observed the territory to the northeast, and its viewshed encompassed both Cabeço de Vaiamonte and the villa of Torre de Palma. While an Iron Age settlement existed at Torre de Palma prior to the establishment of a villa there, the site does not appear to have been intensely occupied until the first century CE after the *fortins* and *recintos-torre* were falling into disuse.[11] Cabeço de

---

[10] For Cabeço de Vaiamonte, see Fabião 1996. The pre-Roman occupation of Torre de Palma is discussed by Langley et al. 2008.

[11] Maloney and Hale 1996: 275–80.

Vaiamonte, originally an indigenous hillfort, was occupied by the Roman military from the second century BCE to around 80 BCE.[12] The date of abandonment roughly coincides with the rebellion lead by the Roman general Q. Sertorius, and the forces stationed here may have been involved in this conflict. The paucity of materials recorded from F2 makes it difficult to establish that F2 was occupied at the same time as Cabeço de Vaiamonte or after its abandonment, although a few sherds late Iron Age pottery from F2 makes this possible.[13]

Nearby, the *recintos-torre* R17 and R18 occupy very different positions within the landscape. Both sites, as described in Chapter 4, occupy positions in the landscape that offer limited surveillance even with the addition of an observation tower. Their viewsheds demonstrate their low topographic prominence (Fig. 6.3). They can see only a limited part of the landscape. Instead of being used for wide-area surveillance, as was the case at F2, the *recintos-torre* at R17 and R18 appear to have observed areas of special importance, in this case the low-lying areas around streams that fed into the viewshed of F2 from the indigenous fortification of Castelo Velho de Veiros that lies to the south.

A similar conscious manipulation of visibility is evident in two other nearby structures to the south, F3 and R19. The F3 viewshed is particularly expansive (Fig. 6.4). While the viewshed suggests that the site had great topographic prominence and thus surveillance potential, F3 is also well positioned to observe a path that runs from east to west through the landscape along a narrow bed of the Ribeira da Colónia. This route was an important artery in the region, and served to link both indigenous settlements like the nearby fortifications of Castelo Velho de Veiros and Serra de Segóvia as well as Roman colonial settlements like Ammaia, Monte da Nora, and Cabeço de Vaiamonte. R19 is located in a depression and surrounded by schist outcrops, and its view of the local territory is limited to the southern course of the nearby river. The R19 viewshed, while limited in comparison, provides a complementary surveillance over additional parts of the landscape outside of F3's vision (Fig. 6.5).

To the southeast of F3 and R19, the course of the Guadiana River is guarded by two *fortins*, F6 and F7 (Fig. 6.6). Their location also serves to screen the approaches to the possible Roman garrison at Monte da Nora. These sites provide surveillance over an important route through the landscape of Monte da Nora, Ammaia, nearby indigenous fortifications, and the course of the Guadiana River. Control over passage on the Guadiana permitted the Romans more readily to access the natural resources of the central Alentejo and central Iberia generally. The large ceramic kilns at the mouth of the Guadiana and Guadalquivir rivers in the south of Iberia are testament to this.[14] They provided the packaging for the vast

---

[12] Fabião 2006: 121; Fabião 1996: 31–34.
[13] Mataloto 2002: 165.
[14] Almeida 2008.

quantities of grain, oil, wine, and other agricultural goods produced in the peninsula. The viewsheds from F6 and F7 demonstrate the vision over the river's course and crossings possessed by these two sites. Each of them is positioned on different branches of the Guadiana and so controls access to the river via those entrance points. Control over the Guadiana River was an essential part of controlling western Iberia. Indeed, the placement of these sites guarding certain passages in the landscape mirrors the placement of structures around Évora.

Taken together, the towers at F1, F2, F3, F6, F7, R17, R18, and R19 may all have been positioned to monitor the approaches and routes between the indigenous fortifications of Castelo Velho de Veiros to the south and Serra de Segóvia to the northeast as well as the routes between this region and the Roman city of Ammaia to the north (Fig. 6.7). The site of Monte da Nora may also have benefited from this surveillance of the local region, and, if it held a Roman military presence, Monte da Nora may have been the central commanding node that coordinated all of the towers in this locality. Together the towers provided a screen on the approaches north to the Roman colonial city of Ammaia and its mineral-rich territory. They dissuaded brigandage on the route from the south to the north and east and along the course of the Guadiana. The complex topography of this part of the Alentejo no doubt lent itself to banditry, and the towers here were potentially meant to counter that form of resistance.

Turning to the west, several sites provide surveillance over the northern approaches to the Roman colonial city of Évora. These include the *fortim* F4 and five *recintos-torre*, R20, R21, R22, R23, and R24. Like the towers south of Ammaia, each of these sites is positioned to monitor the primary approaches to Évora. This city was promoted to the status of *municipium* in the mid-first century BCE and given the name *Liberalitas Iulia Ebora* by Julius Caesar or Augustus.[15] Évora is one of the largest settlements in the region, and eventually, under the provincial reorganization instituted by the emperor Augustus at the end of the first century BCE, it becomes the administratively most important settlement north of *Pax Iulia* (Beja). If Varro's description (1.16.2) of this territory as a place inhospitable to farming because of brigandage is accurate, then the establishment of surveillance over the farms feeding Évora represents an early, cautious step in the colonization and settlement of this region.

The northernmost of this group, F4, provides surveillance over what was once a river crossing between the hilly north and the rolling plains to the south (Fig. 6.8).[16] This outpost represents the first in a series of structures that, taken together, guard the boundary between the territory around the new colonial city, Évora,

---

[15] Simplício 2003: 365–66; Faria 1999, 2001: 355–57; Alarcão 1988: 160. The name and topography of Évora suggest that it has indigenous roots, but no archaeological evidence for a pre-Roman occupation has yet been found in the city.

[16] The original landscape around F4 is now obscured by flooding caused by the Soieros Dam.

and the uncolonized space farther north in the interior of the peninsula. The *recintos-torre*, R20, R21, R22, R23, and R24, play a similar role within the landscape. Their proximity to each other suggests, at first glance, that their viewsheds might overlap. This, however, is not the case. A cumulative viewshed of these five *recintos-torre* reveals that their viewsheds are complementary (Fig. 6.9), as with the towers south of Ammaia. Each is positioned so that it observes a different part of the local landscape. Rather than a communicative network, they are a dispersed patchwork of towers that offer surveillance over their immediate surroundings. This pattern of dispersed distribution appears to have been intended at the majority of the *fortins* and *recintos-torre*.

Together, these six surveillance structures monitor important passes, crossings, and streams and rivers through the landscape to the north of Évora. Indeed, it was along these same paths that Roman roads were constructed in the decades following the city's foundation.[17] When characterizing the landscape around Évora, it is essential to remember the historical context. The second and first centuries BCE had seen repeated bloody conflicts over control of this region. Nor was this area pacified even by the middle of the first century BCE. The six sites discussed above are the physical remnant of the process of territorial control and reorganization that reshaped this region from a landscape of colonial violence to one of imperial administration. Their positions north of Évora served also to claim the city's agricultural hinterland. Surveillance, through the concomitant threat of violent reprisal it represents, could persuade indigenous resistance to cease contesting the colonists' ownership of this territory. Guarding against bandits thus had the additional purpose of claiming territory.

The routes around the Serra d'Ossa, which dominates the rugged central Alentejan landscape, are observed by at least three structures. The Serra d'Ossa rises from the Alentejan plains as a large solitary impediment to movement across this region from north to south (Fig. 2.1). Indeed, it is far easier to simply pass around the mountain than cross over it. Three *fortins*, F5, F8, and F9, like the *recintos-torre* guarding Évora's northern territory, provide visual control over the landscape to the north and south of the Serra d'Ossa. Their viewsheds offer little overlap, but, like the towers south of Ammaia and north of Évora, each serves to monitor a specific, chosen part of the surrounding territory. They were again distributed in a patchwork of surveillance where each viewshed complemented the surveillance potential of its neighbor. Given the importance of this region in terms of both its natural resources and its traversable routes, still more *fortins* and *recintos-torre* may yet lie undiscovered in the shadow of the Serra d'Ossa.

One of these, F9, possesses an especially large field of vision which encompassed not only the landscape to the north but also a fortified indigenous settlement known as Monte Outeiro (Fig. 6.10). F9's placement in the landscape

[17] Bilou 2005.

represents a conscious recognition of the surveillance potential offered by that topographically prominent location. The visual control offered by F9 is complemented by another *fortim*, F8, situated nearby (Fig. 6.11). The viewshed from F8 is comparable in its extent to that from F9. It appears that F8 was positioned to observe the southern and western slopes of the Serra d'Ossa and the path through the landscape just outside the vision of F9. Another *fortim*, F5, completes the surveillance apparatus around the mountain. F5 is positioned on the northern slope of the Serra d'Ossa. Its viewshed encompasses the area to the north of the mountain (Fig. 6.12), thus ensuring that the territory around the mountain, a potential stronghold for indigenous resistance, was effectively surveilled. Additionally, these three structures monitor access to the Guadiana River to the east and to the Estremoz Anticline marble quarries to the northeast. The cumulative viewshed of F5, F8, and F9 reveals the total area under surveillance around the Serra d'Ossa (Fig. 6.13).

Considering the F9 viewshed in this second context is essential for understanding the role of F10, one of the least topographically prominent sites in the central Alentejan landscape. F10 is situated on a steep outcrop above a narrow winding stream. Cliffs taller than even the outcrop prevent observers from F10 from surveilling any region beyond the course of the stream below it. Despite its otherwise excellent viewshed, F9 is unable to observe F10 or the ravine below it (Fig. 6.10). F10, then, appears to have been positioned specifically to make up for this deficiency in F9's otherwise exemplary surveillance potential. The viewshed from F10 confirms this (Fig. 6.14). F10's location was chosen specifically for its ability to monitor this otherwise hidden route through the landscape.

An indigenous shrine and settlement known as Rocha da Mina (discussed above in Chapter 2) also exists near both F9 and F10.[18] Visibility analysis of Rocha da Mina indicates practically no potential for surveillance at the site. As a result, the site is also nearly impossible to see from the surrounding landscape despite being positioned between two *fortins*. Rocha da Mina's viewshed is limited to only its most immediate surroundings, and so it is practically impossible to display the shrine's viewshed on a map as I have done for the neighboring *fortins*. At Rocha da Mina the inhabitants appear to have situated their shrine and settlement in a place that is almost impossible to observe. The settlement at Rocha da Mina is also concealed behind a relatively large dry stone wall. This wall would have provided no practical defense against an attack by the Roman military, but was likely an effective deterrent against bandits. Thus this site seems to avoid violence of colonial resistance as much as it does imperial surveillance. The inhabitants of Rocha da Mina may simply have attempted to navigate the colonial landscape by remaining unnoticed.[19] The shrine and its settlement, however, appear to have been aban-

---

[18] See also Mataloto et al. 2014 and 2016 for discussion of Rocha da Mina and its artifact assemblage.
[19] Mataloto et al. 2014. Other examples of hidden indigenous sites may remain undiscovered in the

doned at roughly the same time as the *fortins* and *recintos-torre* were established, hinting at a policy of surveillance that sought to end even the passive resistance offered by privacy.

Other *fortins* in this region provide ample surveillance over the tributaries of the Guadiana and over the river itself. Like the towers south of Ammaia that lie to their north, this group appears to have been positioned to monitor the course of the Guadiana and its crossings into and out of the central Alentejo. F12's viewshed indicates that the site enjoyed a dominant topographic prominence and field of vision (Fig. 6.15). The viewshed from F13 offers a similar degree of visual control over the northern and eastern tributaries (Fig. 6.16). The viewsheds from F14 (Fig. 6.17) and F15 (Fig. 6.18) complement those of the towers to their north by observing primarily the course of the Guadiana and crossings over it. Together, the surveillance provided by these four sites resembles that offered by F6 and F7. This similarity suggests that these sites were placed consciously, even strategically, within the landscape with an understanding of how each site's vision could complement the others. The cumulative viewshed of this region demonstrates how these structures, working in concert if not within immediate communication, monitored the Guadiana River and access to it from the north and northwest (Fig. 6.19).

The only outlier in this program of observation is F11. This site, positioned to the northeast of F12 on another tributary, possesses relatively little visual access to the surrounding landscape (Fig. 6.20). Nevertheless, F11 may be specifically positioned, like F10, to observe small, specific parts of the landscape that were otherwise beyond the vision of its more topographically prominent neighbors. In this case, F11 appears to observe a crossing of the Guadiana that lies beyond the field of vision of its neighboring towers. Despite its limited viewshed, F11 is a part of the patchwork of surveillance structures that observed this southern course of the Guadiana.

The last *fortim* considered in this chapter is positioned further south along the Guadiana River and its tributaries. Like the sites above, F16 appears to have been positioned in order to observe closely the course of the Guadiana and points of access to it. F16 possesses a somewhat greater viewshed (Fig. 6.21) than its closest neighbor F15. Nonetheless, F16 may appear at first glance as something of an outlier. No other towers are positioned immediately beyond the scope of its viewshed, as is the case with the majority of the sites mentioned above. When understood as part of the same surveillance system implanted along the course of the Guadiana River through the central Alentejo, the reasons behind the construction of F16 and its placement in the landscape are revealed. The viewshed offered by F16 is limited when compared to the cumulative viewsheds available around the Serra d'Ossa, for example, but it, like the others in the region, monitors an important

---

more rugged parts of the Alentejan hinterland.

access point to the area. It may be the case that additional *fortins* or *recintos-torre* once existed around F16 to create the complementary patchwork seen in the distribution of the towers above, but no trace of them exists or else any trace was submerged with the recent damming of the Guadiana River.

The cumulative viewshed of all the towers within the area of study indicates their purpose and function within the landscape as a whole (Fig. 6.22). The sites are arranged in three broad arcs that screen the approaches to valuable natural resources and colonial centers like Évora and Ammaia. They serve to monitor traffic between indigenous centers like Serra de Segóvia, Castelo Velho de Veiros, and Castelo Velho de Degebe, and they observe the routes of transport along the roads, rivers, and streams of the Alentejo. Most of the towers worked in relation to the effective vision of their nearest neighbors. Some few were installed in particular locations away from others in order to surveil a particularly important part of the landscape, such as river crossings. They appear to have been consciously installed in the landscape not to create a network of surveillance but instead to create a patchwork of it.

The *fortins* and *recintos-torre* were not meant to be integrated, intervisible, and able to communicate between the towers. Instead, the surveillance they provided was a patchwork of dispersed sites, many located so that their vision could surveil an area just beyond the vision of its nearest neighbor. Communication and signaling between the towers does not appear to have been the goal (although it may still have been possible between some structures through the use of fire beacons or smoke signaling). The towers were not meant to guard against armies, but rather to stymie the efforts of bandits. They were installed in the landscape to push the lingering active indigenous resistance to the margins of the territory undergoing colonization. The towers encouraged resistance to cede territory where it could be observed and thus put an end to disruptions of travel, trade, farming, and natural resource acquisition. These humble surveillance structures did not provide total panoptic control, and they were never meant to. Instead, their surveillance was focused on areas deemed most vulnerable to brigandage and most valuable to the new Roman administration.

In such a borderless colonial space, the use of these surveillance structures to observe, and so alter, the movement of peoples through the landscape represents an important departure from the traditional method of internal security. For colonial forces, this region was permeated with potential threats, many of which had become all too real in the preceding two centuries. For indigenous Iberians, the central Alentejo was a space where conflict, colonialism, and insecurity were always present. Early colonists may likewise have sought to avoid conflict. The solution for each group was the same: manipulate visibility within the landscape in order either to escape detection or access surveillance. The placement of the towers within the landscape represents the agency of the builders, likely at the behest of the new colonial administration, to structure a system of surveillance that countered attempts at even passive indigenous resistance. A theory of colonial surveillance that draws from all these disparate threads of evidence is put forward in the final chapter.

CHAPTER 7

TOWARD A THEORY OF SURVEILLANCE IN A ROMAN COLONIAL LANDSCAPE

This chapter proposes a model for understanding the use of surveillance in ancient colonial encounters. As the evidence supplied in previous chapters has demonstrated, surveillance structures, both physical and ideological, played an integral role in the negotiation of territorial control in the central Alentejo during the late first century BCE. That the occupation of these first-century BCE surveillance structures was so brief only serves to bolster this interpretation. The impact of surveillance on the central Alentejo was limited in its chronological scope, but it held enormous importance for the sociopolitical reorganization of the landscape. As the previous chapters illustrated, the colonization, pacification, and resettlement succeeded in creating a landscape where the imposition of Roman cadastral systems, roads, and extractive industry was possible. Yet prior to this, the Alentejo was home to resistance to Roman conquest. The viewshed analysis presented in the previous chapter suggests that some *fortins* and *recintos-torre* were positioned to monitor areas prone to such resistance, such as the territory around indigenous settlements or the routes around and over the Serra d'Ossa.

Building on the evidence presented previously, this chapter provides a typology for interpreting Roman surveillance systems on the frontiers of the empire, established around extractive industry and agricultural fields, and embedded in borderless zones of colonial contact like the central Alentejo. A survey of some of the extant archaeological remains of surveillance structures from around the Mediterranean is presented, including the signaling towers constructed beyond Hadrian's Wall, the observation posts guarding the quarries of Mons Claudianus, and examples of the towers that sometimes accompanied farmsteads and villas. Alongside the surveillance structures of early Roman Portugal discussed in prior chapters, those surveyed here provide additional examples for a typology of the surveillance systems employed by the Romans.

By typologizing surveillance, this chapter attempts to understand the ways in which surveillance of landscapes was undertaken in antiquity and how these may be archaeologically identified and theorized. This typology marks a new means through which colonial landscapes may be analyzed by archaeologists. Similarly, recognition that surveillance may play a role in the appropriation and transformation of both physical and cultural landscapes likewise ranks among the contributions offered by this chapter.

The theoretical approaches essential to understanding Roman surveillance systems and colonization are presented as the concluding section of this chapter. The concept of social, political, economic, and material entanglement holds great promise for interpreting zones of ancient Mediterranean cultural contact like the central Alentejo. Surveillance and visibility represent the entanglement of the Alentejan built and natural landscape in the colonial encounter, and one of the ways in which that encounter was negotiated. A theory of surveillance, which draws on a wide variety of approaches to ancient colonialism, surveillance, and empire, is proposed in the first section of this chapter. This interpretive model builds on the concept of the panopticon, but seeks to acknowledge the negotiated nature of power within a colonial landscape.

All generalizing theories, like the panopticon, must be qualified when they are applied to the unsettled, entangled, and composite nature of the colonial encounter. Thus surveillance, while it provided a degree of panoptic control in the Roman colonial situation discussed here, was an imperfect tool. The landscape offered a multitude of opportunities to resist surveillance and empire. Yet surveillance provided one avenue for securing the new Roman administration's hold over territory and resources not only because it expressed power over the landscape through an imperial gaze, but also because it probably incorporated locals into the maintenance of the colonial control. Local collaborators, offered a connection to the colonial elites, manned the towers and helped to embed them within the physical and ideological landscape. It was through their collaboration that the towers provided protection from indigenous resistance in the form of banditry. Surveillance worked not only because it dissuaded the surveilled from active resistance, but also because it invested some within the structures of Roman imperial power. The end of the colonial negotiation of territory is signaled by the abandonment and transformation of the towers in favor of large rural agricultural estates, many of which were constructed at the bases of the same hills that held *fortins* and *recintos-torre*.

ARCHAEOLOGICAL REMAINS OF SURVEILLANCE STRUCTURES

Structures whose primary purpose was the surveillance of their surrounding landscape represent a limited part of the archaeological record. They are often outweighed, both in terms of size and number, by sites intended for habitation, production, worship, or commerce. In some particular contexts, enormous effort was expended to erect structures to monitor contested borders or mines, quarries, and field systems. Hadrian's Wall, for example, served in part to surveil beyond the border of the Roman Empire in order better to control access between the unconquered north and the Roman imperial territory to the wall's south. Other borders were similarly guarded by Roman defensive structures, and many fortifications were built with dedicated watchtowers spaced carefully along their extent. Roman watchtowers were also constructed around valuable mines and quarries in Jordan as part of an effort to control the convict labor that operated them. Still other sites, notably villas or fortified farmhouses, as discussed above, possess towers and other structures meant to observe field systems and those laboring in the fields. Each of these systems of surveillance created spaces where privacy was invaded and behavior curtailed. They expressed a panoptic power over their surveilled territory, and the resistance they received in response was limited by the established structures of authority and power. In a colonial encounter, however, where these systems have yet to be established, surveillance instead provides a means to negotiate the creation of new structures of power in both the physical landscape and the social one.

Two different surveillance landscapes are considered briefly below. The surveillance structures present in each landscape are described, and their similarity to the surveilled central Alentejan landscape is discussed. The social, environmental, military, and political contexts for each of the sites considered below are quite different than those present in the first-century BCE central Alentejo. Consequently, the surveillance utilized in these regions is different in both its form and execution than in the project area presented here. Nevertheless, the contrasts between the different landscapes discussed below and the Alentejan landscapes of the first century BCE and first century CE serve to illuminate further the use of surveillance in the negotiation of the colonial encounter.

Villas and their towers: an archaeology of exploitation

In 2005 S. Morris and J. Papadopoulos proposed that towers associated with Greek farmhouses represented a systemic form of exploitation.[1] The Greek tow-

---

[1] Morris and Papadopoulos 2005. Farmhouses with attached towers are especially common in Greece where they appear in almost every region, especially on the islands of Thasos, Siphnos, and Keos. For a recent list of towers in ancient Greece, see Morris and Papadopoulos 2005: fig. 6.

ers are built from worked stone or, sometimes, mud brick, and are constructed with either circular or rectangular plans.[2] Similar towers are recorded attached to farmhouses throughout the archaeological record of the Mediterranean world.[3] According to R. Osborne, these structures were intended to provide oversight over fields, quarries, vineyards, and mines, as well as the slaves who worked in them.[4] As in Foucault's panopticon, the slaves' knowledge of the tower's potential surveillance restricted their behavior. They were prisoners of the landscape in which they lived. Morris and Papadopoulos, based on the evidence for strong locks on the doors of the towers, suggest that they were instead meant as housing for slaves. With the doors bolted, the enslaved would be locked inside the towers at night when their masters' ability to monitor them was most limited.[5] Thus the towers form the crux of an "archaeology of exploitation," in the words of G. Davies, which may be seen throughout the ancient Greek landscape.[6]

Towers may have been built at Roman villas in the central Alentejo, but few have been identified.[7] They may also have been constructed from temporary materials, especially since observing agricultural work was a seasonal process. Treehouses or similar structures, as described in Pseudo-Cyprian's *De Duobus Montibus Sina et Sion*, were sometimes constructed near villas to watch over olive groves and vineyards.[8] Thus, it is difficult to assess the surveillance potential of any unexcavated villa site since it is unclear just how high any surveillance structure, whether permanent or temporary, might have been. In the visibility analysis below, the height of surveillance towers attached to villas (added as an offset to each villa's entry in ArcGIS) is calculated at 7.75 m, the same height as the *fortins* and *recintos-torre*. This is only an estimate, however, and the height might have been substantially less or may have varied between villas depending on the existence of a tower, its purpose, and its size. With these caveats in mind, the visibility analysis presented here should be taken as an impression of the surveillance potential of these villas rather than as an actual projection of their viewsheds.

A sampling of villas in the heart of the central Alentejo was analyzed as part of this chapter. These sites were chosen for the quality of their available data, for their first-century CE foundation dates, and for their close proximity to the Serra d'Ossa, one of the regions where surveillance was concentrated in the first century BCE. A cumulative viewshed analysis was completed on these villas in order to

---

[2] Morris and Papadopoulos 2005: 156.
[3] For examples see Ober 1985; Ashton and Pantazoglou 1991; Ault 1994: 117–18; Carter et al. 2000; Morris 2001; Pettegrew 2001, 2002; Decker 2006, among others.
[4] Osborne 1987: 78–79.
[5] Morris and Papadopoulos 2005: 188–200.
[6] Davies 1997. See also Renfrew and Wagstaff 1983.
[7] For Lusitanian villas that may possess towers, see Torre de Palma (Maloney and Hale 1996).
[8] Pseudo-Cyprian's text and depictions of treehouses on Roman pottery are discussed further in Chapter 3. See also Tortorella 2005: 192–95.

compare their potential use of surveillance during the colonial encounter of the first century BCE with the new agricultural, territorial, and ideological system imposed during the first century CE (Fig. 7.1). This cumulative viewshed reveals that any towers built among the villas south of the Serra d'Ossa would have possessed generally limited viewsheds, particularly compared to those possessed by *fortins* and *recintos-torre* like Caladinho.

Those in the shadow of the Serra d'Ossa could, as would be reasonably expected, see the southern slopes of the nearby mountain. Most others, however, would have found their visibility curtailed to only their immediate territory. Some, like the two sites on the western side of the viewshed, would have possessed reasonably ample visibility of the surrounding landscape. The southernmost villa even appears to have had the potential for monitoring the north-south course of a stream bed much like the *fortins* and *recintos-torre* along the Guadiana. Yet none of the villas appear to work in concert with the others, and the territory south of the Serra d'Ossa appears no longer to have been surveilled as intensely nor as systematically as before. This is especially clear when the cumulative viewshed of the villas south of the Serra d'Ossa (Fig. 7.1) is compared with that of the *fortins* positioned around the mountain range in the first century BCE (Fig. 6.13). The viewsheds of the villas do not appear to work in concert, nor do they focus on the traversable route immediately south of the Serra d'Ossa. Instead, even if we assume that every villa possessed a tower, they would each be monitoring their own immediate territory rather the wider regional landscape. Most strikingly, even when the villas' viewsheds are combined, they provide neither a comprehensive view over the landscape nor a coherent attempt at monitoring roads, passes, or streams. The villas were not placed in locations that afforded a great deal of vision and visibility, but they also seem unconcerned with security—there are no walls to protect them as there had been at earlier indigenous sites like Rocha da Mina or Monte do Outeiro. The landscape populated with these villas is thus fundamentally different from the one occupied by the *fortins*, *recintos-torre*, and the scattered indigenous sites.

Static defenses of the Hadrianic frontier, northern England

The outposts and peripheral defenses around Hadrian's Wall in northern England present one of the best understood networks of watchtowers in the western provinces of the Roman Empire. The signaling networks in use in Roman Britain, and the structures that make it up, have been the object of study for D. J. Woolliscroft for the last fifteen years. His work primarily concerns methods of signaling information between towers.[9] As static border defenses, the towers and forts along

---

[9] For thorough explorations of Roman military signaling and intelligence gathering, see Woolliscroft 2001; Southern 1990; Donaldson 1988.

Hadrian's Wall depended on the surveillance provided by additional structures operating beyond the established *limes*. These outposts, called "signal" or "series" towers, would be expected to signal, in a manner still debated, to the primary fort or to other towers in the network.[10] Given the simplicity of the technologies available, the messages sent from series tower to fortress must have been both short and uncomplicated. Thus the messages may have been on a simple binary system: one signal fire when the situation was normal, two signals when the situation was not. The outposts would have provided their home fortresses with forewarning of attack and of the direction and distance of the approaching enemy.

In order for signaling to be accomplished, a line of sight must exist between each tower, fort, or camp in the network. Woolliscroft identifies numerous signaling towers in the landscape beyond the Stanegate Milecastle. The intervisibility of these towers was tested with an "elevated camera tower," a camera attached to a rod, and then diagrammed manually on topographic maps.[11] The equivalent of viewsheds was thus produced for the region. These viewsheds revealed an intricate network of towers spanning the area around Stanegate and connecting each of the other milecastles along the Wall.[12] Signaling between these towers and forts connected the surveillance of each structure along Hadrian's Wall into one viewshed. While the amount of information that a primitive signaling systems could pass was undoubtedly limited, the messages needed only to be brief.

The climate in northern England along Hadrian's Wall makes visibility difficult except on the clearest days. Thus surveillance and signaling from the towers in this network would have often been hampered or even impossible.[13] That this network was constructed even without the optimum environmental conditions implies the importance of surveillance along this frontier. It may be that this system of border surveillance developed out of earlier systems of borderless surveillance in other zones of colonial contact. The precision required in the construction of the signaling network along Hadrian's Wall entails both expertise and experience in the construction of systems of surveillance.

Unlike the surveillance system embedded in Alentejo, Hadrian's Wall and its outlying watchtowers were almost certainly manned by professional soldiers year round.[14] These border fortifications provided not only security against whatever

---

[10] Ozawa et al. (1995) reviews the utility of GIS for the analysis of signaling tower networks such as the ones set along the Roman frontiers, yet little work has yet been done along these lines.

[11] Woolliscroft 2001: 15–19.

[12] Woolliscroft 2001: 67–73. The surveillance system established around Hadrian's Wall was likely derived from the one constructed along the German-Raetian frontier. The German-Raetian border possessed more than nine hundred signaling towers constructed in timber and, by late antiquity, in stone. See Baatz 1976: 5; *ORL* A 1–5, 7–10, and 12–15. Another Roman signaling tower, this one made of timber and surrounded by a ditch, is discussed by Van Dierendonck (2004). It is situated near the Roman auxiliary fort of Valkenburg in the Netherlands along the *limes* of *Germania Inferior*.

[13] Woolliscroft 2001: 63.

[14] Given that civilians likely manned the watchtowers around the Mons Claudianus quarries in

lay to the north, but also represented an imposing manifestation of imperial power and military might to anyone approaching them. The presence of a series of towers situated to the north of Hadrian's Wall itself suggests that the region even beyond the border was reasonably pacified. While more vulnerable than the soldiers in the milecastles, those stationed in the watchtowers were safe enough that such towers could be built in the first place. Thus the towers are better described as artifacts of the panopticon—or an attempt at one—with the borderland north of Hadrian's Wall in its gaze, rather than as part of the security apparatus itself. The towers provide visibility to the Roman soldiers garrisoning the Wall and the knowledge of surveillance to those living beyond it.

Surveillance and the quarries at Mons Claudianus, Egypt

Like the imperial border in northern England, the Roman quarries at Mons Claudianus, Egypt were guarded by a system of forts and watchtowers.[15] The lookout posts, known as *skopeloi* in *ostraka* from the site, are much smaller than the *fortins* and *recintos-torre* of the central Alentejo. Peacock and Maxfield suggest that they provided a means of communication between the fort and quarries around Mons Claudianus.[16] They are placed both along roads and across the countryside in two parallel lines.[17] Each is positioned at a maximum distance of 650 m from either another *skopelos* or from a quarry. Some, with extant walls, possess windows that look out directly at the position of other *skopeloi*, thus allowing the occupants to stay cool indoors and still take part in the signaling network. Peacock and Maxfield suggest that "the system was not designed for advance warning of personnel approaching down the wadis, but was rather a system of internal communication."[18] The *skopeloi* provided surveillance of the quarries and their workers, but this surveillance was intended to promote communication rather than security.

Other surveillance structures were built around Mons Claudianus with security in mind. These include the larger tower constructed near the *hydreuma* that supplied the *skopeloi* and the fort and another tower positioned over quarries west of Mons Claudianus. The larger of the two towers is roughly equivalent to Caladinho in size, but far different in its manner of construction. It is located in a position that affords it visual control over the *hydreuma*, the *skopeloi*, the fort, and several

---

Egypt and the Roman imperial mines in Jordan, it is not impossible that civilians, operating under military jurisdiction, manned the towers north of Hadrian's Wall as well. This seems unlikely, however, because of the far more substantial size and martial character of these British towers. For a discussion of one of the series towers north of the Wall, see Woolliscroft 2000.

[15] The surveillance and signaling system at Mons Claudianus, particularly the evidence from *ostraka*, is discussed above in Chapter 5 where it is placed in comparison with the remains of the Caladinho watchtower from Portugal.

[16] Peacock and Maxfield 1997: 254.

[17] Jackson 2002: 56.

[18] Peacock and Maxfield 1997: 254.

wadis to a distance of roughly 7 km.[19] Like the towers positioned north of Hadrian's Wall, it is thought that the towers at Mons Claudianus were constructed to provide forewarning in the case of an attack. The reason for their position within the landscape, however, would also have been apparent to every desert traveler.

As a defensive system, the towers (and perhaps *skopeloi*) at Mons Claudianus served more as a deterrent than a physical defense. The fort, where the majority of the Roman soldiers resided, presented the primary means of defense for the quarries in case of an uprising among the workers or in the very unlikely event of an external attack. In this way, the towers express a panoptic power that is far more similar to the kind envisioned by Foucault. Since it is very likely that many of the workers in the quarries were enslaved, perhaps even *servi poenae* (enslaved criminals), characterizing their surveillance as a panopticon is particularly apt. With the tower and *skopeloi* continuously in sight, the quarry workers would have known that they were being watched. Any attempt at rebellion in the quarries would be easily spotted, and, thanks to the *skopeloi*, the fort would be quickly notified of the disturbance.

TOWARD A TYPOLOGY OF SURVEILLANCE
Border control

Here I offer a typology of three modes of surveillance utilized in the Roman Empire to monitor frontiers, colonized landscapes, and forced and punitive labor. The first, a purely military system, guards established borders, whether it is the border of the Empire itself or merely the perimeter of a camp in hostile territory. This system can be seen in the networks of watchtowers established beyond Hadrian's Wall, for example, or along the Gask Ridge in Scotland, or along the *limes* in *Germania Superior* and *Inferior*. Indeed, the presence of surveillance systems along borders represents an especially commonplace element of Roman imperial control over these frontiers. These towers and garrisons not only guarded the provinces against raiders and bandits, but also provided a check on those passing through the empire's borders.

In this system, the imperial gaze is turned outward. Those under the surveillance of the border fortifications must have realized their potential for reporting threats, and so altered their behavior in response. This reaction was likely the desired response to the *burgi* and other fortifications constructed across Rome's borders in the second century CE under the emperor Commodus.[20] At Hadrian's Wall, the presence of an extra-mural system of watch and signal towers suggests a garrison that was prepared for an attack by an organized enemy military. Yet

---

[19] Peacock and Maxfield 1997: 254–55.

[20] See discussion of the inscriptions relating to the *burgi specularii Commodiani* in Chapter 3.

no such attack ever befell the Wall. The purpose of these towers was, perhaps, not merely for the defense of the wall but also for the surveillance of the territory beyond it. With the projection of surveillance into this territory came also the projection of empire itself. The potential for observation in the areas north of Hadrian's Wall may have served to curtail acts of resistance there. The same might be said for any other region of the Roman Empire where borders were provisioned with watchtowers and the garrisons to man them. Indeed, the longest Roman border, the German-Raetian *limes*, possessed over nine hundred timber and stone watchtowers.

Oversight

A second system of surveillance exists in many parts of the Roman world where large agricultural or extractive industries were worked by carceral, enslaved, or punitive labor. This system of oversight can be seen in the Roman mines in Jordan, amid the mines and plantations of Roman Israel, and among the field systems of many Roman villas outfitted with towers. The Jordanian mines, operated by condemned convicts and other forced laborers, were monitored by watchtowers so that none of the laborers might escape. The potential for resistance among the laborers was limited, and we must assume those under observation existed under a constant threat of violence from their civilian and military overseers. The surveilled in this particularly brutal industrial context have little hope of resistance. They were held within a system which relied on surveillance to disempower, even dehumanize, its subjects.

Not even indigenous people were subjected to this surveillance, only the condemned, declared enemies of the state, were sent to work the mines. Trapped between the vision of multiple watchtowers, the enslaved laborers were forced to toil to produce precious metals for the Roman state. The projection of power in this system, which was instituted well after the region was colonized and reorganized, was truly panoptic in its scope. Similar systems of ancient labor surveillance can be found in other industries, other regions, and on different scales, yet they all retain some similar features. For example, each turns surveillance inward to observe a low status, often enslaved, population of laborers. They make use of individuals of a middle status to observe the enslaved and report back to overseers.[21] And finally, the surveillance present in these systems is ubiquitous in the lives of the observed. It defines their relationships with those of higher social status and with their peers. Surveillance, and the potential of being watched at any time, limits the ability of the enslaved to resist either actively or passively his or her enslavement.

This system of labor oversight, operating on a smaller scale than in imperial

---

[21] In the case of the mines in Mons Claudianus, Egypt, local civilians engaged in surveillance reported to Roman military officers. At Roman agricultural estates, individual slaves were given supervisory roles over forced laborers and made to report to their masters.

mining areas, can be observed in the central Alentejo by the first century CE.[22] With the *fortins* and *recintos-torre* largely abandoned and replaced with villas, which in some cases were constructed within meters of the older surveillance structures, the use of surveillance in the now pacified territory was greatly altered. The viewsheds of the villas do not appear to act in concert, even when they possess relatively good vision of the landscape. And only a few early villas, like Castelo da Lousa, are positioned in especially defensive positions. Instead, they largely monitor their immediate surroundings where each possessed farmland. In doing so, these villas demonstrate that, where surveillance was present in the first century CE, it was directed at the control over forced laborers rather than the expression of power over either a demarcated border or a conquered zone. By the first century CE, control over the central Alentejo was settled, and surveillance was repurposed in the pursuit of agricultural and industrial production.

Borderless surveillance

The interpretation of surveillance as a unidirectional, oppressive panopticon is an inadequate model for understanding the central Alentejo in the first century BCE. In this borderless zone of cultural contact, the population of colonists, soldiers, and collaborators was likely greatly outnumbered by indigenous groups. No system of surveillance could have stamped out all resistance. Further, the existence of large fortified indigenous settlements—such as Monte do Outeiro, Castelo Velho de Degebe, Castelo Velho de Veiros, and Serra de Segóvia—suggests that physical and ideological control over the landscape remained unsettled. In response to both passive resistance and the threat of further unrest, the Romans established a system of surveillance that took advantage of the fluid nature of the borderless zone. Rather than a network of signaling towers like that established beyond Hadrian's Wall, the towers in Alentejo were dispersed through the landscape with their vision focused on specific valuable or vulnerable locations.

Rather than a surveillance network, the towers of the central Alentejo are better characterized as a surveillance patchwork. This patchwork system appears to have been consciously constructed since most of the towers are situated so that their viewsheds complement their nearest neighbors. Communication between the *fortins* and *recintos-torre* was not a priority. Instead, this system of borderless surveillance was directed at the most overt form of lingering indigenous resistance: brigandage. The towers in this borderless zone monitored valuable territory both to protect colonial investments and to dissuade indigenous claim to it. Without banditry there to resist Roman colonists and hinder their control over

---

[22] It is unclear how labor in the central Alentejan marble quarries was organized. It is likely that, judging from the organization of other mines and quarries in the Roman world, including the mines in nearby Aljustrel (ancient Vipasca), that the Alentejan quarries made use of enslaved laborers under the observation of Roman administrators and a military garrison.

land and resources, Roman control over the landscape became a certainty. Within decades, surveillance helped to settled the negotiation of this colonial encounter. By guarding against bandits and offering the promise of violence against those caught in the gaze of the towers, Roman colonial forces expanded their control over both natural resources and territory. The new reality of life in this colonial landscape solidified in the shadows of the many *fortins* and *recintos-torre*.

The third form of surveillance affects the reordering of the physical and natural surroundings of a conquered, colonized territory by situating surveillance throughout the landscape. In this borderless system, surveillance is entangled within the processes of the colonial encounter. It also, while still connected with the Roman military, allows for the *fortins* and *recintos-torre* to be inhabited by non-soldiers, a situation supported by the artifact assemblage at many of these sites. Further, this borderless surveillance exists in a landscape where control is uncertain. Active resistance may have been the cause for the creation of the surveillance system, and its implementation in the landscape served both to protect new colonial investments and to curtail lingering resistance.

It is this third system of surveillance that fits best with the landscape of the central Alentejo and the archaeological remains there. The *fortins* and *recintos-torre* which surveilled the landscape did so to protect important urban centers, natural resources, or transportation routes.[23] In this way, borderless surveillance combines the defensive posture of border surveillance with the inward gaze of oversight. More than that, though, borderless surveillance represents an attempt at reordering the landscape per an imperial vision, in both senses of the word. This third theory, which recognizes surveillance in the context of a contested, colonized landscape, functions, I hope, as an adequate interpretive model for the changes in the central Alentejo that occurred during the first century BCE.

DEFINING SURVEILLANCE IN ANCIENT COLONIAL LANDSCAPES

The formation of a post-panopticon theory of surveillance in ancient colonial contexts, one that recognizes the agency of the colonized to avoid surveillance as much as the ability of the colonizer to surveil, is necessary to understand the nature of the central Alentejo in the first century BCE.[24] Indeed, since surveillance networks appear to be common throughout the Roman world—especially in

---

[23] Hints of a similar, but much later, system of surveillance can be seen in the inscription (*CIL* VIII.2495), suggesting that watchtowers were constructed to observe the roads of Roman Numidia. See Chapter 3 for further discussion of this inscription.

[24] Foucault (1980: 156) acknowledged that the observer was exposed to surveillance, and so had their behavior restricted, as much as the observed, writing, "this machine is one in which everyone is caught, those who exercise this power as well as those who are subjected to it."

those areas with histories of indigenous resistance or with significant numbers of individuals pressed into industrial activity—a nuanced theory of surveillance holds promise for our understanding of many colonial encounters under the Roman Empire. In order to build such a theory, the particular cultural context in which surveillance was utilized and resisted must be examined. The archaeology of the central Alentejo during the mid- to late first century BCE points to a colonial encounter where both indigenous and Roman societies were culturally entangled in both the material culture they created and consumed as well as the landscape they altered.

Entangled landscapes

The study of cultural entanglement is predicated on the presence of agency among both indigenous and non-indigenous societies involved in a colonial encounter. The entanglement of cultures begins with the "intercultural consumption of objects or practices," according to M. Dietler's recent definition. The choices involved in consumption of local and foreign-made products represent active and individual appropriations, transformations, and manipulations of material culture, cultural practices, and perceptions of them.[25] The processes of cultural entanglement incipient during any colonial encounter are contingent on the local social, economic, and political situation. Thus the Roman colonization of the central Alentejo involved not only the introduction (and so entanglement) of imported products and practices, but also an entanglement of a landscape populated by groups recognized for their potential to resist colonialism. This landscape, with its long history of violence, was implicated in the colonial encounter as it was appropriated, transformed, and manipulated in the same manner as the material products consumed in the central Alentejo. Its entanglement relied on the use of surveillance to demarcate newly claimed territory, to reorganize settlements, to control natural resources, and to dissuade active resistance to Roman rule in the form of brigandage. This last element of surveillance, guarding against bandits, was also a method of claiming territory since the surveilled could not effectively operate as bandits when the towers promised recognition and reprisal. Effectively, the towers were a way of claiming the territory within their viewsheds since any groups seeking to reclaim that territory or disrupt its colonization would have been encouraged instead to cede it and operate in areas outside of the system of surveillance.

Any archaeological analysis of the central Alentejo must take into account the entanglement of both the physical and ideological artifacts of colonialism present in the region. A number of examples of this process can be identified at Caladinho and the other sites in the region. Foremost among these are the ceramics both im-

[25] Dietler 2010: 55.

ported to the central Alentejan *fortins* and *recintos-torre* and those made in the region during the latter half of the first century BCE. The amphorae produced in the new Roman colonial possessions along the southern and western Iberian litoral represent the majority of the transport pottery imported to the central Alentejo (although some Italian amphorae also appear in some assemblages from the first century BCE). These large transport vessels brought Roman products—namely olive oil, wine, and fish sauce—to the region. The amphorae from the bay of Cadiz were primarily of the Haltern 70 type, and, as in other contexts in Europe and the Mediterranean, were likely originally intended to supply the Roman military with wine. The Lusitanian amphorae, used for the distribution of *garum* produced along the southwestern coast of Portugal, are also found in the central Alentejo.

The perception of these amphorae and the food products they contained as elements of the Roman occupation of the province perhaps shaped their patterns of consumption. Those who sought to ally themselves with the new colonial order might adopt Roman (or simply Mediterranean) culinary practices. Locally produced amphorae are of particular interest to the question of the perception of Roman products in the central Alentejo. These amphorae, while few in number and as yet poorly understood, first appear in the middle of the first century BCE. The techniques of their manufacture, as discussed above, betray an ignorance among central Alentejan potters as to the correct way to form an amphora. Additionally, the region is particularly ill-suited to the use of amphorae as containers for transport since the only navigable body of water, the Guadalquivir River, lies at the border of this region.[26] Instead, these local amphorae seem to have been a response to the perceived need of amphorae to hold wine (or oil or *garum*) rather than their intended use as transport pottery. The form of a Roman amphora was thus appropriated and transformed in order to suit the local social needs of the colonial encounter.

The entanglement of Roman and indigenous cultures in the central Alentejo may also be observed in the importation of Italian finewares and the local production of imitations of Italian finewares. Pottery of these types was intended for dining, and the forms are distinctly Italian in their origins. Italian terra sigillata, found in the assemblage of Caladinho and other *fortins* and *recintos-torre* in the central Alentejo, suggest a connection with a wider Mediterranean economy and the entanglement of foreign ways of cooking and dining in the central Alentejo. The desire for Roman-style finewares in the central Alentejo is further evidenced by the presence of local imitations of Campanian black gloss ware. This production of black gloss ware was in decline by the end of the first century BCE as terra sigillata began to dominate the market in both Italy and the provinces. Yet in

---

[26] Funari (1986) and Rodriguez et al. (1991) discuss the exploration and colonization of the Guadalquivir in the Roman period. Although it had some commercial impact on the central Alentejo, the Roman colonization of the Guadalquivir river valley largely lies beyond the scope of this work.

the central Alentejo, the consumption of this older style of Roman fineware continued. The presence of a remnant imitation black gloss industry in the central Alentejo suggests that these wares had become appropriated and the perception of their use manipulated to fit a local understanding. Just how these wares fit within the entangled society of the central Alentejo remains unclear, but their continued production long after the introduction of new Roman-style pottery indicates that they possessed an important local cachet.

The architecture of sites within the central Alentejo also suggests cultural entanglement between indigenous and Roman societies. At Castelo da Lousa, for example, Alentejan dry schist masonry was utilized to construct an atrium-style house in the middle of the first century BCE. Its material culture encompasses a wide range of imported Roman artifacts, local imitations of Italian pottery, and some indigenous wares. The house, perhaps best described as a fortified villa, was situated overlooking the Guadiana River and so well placed to observe its traffic. The *fortins* and *recintos-torre* of the central Alentejo make use of similar masonry techniques, date to roughly the same period, possess comparable artifact assemblages, and are often positioned to observe traversable routes through the landscape. Both the physical nature of these sites—their architecture and material culture—and their functional roles suggest that they played a role in the social, economic, and ideological entanglement of the region's physical and cultural landscape.

The careful positioning of these sites to take advantage of their ability to surveil, often in concert with other sites, embeds surveillance in the appropriation and transformation of this landscape. Surveillance, however, was not used merely to demarcate and monitor borders, especially since so few formal borders existed in this zone of colonial contact. Instead, it was likely the reaction to another part of the colonial process, violence and insecurity. Surveillance towers provided the ability to police the colonized landscape, which was, Roman sources tell us, rife with banditry and prone to armed uprisings. Indeed, during the middle of the first century BCE, violence, both between Romans and indigenous Lusitanians and between factions of each, had played an integral role in the negotiation of the colonial encounter. It was this perception of the central Alentejo as a landscape of violence that, perhaps, initiated the construction of a system of surveillance within the region. As a tool of empire, surveillance provides a ready means to confront, both physically and psychologically, active modes of resistance through the potential for observation. Surveillance is by nature both visible and invisible to the surveilled. They may know that a surveillance tower is within sight, but they cannot know if they are, at any given moment, under observation. Thus the landscape under surveillance may be controlled, and resistance pushed to those regions where surveillance has not or can not yet reach.

Local groups chose to ignore, resist, or collaborate with foreign incursions, and various Roman armies, including those of both the anti-senatorial Sertorians and the pro-senatorial Pompeians, made use of Lusitanians in Rome's many civil wars. Banditry, which in the case of Viriathus exploded into a bloody colonial war, is one such attempt to realign access to power in a colonial encounter through violence. We are told, as discussed above in Chapter 2, that western Iberia was filled with bandits. While such accounts cannot be accepted uncritically, the presence of so many fortified structures suggests that small-scale violent resistance to Roman imperial appropriation of indigenous Iberian territory likely continued during the first century BCE, even if such resistance often acted in conjunction the goals of one faction of the late republican government or another. In such an insecure landscape, where bandits or rumor of bandits persisted and warfare seemed endemic, surveillance represented an attempt to police and control violence and thus to curtail resistance to imperial power.

Empire and surveillance beyond the panopticon

Many previous explorations of surveillance have looked to Foucault's theory of the panopticon to explain the role of watching and being watched in the expression of power. Foucault's panopticon was derived from early modern designs for prisons, conceived by J. Bentham, where a single guard could observe an entire population of prisoners.[27] Since the late twentieth century, this theory of vision, surveillance, and the perception of being seen has found application in both the humanities and social sciences. Foucault's theory holds that those in power persuade those they dominate that they could, at any moment, be under surveillance. The perception of being observed, or the mere potential of being observed, by those in power alters the behavior of the subjugated to better fit the desires of the powerful. The crux of this theory of surveillance rests on the recognition by the powerless that acts of resistance to power may be observed and met with severe repercussions. Indeed, surveillance in the panopticon is concomitant not only with the threat of censure but also of violence. It is through this threat that active resistance to imperial domination may be disempowered.

The panopticon has been used even in discussions of the archaeology of surveillance particularly among Roman imperial mining and agricultural production in Israel and Jordan.[28] In these contexts, where surveillance is established over a group of laborers condemned to the mines or enslaved to work in the fields, the panopticon provides a ready explanation for the expression of power over a subjugated population. Those forced to work in the mines and fields could never be certain whether they were being watched or not, but must assume that they were whenever a surveillance structure was within sight. As in a Bentham's prison, sur-

[27] Bentham 1787.
[28] Friedman 2008, 2009a, 2009b; Yekutieli 2006. Farther afield, Romero (2002) has applied Foucault's approaches to power and space in his analysis of the archaeology of colonial Argentina.

veillance defines the social relationships between individuals in these contexts and limits their potential actions.

Its application in the interpretation of archaeologies of forced labor, imprisonment, and industry is apt, but the panopticon possesses some deficiencies when used to explain power relationships within a colonial encounter. In the panopticon, vision, and thus power, is unidirectional. It does not matter to the powerful if the subjugated look back, nor is hiding from the panoptic gaze possible. Yet in an entangled, colonial landscape, where surveillance is often met with resistance and where local perceptions reshape imported cultural materials and practices, the panopticon fails to account for the agency of indigenous actors.

In order to understand a system of surveillance embedded within a colonized landscape, we must recognize the ability of a colonized (rather than subjugated) population to appropriate, transform, and manipulate vision and visibility. Surveillance of such a landscape by a colonizing, imperialist power like Rome certainly helped to reshape the social, political, and economic realities of the region, yet this reshaping was met with resistance. Banditry provides the primary example of resistance which surveillance may counter. We may assume that resistance to surveillance was met with violence, as it would have been under the panopticon, but, as was discussed above, this colonial landscape was already prone to acts of violence both in the pursuit of empire and in resistance to it. Instead, surveillance serves to mark claims to territory and resources, to curtail the landscape's potential for harboring violent resistance, and to contribute to the sociopolitical reordering of the region.

Surveillance in a colonial context represents the embedding of a new order within the landscape itself. As with any element introduced to an indigenous landscape during a colonial encounter, particularly a prolonged one, surveillance was inevitably entangled within the matrix of the local society and its own political and economic hierarchies. This promotes a process of control that Foucault termed "normalization," and an expression of power which "needs continuous regulatory and corrective mechanisms.... Such a power has to qualify, measure, appraise, and hierarchize, rather than display itself in its murderous splendor."[29] The expression of power through surveillance serves to normalize political relationships as much as it attempts to control the behavior of its subjects. The spatial and temporal ubiquity of power's expression over a surveilled landscape serves to habituate colonizer and colonized to new social, political, territorial, and economic relationships within the landscape.

In the central Alentejo, the ability to surveil became, as with imported and imitation pottery, appropriated by locals and transformed to meet their social needs. Individual agency during the colonial encounter was open to those who may have held power prior to colonization or those who were marginalized. The

[29] Foucault 1978: 144.

manipulation of surveillance permitted individuals either to (re)assert claims to power or simply to avoid expressions of it. Whether observing or under observation, the use of surveillance in the colonized landscape served to normalize the new sociopolitical hierarchies. Surveillance represents both an imperial power to subdue, police, and regulate a landscape as well as the opportunity for locals to transform expressions of colonialism to meet the immediate social needs of their cultural landscape.

Surveillance there was predictable, non-specific in its object, and a patchwork in its dispersion throughout the landscape. It was not a panopticon, but like the imperfect surveillance systems of the modern world, it still provided a useful tool for monitoring and controlling dissent, resistance, and criminality. The system of surveillance in Alentejo was far from total, but it served to entangle the landscape itself in the colonial encounter. The imperial gaze could monitor the territory and resources it valued and could protect its claim from indigenous resistance through the threat of violence concomitant with being watched. It was not a network of towers, as might be seen on the borders of the Roman Empire, but a borderless system that held many objects of its gaze. It could certainly be avoided by leaving the viewsheds of the towers, but doing so effectively ceded control over the landscape within the towers' view. Avoiding surveillance was a capitulation to the new social and political realities of Roman colonization as much as it was a form of passive resistance. Surveillance thus had a powerful role in negotiating the physical and ideological reorganization of the cultural landscape of the central Alentejo under the Romans.

Thus the panopticon, while it offers an explanation for other uses of surveillance, fails to account for the agency, adaptability, and entanglement present in a colonial encounter.[30] Surveillance in a colonized landscape requires the recognition that expressions of power are rarely unidirectional, and thus vision, visibility, and surveillance structures become, like other cultural practices and their material expressions, entangled within multiple competing perspectives. Archaeological analyses of ancient colonial landscapes, be they in Roman Iberia or beyond, benefit from the recognition of cultural entanglement within the material record. Surveillance is only a single element of a colonial encounter, yet its material presence points to an expression of imperial power, attempts to resist this power, and the conceptual transformation of a natural and built landscape. After surveillance, the surveilled landscape is no longer one where empire and resistance meet, but one where the landscape itself has been appropriated, reordered, and transformed by both indigenous and foreign agency following the rupture caused by colonialism. In the central Alentejo, the colonial processes brought about by surveilling the landscape end with the redistribution of resources to the inhabitants of a new

---

[30] Haggerty (2006: 29–34) provides a similar critique of the panopticon's use in analyses of surveillance in modern society.

social, political, religious, and economic landscape. Those who benefit most are the individuals, among both the colonizers and the colonized, who most deftly negotiate the reordering of this landscape.

CONCLUSIONS AND FUTURE DIRECTIONS

In her seminal *Private Matters: In Defense of the Personal Life*, J. M. Smith describes the ability of surveillance to express power over a subject people:

> The totalitarian state watches everyone, but keeps its own plans secret. Privacy is seen as dangerous because it enhances resistance. Constantly spying and then confronting people with what are often petty transgressions is a way of maintaining social control and unnerving and disempowering opposition. While spying efforts sometimes backfire and increase the loyalty of friends and intimates, too often they succeed. And even when one shakes real pursuers, it is often hard to rid oneself of the feeling of being watched—which is why surveillance is an extremely powerful way to control people.... Feeling watched, but not knowing for sure, nor knowing if, when, or how the hostile surveyor may strike, people often become fearful, constricted, and distracted.[31]

While her work deals primarily with the role of surveillance in modern societies, this analysis seems applicable to ancient society given the prominence of surveillance in Rome's control over its borders, the supervision of enslaved labor, and the colonization of conquered provincial territory. Imperial authorities in zones of colonization, such as the central Alentejo during the first century BCE, may have sought to use surveillance in order to halt, censure, or deaden long-lived resistance movements. The installation of surveillance structures within the central Alentejo prevented the rise of another Viriathus, another Sertorius, or another Pompey.

Yet in landscapes entangled in the colonial encounter we must acknowledge the ability of the surveilled to resist, counter, and usurp visibility. Such is also the case among modern societies under surveillance of all kinds. For example, citizens in many countries turn surveillance against the authorities by recording the actions of police during public encounters. Others seeking digital anonymity create local "mesh" networks separate from the larger and decidedly surveilled global Internet. And a growing movement emphasizes the role of the body in resisting surveillance.[32] But despite these and other measures, surveillance is pervasive in our society, and it remains an effective means of control. Such can also be said for the Roman world where the landscape of the central Alentejo was colonized, reorganized, and settled through the use of watchtowers and their imperfect, dis-

---

[31] Smith 1997: 29–30. The influence of Foucault's panopticon on Smith's critique is clearly present here.

[32] Ball 2006: 309–12.

persed, non-panoptic form of surveillance.

Rome's surveillance systems appear to have their beginnings in her first steps towards empire in Iberia. From there, surveillance begins to play an essential role in the control over conquered territories both by observing borders and by controlling traffic within the provinces. Surveillance even becomes integral to the administration of Roman agricultural and industrial production. It defines the relationship between enslaved laborers, their supervisors, and their masters. The imperial gaze was pervasive in both its physical and its ideological manifestations. Indeed, surveillance seems to be an important element in the sociopolitical relationships both within the Roman Empire's borders and outside them.

Thus, if we wish to better understand surveillance and its role in empire during our own time, we have perhaps no better prototype than its use, as well as its opposition, within the history of Rome and her provinces. Much of ancient surveillance remains to be understood, and the evidence, while diverse, is often scarce. Yet systems of surveillance, whether they are engaged in the observation of borders, laborers, or contested colonial encounters, form an essential part of the Roman state and its relationship to both its own inhabitants and those beyond its borders. In order to understand surveillance in a provincial context, we must acknowledge that it, like other expressions of power, swiftly became entangled in the processes of the colonial encounter. It is this very entanglement that makes understanding surveillance all the more valuable as it opens a window into the negotiation of territory and power among the various factions involved in the encounter.

SELECT FIGURES AND ILLUSTRATIONS

SELECT FIGURES

NOTE: The entire set of figures is available in open access online at eScholarship.org (search for the title of this book to locate the page for this book, which will have a link to the Supplement of images). Only a select set of figures listed here is printed here for the convenience of the reader.

Fig. 1.1. The central Alentejo, Portugal
Fig. 1.2. Map of small fortified structures in the central Alentejo
Fig. 3.1. Watchtower on the Column of Trajan
Fig. 3.2. Watchtowers on the Column of Trajan
Fig. 5.2. Plan of the tower at Caladinho (F9), Sector 1, as of 2010

Fig. 1.1. The central Alentejo, Portugal

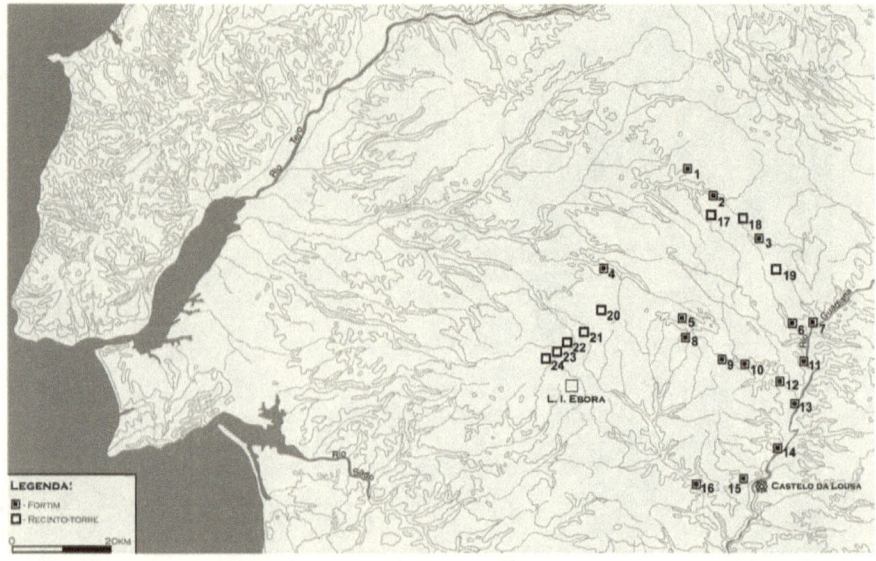

Fig. 1.2. Map of small fortified structures in the central Alentejo
(After Williams and Mataloto 2011, fig. 5)

1 – Malhada das Penas 1 and 2 (F1)
2 – Beiçudos (F2)
3 – Penedo do Ferro (F3)
4 – Soeiros (F4)
5 – Cortes (F5)
6 – Outeiro Pintado (F6)
7 – Três Moinhos (F7)
8 – Monte do Almo (F8)
9 – Caladinho (F9)
10 – Castelinho (F10)
11 – Rocha de Províncios (F11)
12 – Castelinhos do Rosário (F12)
13 – Castelo da Pena de Alfange (F13)
14 – Monte do Gato 2 (F14)
15 – Defensinha (F15)
16 – Moinho do Tojal (F16)
17 – Mariano (R16)
18 – Outeiro da Mina (R18)
19 – Terrugem (R19)
20 – Castelo do Mau Vizinho (R20)
21 – Santa Justa (R21)
22 – Sempre-Noiva (R22)
23 – Castelo dos Mouros (R23)
24 – Vale d'El-Rei de Cima (R24)

Fig. 3.1. Watchtower on the Column of Trajan
Public domain image (After Cichorius 1896, pl. IV)

Fig. 3.2. Watchtowers on the Column of Trajan
Public domain image (After Cichorius 1896, pl. V)

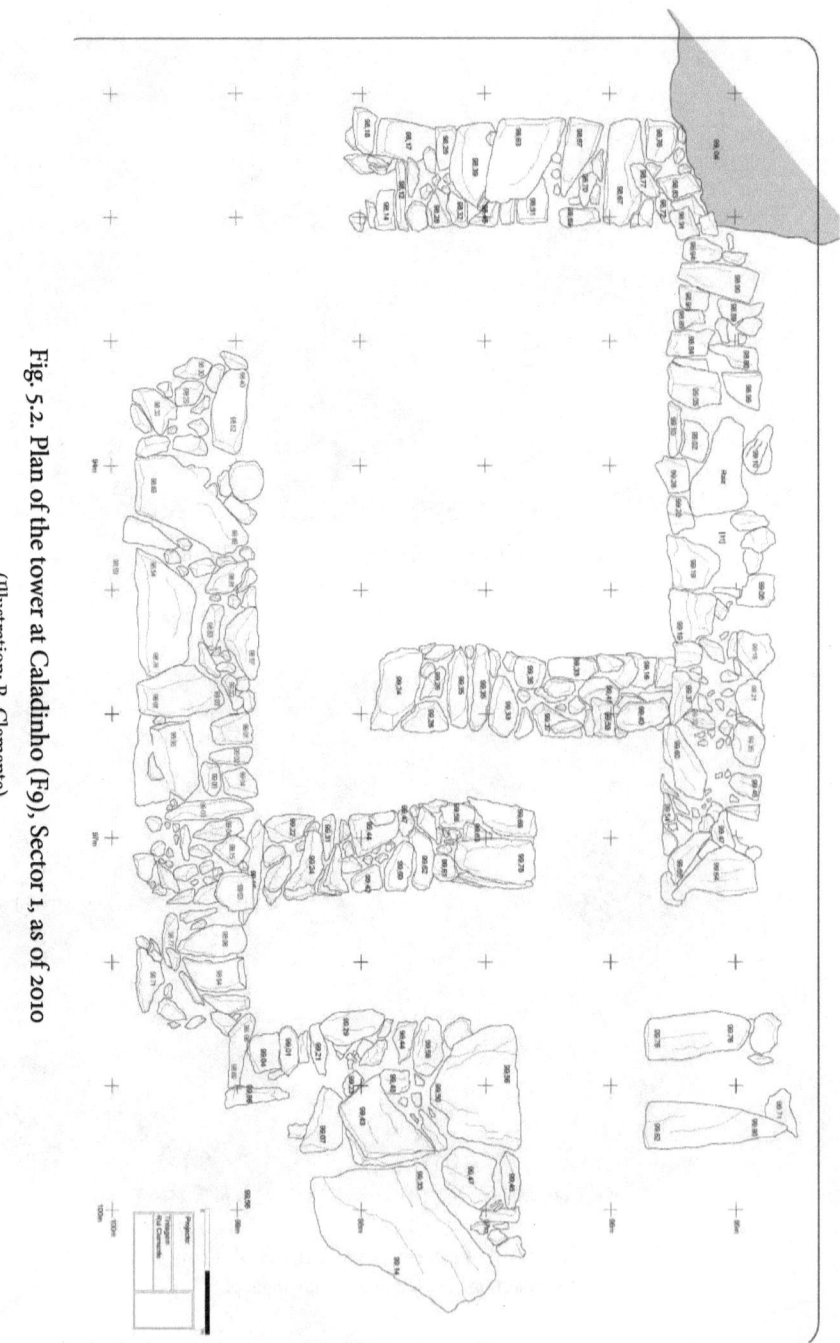

Fig. 5.2. Plan of the tower at Caladinho (F9), Sector 1, as of 2010
(Illustration: R. Clemente)

BIBLIOGRAPHY AND ABBREVIATIONS

Abascal, J., and U. Espinosa. 1989. *La Ciudad Hispano-Romana: Privilégio y Poder*. Logroño: Colegio Oficial de Aparejadores.
AE = *L'Année Epigraphique*.
Alarcão, J. 1988. *Roman Portugal*. 3 vols. Warminster: Aris and Philips.
— . 1990a. "Identificação das Cidades da Lusitânia Portuguesa e dos seus Territórios." In Gorges 1990, 21–34.
— . 1990b. *Nova História de Portugal, I - Portugal das origens à romanização*. Lisboa: Ed. Presença.
— . 1998. "A paisagem rural romana e alto-medieval em Portugal." *Conimbriga* 37: 89–119.
— . 2001. "A localização de *Dipo* e *Evandriana*." *Al-madan* 2.10: 39–42.
Alarcão, J., P. C. Carvalho, and A. Gonçalves. 2010a. "História das escavações e da interpretação do monumento." In Alarcão et al. 2010c, 27–35.
Alarcão, J., P. C. Carvalho, and A. Gonçalves. 2010b. "Estratigrafia, estruturas e materiais." In Alarcão et al. 2010c, 65–110.
Alarcão, J., P. C. Carvalho, and A. Gonçalves, eds. 2010c. *Castelo da Lousa—Intervenções Arqueológicas de 1997 a 2002*. Studia Lusitana 5. Mérida: Museo Nacional de Arte Romano.
Alarcão, J., J.-G. Gorges, V. Mantas, M. Salinas de Frías, P. Sillières, and A. Tranoy. 1990. "Appendice: Propositions pour un nouveau tracé des limites anciennes de la Lusitanie romaine." In Gorges 1990, 319–29.
Aldenerfer, M., and H. Maschner, eds. 1996. *Anthropology, Space, and Geographic Information Systems*. Oxford: OUP.
Almeida, J. 1945. *Roteiro dos Monumentos Militares Portugueses*. 3 vols. Lisbon: Império.
Almeida, R. 2008. *Las ánforas del Guadalquivir en Scallabis (Santarém, Portugal): Una aportación al conocimiento de los tipos minoritarios*. Barcelona: Edicions Universitat Barcelona.
Alonso Sánchez, A. 1988. *Fortificaciones romanas en Extremadura: La defensa del territorio*. Salamanca: Universidad de Extremadura.
Alonso Sánchez, A., and F. Corrales. 2000. "El processo de romanización de la Lusitania Oriental: La creación de assentamientos militares." In Gorges and Nogales Basarrate 2000, 85–100.

Álvarez, J. A. A., M. L. G. Fernández, and B. M. Serrano. 2008. "Recientes investigaciones en el Campamento de Cáceres el Viejo." In *Arqueología urbana en Cáceres. Investigaciones e intervenciones recientes en la ciudad de Cáceres y su entorno*, edited by P. J. S. Marcos, 115–43. Cáceres: Actas de las Jornadas de Arqueología del Museo de Cáceres.

Álvarez-Sanchís, J. R. 2000. "The Iron Age in Western Spain (800 BC–AD 50): An Overview." *Oxford Journal of Archaeology* 19.1: 65–89.

Alves, C. S. A. 2010. "A Cerâmica Campaniense de Mesas do Castelinho." M.A. thesis. Universidade de Lisboa.

Aquilué Abadías, X., J. García Rosello, and J. Guitart Duran, eds. 2000. *La ceràmica de vernís negre dels segles II i I a.C.: Centres productors mediterranis i comercialització a la Península Ibèrica*. Mataró: Museu de Mataró.

Arnaud, J. M. 1970. "O 'Castelo Velho' de Veiros (Estremoz). Campanha Preliminar de Escavações de 1969." *Actas das I Jornadas Arqueológicas da Associação dos Arqueólogos Portugueses* 2: 311–28.

Arruda, A., and R. Almeida. 1999. "As importações de vinho itálico para o território actualmente português. Contextas, cronologias e significado." In Gorges and Rodríguez Martín 1999, 307–37.

Arruda, A., C. Viegas, and P. Bargão. 2006. "Ânforas lusitanas da Alcáçova de Santarém." *Setúbal Arqueológica* 13: 153–76.

Ashton, N. G., and E. Th. Pantazoglou. 1991. *Siphnos: Ancient Towers B.C.* Athens: Eptalofos Abee.

Aubet, M. E. 2001. *The Phoenicians and the West: Politics, Colonies, and Trade*. 2nd edition. Cambridge: CUP.

Ault, B. 1994. *Classical Houses and Households: An Architectural and Artifactual Case Study from Halieis, Greece*. Ph.D. diss., Indiana University.

Austin, N. J. E. 1987. "What Happened to Intelligence Information from the Frontiers?" *Prudentia* 19.2: 28–33.

Austin, N. J. E., and N. B. Rankov. 1995. *Exploratio: Military and Political Intelligence in the Roman World*. London: Routledge.

Baatz, D. 1976. *Die Wachttürme am Limes*. Stuttgart: Württembergisches Landesmuseum.

Bagnall, R. S. 1977. "Army and Police in Roman Upper Egypt." *Journal of the American Research Center in Egypt* 14: 67–86.

Ball, K. 2006. "Organization, surveillance and the body: Towards a politics of resistance." In Lyon 2006, 296–317.

Barker, G., and J. Lloyd, eds. 1991. *Roman Landscapes: Archaeological Survey in the Mediterranean Region*. London: British School at Rome.

Barker, P. 2005. *Techniques of Archaeological Excavation*. 3rd edition. New York: Routledge.

Bender, B. 1993. "Introduction: Landscape—meaning and action." In *Landscape: Politics and Perspectives*, edited by B. Bender, 1–18. Oxford: Berg.

Bentham, J. 1787. "Panopticon." In Bozovic 1995, 29–95.

Berlin, A. 1997. *Tel Anafa II: The Hellenistic and Roman Pottery*. Journal of Roman Archaeology Supplementary Series 10, 2. Ann Arbor: University of Michigan Press.

Berrocal, L. 1992. *Los Pueblos Celticos del Suroeste de la Peninsula Iberica*. Complutum-Extra 2. Madrid: Ed. Complutense.

—. 1996. "Fortificación, guerra y poblamiento en la Beturia: Consideraciones sobre el altar de Capote y la conquista del suroeste." *Revista de Estudios Extremeños* 52.2: 411- 40.

Bilou, F. 2005. *Sistema viário antigo na região de Évora*. Lisbon: Edições Colibri.

Bingen, J., A. Bülow-Jacobsen, W. Cockle, H. Cuvigny, L. Rubenstein, and W. van Rengen. 1992. *Mons Claudianus: Ostraca Graeca et Latina* I. Cairo: Institut Français d'Archéologie Orientale.

Birley, E. 1961. *Research on Hadrian's Wall*. Kendal: Titus Wilson and Son.

Blázquez Martínez, J. M. 2002. "Las calzadas: Arterias de la guerra en la Hispania romana republicana." In Morillo 2002, 493–501.

Boaventura, R., and C. Banha. 2006. "Ânforas da região de Monforte: Contributo para o conhecimento do comércio rural romano." *O Arqueólogo Português* 4.24: 360–99.

Boaz, J. S., and E. Uleberg. 1995. "The Potential of GIS-Based Studies of Iron Age Cultural Landscapes in Eastern Norway." In Lock and Stančič 1995, 249–59.

Bowes, K. 2012. "Excavating the Roman Peasant." Paper read at the 2012 Annual Meeting of the Archaeological Institute of America, 5–8 January, Philadelphia.

Bozovic, M., ed. 1995. *The Panopticon Writings*. London: Verso.

Bucher, G. S. 2000. "The Origins, Program, and Composition of Appian's *Roman History*." *TAPA* 130: 411–58.

Burgess, C. 1987. "Fieldwork in the Évora District, Alentejo, Portugal, 1986–1988: Preliminary report." *Northern Archaeology* 8: 35–105.

Burgess, C., C. Gibson, V. Correia, and I. Ralston. 1999. "Hillforts, *oppida* and vitrification in the Évora area, central Portugal." In *"We Were Always Chasing Time": Papers Presented to Keith Blood*, edited by P. Frodsham, P. Topping, and D. Cowley. *Northern Archaeology* 17/18: 129–47.

Burini, C. 1994. *Pseudo Cipriano: I due monti Sinai e Sion*. Biblioteca Patristica 25. Florence: Nardini.

Burnett, A., M. Amandry, and P. P. Ripollès, eds. 1992. *Roman Provincial Coinage: From the Death of Caesar to the Death of Vitellius (44 BC–AD 69)*. Vol. 1. London: British Museum Press.

Burrough, P. A. 1986. *Principles of Geographical Information Systems for Land Resource Assessment*. Oxford: Clarendon Press.

Calado, M. 1993. *Carta Arqueológica do Alandroal*. Alandroal: Câmara Municipal de Alandroal.

—. 1994–1995. "Recintos ciclópicos do Alentejo central." *A Cidade de Évora*. 2.1: 275–85.

—. 1996a. *Carta Arqueológica do Concelho de Évora*. Évora: Câmara Municipal de Évora.

—. 1996b. "Recintos ciclópicos do Alentejo central." *A Cidade de Évora—Boletim Cultural da Câmara Municipal de Évora*. 2.1: 275–85.

Calado, M., M. Deus, and R. Mataloto. 2000. "O sítio dos Soeiros (Arraiolos): Uma abordagem preliminar." *Revista de Guimarães* 2: 759–74.

Calado, M., and R. Mataloto. 2001. *Carta Arqueológica do Concelho do Redondo*. Redondo: Câmara Municipal de Redondo.

Calado, M., and L. Rocha. 1997. "Povoamento da Idade do Ferro no Alentejo Central." *Cadernos de Cultura de Reguengos de Monsaraz* 1: 99–130.

Carreras Monfort, C. 2003. "Haltern 70: A Review." *Journal of Roman Pottery Studies* 10: 85–91.

Carrión, J. S., C. Navarro, J. Navarro, and M. Munuera. 2000. "The distribution of cluster pine (*Pinus pinaster*) in Spain as derived from palaeoecological data: Relationships with phytosociological classification." *The Holocene* 10: 243–52.

Carter, J. C. 2003. *Crimean Chersonesos: City, Chora, Museum and Environs*. Austin: National Preserve of Tauric Chersonesos and Institute of Classical Archaeology.

Carter, J. C., M. Crawford, P. Lehman, G. Nikolaenko, and J. Trelogan. 2000. "The Chora of Chersonesos in Crimea, Ukraine." *AJA* 104.4: 707–41.

Carvalho, P. C., and R. Morais. 2010. "Terra Sigillata de tipo itálico." In Alarcão et al. 2010c, 139–52.

Castro López, M., and L. Gutiérrez Soler. 2001. "Conquest and Romanization of the upper Guadalquivir valley." In Keay and Terrenato 2001, 146–60.

Castro Martínez, P. V., V. Lull, and R. Mico. 1996. *Cronologia de la prehistoria reciente de la Peninsula Iberica y Baleares (c. 2800–900 cal ANE)*. BAR-IS 652. Oxford.

Chapman, H. 2006. *Landscape Archaeology and GIS*. Stroud: Tempus.

Christopherson, G. L., and P. D. Guertin. 1996. "Visibility analysis and ancient settlement strategies in the region of Tall al-Umayri, Jordan." *Madaba Plains Project Hinterland Survey*. http://www.casa.arizona.edu/MPP/viewshed/vspaper.html

Cichorius, C. 1896. *Die Reliefs des Ersten Dakischen Krieges*. Berlin: Verlag von Georg Reimer.

CIL = Corpus Inscriptionum Latinarum.

CIMAC = *Comunidade Intermunicipal do Alentejo Central*. http://www.cimac.pt/

CIMAC. 2014. "Ambiente: Modelo Territorial e Ambiente."

Clark, V., and T. Parker. 1987. "The late Roman observation and signalling system." In *The Roman Frontier in Central Jordan: Interim Report on the Limes Arabicus Project, 1980–1985. Part I and Part II*, edited by T. Parker, 165–82. BAR-IS 134. Oxford: Archaeopress.

Conolly, J., and M. Lake. 2006. *Geographical Information Systems in Archaeology*. Cambridge: Cambridge University Press.

Consp. = Ettlinger, E., B. Hedinger, B. Hoffmann, P. Kenrick, G. Pucci, K. Roth-Rubi, G. Schneider, S. von Schnurbein, C. M. Wells, and S. Zabehlicky-Scheffenegger. 1990. *Conspectus Formarum Terrae Sigillatae Italico Modo Confectae*. Bonn: Dr. Rudolf Habelt GmbH.

Corsi, C. 2014. *Ammaia II: The Excavation Contexts 1994–2011*. ARGU 9. Gent: Academia Press.

Corsi, C., and F. Vermeulen. 2009. "Archaeology of a Roman Landscape in Central Portugal." *The Egyptian Journal of Environmental Change* 1: 1–5.

Corsi, C., and F. Vermeulen, eds. 2010. *Changing Landscapes: The Impact of Roman Towns in the Western Mediterranean*. Bologna: Ante Quem.

Corsi, C., and F. Vermeulen, eds. 2012. *Ammaia I: The Survey. A Romano-Lusitanian Townscape Revealed*. ARGU 8. Gent: Academia Press.

CSEL = Corpus Scriptorum Ecclesiasticorum Latinorum.

Curchin, L. 1991. *Roman Spain: Conquest and Assimilation*. London: Routledge.

— . 2004. *The Romanization of Central Spain: Complexity, Diversity and Change in a Provincial Hinterland*. London: Routledge.

Daveau, S., O. Ribeiro, and H. Lautensach. 1987. *Geografia de Portugal I: A Posição Geográfica e o Território*. Lisboa: Sá da Costa.

Davies, G. 1997. *Studies on the Social and Economic History of an Island Polis: Siphnos in Classical Antiquity.* Ph.D. diss., Oxford University.

Decker, M. 2006. "Towers, refuges, and fortified farms in the Late Roman East." *Liber Annus* 56: 449–520.

Deprez, S., M. De Dapper, and F. Vermeulen. 2007. "Geoarcheologisch onderzoek van een historische goudmijnsite in de noordoostelijke Alentejo, Portugal." *Tijdschrift voor Mediterrane Archeologie* 37: 33–41.

Dias, M. I., M. J. Trindade, C. Fabião, A. Sabrosa, J. Bugalhão, J. Raposo, A. Guerra, A. L. Duarte, and M. I. Prudêncio. 2012. "Arqueometria e o estudo das ânforas lusitanas do Núcleo Arqueológico da Rua dos Correeiros (Lisboa) e de centros produtores do Tejo." *Estudos Arqueológicos de Oeiras* 19: 57–70.

Dietler, M. 1998. "Consumption, agency, and cultural entanglement: Theoretical implications of a Mediterranean colonial encounter." In *Studies in Culture Contact: Interaction, Culture Change, and Archaeology,* edited by J. Cusick, 288–315. Carbondale: Southern Illinois University Press, Center for Archaeological Investigations.

— . 2010. *Archaeologies of Colonialism: Consumption, Entanglement, and Violence in Ancient Mediterranean France.* Berkeley: University of California Press.

Diogo, A. M. D. 1987. "Quadro tipológico das ânforas de fabrico lusitano." *O Arqueólogo Português* 4.5: 179–91.

Diosono, F. 2005. "El *castellum* romano el Cerro del Trigo (Puebla Dom Fradique, Granada) y el control del território en época republica." *Archivo Español de Arqueología* 78: 119–28.

Dobson, M. J. 2008. *The Army of the Roman Republic: The Second Century BC, Polybius and the Camps at Numantia, Spain.* Oxford: Oxbow.

— . 2013. "No Holiday Camp: The Roman Republican Army Camp as a Fine-Tuned Instrument of War." In Evans 2013, 214–34.

Domergue, C. 1983. *La mine antique d'Aljustrel (Portugal) et les tables de bronze de Vipasca.* Paris: Boccard.

— . 1987. *Catalogue des Mines et des Fonderies Antiques de la Péninsule Ibérique.* Madrid: Diffusion de Boccard.

— . 1990. *Les mines de la péninsule ibérique dans l'Antiquité romaine.* Rome: École française de Rome.

Domínguez, A. J. 2002. "Greeks in Iberia: Colonialism without colonization." In *The Archaeology of Colonialism: Issues and Debates,* edited by C. L. Lyons and J. K. Papadopoulos, 65–95. Los Angeles: Getty Research Institute.

Donaldson, G. H. 1988. "Signaling Communications and the Roman Imperial Army." *Britannia* 19: 349–56.

Eckstein, A. M. 1987. *Senate and General: Individual Decision Making and Roman Foreign Relations, 264–194 BC.* Berkeley: University of California Press.

EDIA = *Empresa de Desenvolvimento e Infra-estruturas do Alqueva.*

EDIA. 1996. *Património Arqueológico no Regolfo de Alqueva: Quadro Geral de Referência.* Beja: EDIA.

— . 1999. *Plano de Minimização de Impactes sobre o Património Arqueológico.* Beja: EDIA.

Edmondson, J. C. 1987. *Two Industries in Roman Lusitania: Mining and Garum Production.* BAR-IS 362. Oxford: Archaeopress.

——. 1990. "Romanization and Urban Development in Lusitania." In *The Early Roman Empire in the West*, edited by T. Blagg and M. Millett, 151–78. Oxford: Oxbow Books.
——. 1992–1993. "Creating a provincial Landscape: Roman imperialism and rural change in Lusitania." *Studia Historica: Historia Antigua* 10–11: 13–30.
——. 1996. "Roman power and the emergence of provincial administration in Lusitania during the Republic." In *Pouvoir et Imperium. L'exercice du pouvoir et l'administration provinciale dans l'Empire romain républicain*, edited by E. Hermon, 163–211. Quebec: Université Laval.
Ettlinger, E., B. Hedinger, B. Hoffmann, P. Kenrick, G. Pucci, K. Roth-Rubi, G. Schneider, S. von Schnurbein, C. M. Wells, and S. Zabehlicky-Scheffenegger. 1990. *Conspectus Formarum Terrae Sigillatae Italico Modo Confectae*. Bonn: Dr. Rudolf Habelt GmbH.
Evans, J. D., ed. 2013. *A Companion to the Archaeology of the Roman Republic*. Oxford: Wiley-Blackwell.
Fabião, C. 1996. "O povoado da Cabeça de Vaiamonte (Monforte)." *A Cidade-Revista Cultural de Portalegre* 11: 31–80.
——. 1998. *O Mundo indígena e a sua romanização na área céltica do território hoje português*. Ph.D. diss., Universidade de Lisboa.
——. 2001. "Mundo indígena, romanos e sociedade provincial romana: Sobre a percepção arqueológica da mudança." *Arqueología* 3: 108–31.
——. 2004. "Arqueologia militar romana da Lusitania: Textos e evidências." In Pérez González and Illarregui Gómez 2004, 53–74.
——. 2006. "The Roman army in Portugal." In Morillo and Aurrecoechea 2006, 107–26.
——. 2012. "Os chamados *castella* do Sudoeste peninsular, no quadro do povoamento romano da viragem da Era." Paper read at the II Reunião Científica as Paisagens da Romanização: Fortins e Ocupação do Territórionos séc. II a.C.–I d.C., 24–25 May, Redondo and Alandroal, Portugal.
Fabião, C., and A. Guerra. 1987. "Considerações preliminares sobre a cerâmica comum do acampamento militar romano da Lomba do Canho (Arganil)." *Da pré-história à história: Homenagem a Octávio da Veiga Ferreira*, 287–308. Lisbon: Delta.
Fabião, C., and A. Guerra. 2010. "Mesas do Castelinho (Almodôvar): A case of a failed Roman town in southern *Lusitania*." In Corsi and Vermeulen 2010, 324–46.
Fabião, C., J. Norton, and J. L. Cardoso. 1997. "O recinto fortificado de Casa Branca (Ferreira do Alentejo)." *Al-madan* II.6: 38–42.
Fabricius, E., F. Leonhard, F. Hettner, and O. von Sarwey. 1894–1937. *Der obergermanischraetische Limes des Roemerreiches*. Section A. Volumes 1–15. Heidelberg: Verlag von O. Petters.
Faria, A. M. 1984–1985. "As Moedas do Acampamento Romano da Lomba do Canho (Arganil)." *Nummus* 2.7–8: 37–42.
——. 1999. "Colonização e municipalização nas províncias hispano-romanas: Reanálise de alguns casos polémicos." *Revista Portuguesa de Arqueologia* 2.2: 29–50.
——. 2001. "Pax Iulia, Felicitas Iulia, Liberalitas Iulia." *Revista Portuguesa de Arqueologia* 4.2: 351–62.
Fernandes, C. S. A., and F. J. M. Neto. 1997. "Povoados da Idade do Ferro do Concelho do Alandroal: Uma aproximação espacial I." *Al-Madan* 2.6: 19–32.
Fernandes, C. S. A., and F. J. M. Neto. 1998. "Povoados da Idade do Ferro do Concelho do

Alandroal: Uma aproximação espacial II." *Al-Madan* 2.7: 45–52.
Fernandes, L. 1997. *Capitéis romanos da Lusitânia ocidental. Vol IV*. M.A. thesis. Lisboa: Universidade Nova de Lisboa.
Ferrill, A. 1992. "Roman Military Intelligence." In *Go Spy the Land: Military Intelligence in History*, edited by K. Nelson and B. J. C. McKercher, 17–29. Westport, Conn: Praeger.
Fleming, A. 2006. "Post-processual Landscape Archaeology: A Critique." *Cambridge Archaeological Journal* 16.3: 267–80.
Fortea, J., and J. Bernier. 1970. *Recintos y fortificaciones ibéricos en la Bética*. Salamanca: Universidad de Salamanca.
Foucault, M. 1978. *The History of Sexuality*. New York: Pantheon.
— . 1980. "The eye of power." In *Power/Knowledge*, edited by C. Gordon, 146–65. New York: Pantheon.
— . 1991. *Discipline and Punish: The Birth of the Prison*. Translated by A. Sheridan. London: Penguin.
Friedman, H. 2008. *Industry and Empire: Administration of the Roman and Byzantine Faynan*. Ph.D. diss., University of Leicester.
— . 2009a. "Forced Labour, Mines, and Space: Exploring the Control of Mining Communities." In *TRAC 2008: Proceedings of the Eighteenth Annual Theoretical Roman Archaeology Conference*, edited by M. Driessen, S. Heeren, J. Hendriks, F. Kemmers, and R. Visser, 1–11. Oxford: Oxbow Books.
— . 2009b. "Imperial Industry and Observational Control in the Faynan Region, Southern Jordan." *Internet Archaeology* 27. http://intarch.ac.uk/
Fugate, S. 2000. "A New Look at the Baths at Torre de Palma." In *Termas romanas en el occidente del imperio: Il Coloquio Internacional de Arqueología en Gijón*, 361–64. Gijón: VTP Editorial.
Funari, P. P. A. 1986. "As estrategias de exploraçao de recursos do Vale do Guadalquivir em época romana." *Revista Brasileira de História* 12: 169–98.
Fusco, A., and I. Mañas Romero. 2006. *Mármoles de Lusitania*. Mérida: Museo Nacional de Arte Romano.
Gaffney, V., and M. van Leusen. 1995. "Postscript—GIS, Environmental Determinism and Archaeology: A Parallel Text." In Lock and Stančič 1995, 367–81.
Gaffney, V., Z. Stančič, and H. Watson. 1996. "Moving from catchments to cognition: Tentative steps towards a larger archaeological context for GIS." In Aldenerfer and Maschner 1996, 132–54.
Gamito, M. T. J. 1981. "A propósito do castro de Segóvia (Elvas): Resistência a Roma no sudoeste peninsular." *História* 29: 32–43.
— . 1987. "O Castro de Segóvia (Elvas, Portugal), ponto fulcral na primeira fase das Guerras de Sertório." *O Arqueólogo Português* 4.5: 149–60.
García-Bellido, M. P. 1994–1995. "Las torres-recinto y la explotación militar del plomo en Extremadura: Los lingotes del pecio de Comacchio." *Anas* 7/8: 187–218.
García y Bellido, A. 1945. "Bandas y Guerrillas en las Luchas con Roma." *Hispania* 5: 546–604.
Gibson, C., V. H. Correia, and C. Burgess. 1998. "Alto do Castelinho da Serra (Montenoro Novo, Évora, Portugal). A Preliminary Report on the Excavations at the Late Bronze Age to Medieval Site, 1990–93." *Journal of Iberian Archaeology* 0: 191–244.

Gibson, J. J. 1986. *The Ecological Approach to Visual Perception.* Hillsdale, N.J.: Lawrence Erlbaum Associates.

Gichon, M. 1989. "Military Intelligence in the Roman Army." In *Labor Omnibus Unus: Festschrift Gerold Walser,* edited by H. E. Herzig and E. Frei-Stolba, 154–70. Historia Einzelschriften 60. Stuttgart: Steiner-Verl.-Wiesbaden-GmbH.

Gillings, M., and D. Wheatley. 2001. "Seeing is not believing: Unresolved issues in archaeological visibility analysis." In *COST Action G2: Ancient Landscapes and Rural Structures. On the Good Use of Geographic Information Systems in Archaeological Landscape Studies,* edited by B. Slapsak, 25–36. Luxembourg: Office for Official Publications of the European Communities.

Gomes, S. M., S. Brazuna, and M. Macedo. 2002. "Ocupações romanas na margem direita do Guadiana. Um território em estudo." *Al-Madan* 2.11: 134–38.

Gonçalves, A., and P. C. Carvalho. 2002. "Intervenção arqueológica no Castelo da Lousa (1997–2002): Resultados preliminares." *Al-Madan* 2.2: 181–88.

Gonçalves, A., E. Moran, M. Posselt, and F. Teichner. 1999. "New aspects of the romanization of the Alto Alentejo (Portugal): Evidence from a geophysical and archeological survey at the Monte da Nora (Terrugem)." *Arqueologia* 24: 101–10.

González Román, C. 1981. *Imperialismo y Romanización en la Provincia Hispania Ulterior.* Granada: Universidad de Granada.

González-Ruibal, A. 2006. "Past the Last Outpost: Punic Merchants in the Atlantic Ocean (5th–1st centuries BC)." *JMA* 19.1: 121–50.

Goodchild, R. G. 1950. "Roman Tripolitania: Reconnaissance in the Desert Frontier Zone." *The Geographical Journal* 115.4/6: 161–71.

Gorges, J.-G., ed. 1990. *Les Villes de Lusitanie romaine: Hierarchies et territoires. Table ronde internationale du CNRS, Talence, le 8–9 decembre 1988.* Paris: Éditions du Centre National de la Recherche Scientifique.

Gorges, J.-G., and T. Nogales Basarrate, eds. 2000. *Sociedad y Cultura en la Lusitania romana.* Mérida: Editora Regional de Extremadura.

Gorges, J.-G., and F. Rodríguez Martín, eds. 1999. *Économie et Territoire en Lusitanie Romaine.* Collection de la Casa de Velázquez 65. Madrid: Casa de Velázquez.

Gorges, J.-G., and M. Salinas, eds. 1994. *Les campagnes de la Lusitanie romaine.* Madrid: Casa de Velázquez.

Green, S. W. 1990. "Approaching archaeological space: An introduction to the volume." In *Interpreting Space: GIS and Archaeology,* edited by K. M. S. Allen, S. W. Green, and E. B. W. Zubrow, 3–8. London: Taylor and Francis.

Groenman-van Waateringe, W., B. L. van Beek, W. J. H. Willems, and S. L. Wynia, eds. 1997. *Roman Frontier Studies 1995.* Oxford: Oxbow.

Gros, P. 2001. *L'architecture romaine II: Maisons, palais, villas et tombeaux.* Paris: Picard.

Haggerty, K. D. 2006. "Tear down the walls: On demolishing the panopticon." In Lyon 2006, 23–46.

Hanel, N. 2006. "Cáceres el Viejo Camp." In Morillo and Aurrecoechea 2006, 224–27.

Harris, E. 1989. *Principles of Archaeological Stratigraphy.* 2nd edition. London: Academic Press.

Harris, T., and G. Lock. 1995. "Toward an evaluation of GIS in European archaeology: The past, present and future of theory and application." In Lock and Stančič 1995, 349–66.

Hayes, J. W. 2008. *The Athenian Agora, Volume XXXII: Roman Pottery: Fine-ware Imports.* Princeton, N.J.: American School of Classical Studies at Athens.

Heras Mora, F. J. 2009. "El Santo de Valdetorres (Badajoz, España): Un Nuevo Enclave Militar Romano en la Linea del Guadiana." In Morillo, Hanel, and Morillo 2009, 315–27.

——. 2010. "Paisaje militarizado en Extremadura: Secuencia arqueológica en los primeros tiempos de la romanización." In Mayoral Herrera and Celestino Pérez 2010, 115–40.

Higuchi, T. 1988. *The Visual and Spatial Structures of Landscapes.* Translated by C. Terry. Cambridge, Mass.: Massachusetts Institute of Technology.

Hirt, A. M. 2010. *Imperial Mines and Quarries in the Roman World: Organizational Aspects, 27 B.C.–A.D. 235.* Oxford: OUP.

Hoyos, D., ed. 2011. *A Companion to the Punic Wars.* Blackwell Companions to the Ancient World. Oxford: Wiley-Blackwell.

ILS = *Inscriptiones Latinae Selectae.*

Ingold, T. 2000. *The Perception of the Environment: Essays in Livelihood, Dwelling and Skill.* London: Routledge.

Jackson, R. B. 2002. *At Empire's Edge: Exploring Rome's Egyptian Frontier.* New Haven: Yale University Press.

Jérez Linde, J. M. 2005. *La Terra Sigillata Itálica del Museo Nacional de Arte Romano Mérida.* Cuadernos Emeritenses 29. Mérida: Museo Nacional de Arte Romano.

Jimeno, A. 2005. "Numancia y los campamentos romanos: Investigación y recuperación del pasado." In Pérez González and Illarregui Gómez 2005, 237–49.

Kalb, P., and M. Hock. 1984. "O Alto do Castelo, Apiarça (Distrito de Santarém)—Acampamento Romano ou Fortificação Pré-Romana?" In *Livro do Segundo Congresso sobre Monumentos Militares Portugueses,* 239–45. Lisbon: Patrimônio XXI.

Keay, S. J. 1988. *Roman Spain.* Berkeley: University of California Press.

——. 2001. "Romanization and the Hispaniae." In Keay and Terrenato 2001, 117–39.

Keay, S. J., and N. Terrenato, eds. 2001. *Italy and the West: Comparative Issues in Romanization.* Oxford: Oxbow.

Knapp, R. C. 1977. *Aspects of the Roman Experience in Iberia, 206–100 B.C.* Anejos de Hispania Antiqua 9. Valladolid: Universidad DL.

Knauer, E. 1990. "Wind Towers in Roman Wall Paintings?" *Metropolitan Museum Journal* 25: 5–19.

Koenen, K. 1929. "Die Keramik aus den Lagern des Scipio und den Lagern bei Renieblas." In *Numantia IV: Die Ergebnisse der Ausgrabungen 1905–1912: Die Lager bei Renieblas,* edited by A. Schulten, 284–305. Munich: F. Bruckmann.

Kvamme, K. L. 1989. "Geographic Information Systems in Regional Archaeological Research and Data Management." In *Archaeological Method and Theory,* edited by M. B. Schiffer, 139–203. Tucson: University of Arizona Press.

Lake, M. W., and P. E. Woodman. 2003. "Visibility Studies and Archaeology: A Review and Case Study." *Environment and Planning B: Planning and Design* 30: 689–707.

Lake, M. W., P. E. Woodman, and S. J. Mithen. 1998. "Tailoring GIS Software for Archaeological Applications: An Example Concerning Viewshed Analysis." *JAS* 25: 27–38.

Lamberto, V., and P. S. Caetano. 2008. "Marble Stones from *Lusitania*: The Quarries of the Estremoz Anticline." In Nogales and Beltrán 2008, 467–81.

Lamboglia, N. 1952. "Per una classificazione preliminare della ceramica campana." *Atti del*

Primo Congresso Internazionale di Studi Liguri (1950): 139-206.
Lancha, J., P. André, and F. Abraços. 2000. *La Villa de Torre de Palma*. Lisbon: Instituto Portugues de Museus.
Langley, M. M. 2006. "*Est in agris*: A spatial analysis of Roman *uillae* in the region of Monforte, Alto Alentejo, Portugal." *Revista Portuguesa de Arqueologia* 9.2: 317-28.
Langley, M. M., R. Mataloto, and R. Boaventura. 2008. "A Necrópole Sidérica de Torre de Palma (Monforte, Portugal). *Anejos de Archivo Español de Arqueología* 39: 283-303.
Lazzarini, S. 2001. *Lex Metallis Dicta: Studi Sulla Seconda Tavola di Vipasca*. Rome: "L'Erma" di Bretschneider.
Le Roux, P. 1982. *L'Armée romaine et l'organisation des provinces ibériques d'Auguste à l'Invasion de 409*. Paris: Diffusion de Boccard.
Lee, A. D. 2006. *Information and Frontiers: Roman Foreign Relations in Late Antiquity*. Cambridge: CUP.
Leighton, A. C. 1969. "Secret Communications among the Greeks and Romans." *Technology and Culture* 10.2: 139-54.
Llobera, M. 1996. "Exploring the topography of mind: GIS, social space and archaeology." *Antiquity* 70: 612-22.
— . 2001. "Building Past Landscape Perception with GIS: Understanding Topographic Prominence." *JAS* 28: 1005-14.
— . 2003. "Extending GIS-based visual analysis: The concept of visualscapes." *International Journal of Geographical Information Science* 17.1: 25-48.
— . 2007. "Reconstructing visual landscapes." *World Archaeology* 39.1: 51-69.
Llobera, M., D. Wheatley, J. Steele, S. Cox, and O. Parchment. 2010. "Calculating the inherent visual structure of a landscape ('total viewshed') using high throughput computing." In *Beyond the Artefact: Digital Interpretation of the Past: Proceedings of CAA 2004, Prato, 13-17 April 2004*, edited by F. Niccolucci and S. Hermon, 146-51. Budapest: Archaeolingua.
Lloyd, J. 1991. "Forms of rural settlement in the Early Roman Empire." In Barker and Lloyd 1991, 233-40.
Lock, G., ed. 2000. *Beyond the Map: Archaeology and Spatial Technologies*. Oxford: ISO Press.
Lock, G., and T. M. Harris. 1996. "Danebury Revisited: An English Iron Age Hillfort in a Digital Landscape." In Aldenerfer and Maschner 1996, 214-40.
Lock, G., and Z. Stančič, eds. 1995. *Archaeology and Geographic Information Systems: A European Perspective*. London: Taylor and Francis.
Loots, L. 1997. "The Use of Projective and Reflective Viewsheds in the Analysis of the Hellenistic City Defence System at Sagalassos, Turkey." *Archaeological Computing Newsletter* 49: 12-16.
Lopes, M. C. 1996. "O Território de *Pax Iulia*: Limites e caracterização." *Arquivo de Beja* 3.2/3: 63-74.
— . 2003. *A Cidade Romana de Beja: Percursos e Debates Acerca da "Civitas" de Pax Iulia*. 2 vols. Coimbra: Faculdade de Letras de Coimbra, Instituto de Arqueologia.
López García, P. 1986. "Estudio palinológico del Holoceno español a través del análisis de yacimientos arqueológicos." *Trabajos de Prehistoria* 43: 143-58.
López Merino, L., S. P. Díaz, D. A. Schaad, F. A. Sánchez, and J. A. López Sáez. 2010. "El

Paisaje de la Serena (Badajoz) en el Cambio de Era: Análisis Polínico de Cerro del Tesoro." In Mayoral Herrera and Celestino Pérez 2010, 271-85.

López Sáez, J. A., and L. López Merino. 2005. "Precisiones metodológicas acerca de los indicios paleopalinológicos de agricultura en la Prehistoria de la Península Ibérica." *Portugalia* 26: 53-64.

Lowe, B. 2009. *Roman Iberia: Economy, Society, and Culture*. London: Duckworth.

Luís, L. 2010. "Cerâmica Campaniense." In Alarcão et al. 2010c, 111-38.

Lyon, D. 2006. "The search for surveillance theories." In Lyon 2006, 3-20.

Lyon, D., ed. 2006. *Theorizing Surveillance: The Panopticon and Beyond*. Portland: Willan.

Maia, M. 1974a. "1ª Campanha de escavações Realizada no Cerro do Castelo de Manuel Galo (Mértola): Uma Possível Fortaleza Romana." In *Actas das II Jornadas Arqueológicas (Lisboa, 1972)*, vol. 2, 139-55. Lisbon: Associação dos Arqueologos Portugueses.

——. 1974b. "Fortalezas Romanas do Monte de Manuel Galo (Mértola)." In *Actas do III Congresso Nacional de Arqueologia (Porto, 1973)*, vol. 1, 325-31. Porto: Ministério da Educação Nacional, unta Nacional de Educação.

——. 1978. "Fortalezas romanas do Sul de Portugal." *Zephyrus* 28-29: 279-85.

——. 1986. "Os Castella do Sul de Portugal." *Madrider Mitteilungen* 27: 195-223.

Maia, M., and M. Maia. 1996. "Os Castella do Sul de Portugal e a mineração da prata nos primórdios do Império." In *Mineração no Baixo Alentejo*, edited by M. Rego, 60-81. Castro Verde: Câmara Municipal de Castro Verde.

Malm, W. 1999. *Introduction to Visibility*. Cooperative Institute for Research in the Atmosphere (CIRA) NPS Visibility Program. Fort Collins: Colorado State University.

Maloney, S. J., and M. da Luz Hoffstot. 2002. "Torre de Palma: Fact or Fiction?" *O Arqueólogo Português* IV.20: 135-46.

Maloney, S. J., and J. R. Hale. 1996. "The villa of Torre de Palma (Alto Alentejo)." *Journal of Roman Archaeology* 9: 275-94.

Mantas, V. G. 1996a. "Teledetecção, cidade e território: Pax Iulia." *Arquivo de Beja* 3.1: 5-30.

——. 1996b. "Em Tornodo Problemada Fundação e Estatuto de Pax Iulia." *Arquivo de Beja* 3.2/3: 41-62.

——. 2000. "A sociedade luso-romano do município de Ammaia." In *Sociedad y Cultura en Lusitania Romana*, edited by J.-G. Gorges and T. N. Basarrate, 391-420. Mérida: Editora Regional de Extremadura.

——. 2003. "Indícos de um campo romano na Cava de Viriato?" *Al-Madan* 2.12: 40-42.

——. 2011. *As Vias Romanas da Lusitânia*. Studia Lusitana 7. Mérida: Museo Nacional de Arte Romano.

Marcos, P. J. S., ed. 2008. *Arqueología urbanaen Cáceres. Investigaciones e intervenciones recientesen la ciudad de Cáceres y su entorno*. Cáceres: Actas de las Jornadas de Arqueología del Museo de Cáceres.

Marzano, A. 2007. *Roman Villas in Central Italy: A Social and Economic History*. Leiden: Brill.

Mataloto, R. 2002. "Fortins e recintos-torre do Alto Alentejo: Antecâmara da 'romanização' dos campos." *Revista Portuguesa de Arqueologia* 5.1: 161-220.

——. 2004a. "Fortins romanos do Alto Alentejo (Portugal): Fortificação e povoamento na segunda metade do séc. I a.C." In Moret and Chapa 2004, 31-54.

—. 2004b. Um "monte" da Idade do Ferro na Herdade de Sapatoa: Ruralidade y povoamento no 1° milénio a.C. do Alentejo Central. Trabalhos de Arqueologia 37. Lisbon: Universidade de Lisboa.

—. 2008. "O Castelo dos Mouros (Graça do Divor, Évora): A arquitectura 'ciclópica' romana e a romanização dos campos de Liberalitas Iulia Ebora." Revista Portuguesa de Arqueologia 11.1: 123–47.

—. 2010. "Do Campo ao Ager: A ocupação tardo republican do território Alto Alentejo." In Mayoral Herrera and Celestino Pérez 2010, 59–88.

Mataloto, R., and C. Alves. 2008. "Relatório da Campanha 1/2008 em Évoramonte." Field report. Lisbon: Instituto de Gestão do Património Arquitectónico e Arqueológico.

Mataloto, R., C. Alves, and C. Carvalho. 2007. "De Serra em Serra—instabilidade e conflito no final da Idade do Ferro do Alentejo Central." Vipasca 2.2: 242–49.

Mataloto, R., C. Alves, and R. Clemente. 2010. "As ocupações antigas do Castelo de Évoramonte." Paper read at the V Encontro de Arqueologia do Sudoeste Peninsular, 18 November, Almodôvar, Portugal.

Mataloto, R., S. Estrela, and C. Alves. 2007. "As fortificaçoes calcolíticas de São Pedro (Redondo, Alentejo Central, Portugal)." In Los primeros campesinos de La Raya: Aportaciones recientes al conocimiento del neolitico y calcolítico en Extremadura y Alentejo, edited by E. Cerrillo Cuenca and J. M. Valadés Sierra, 113–41. Cáceres: Jornadas de Arqueología del Museo de Cáceres.

Mataloto, R., C. Roque, and J. Williams. 2014. "'E dahí desceo a dar-lhe batalha...': A ocupação prerromana e a romanização da região da Serra d'Ossa (Alentejo Central, Portugal)." In Mayoral 2014, 17–43.

Mataloto, R., and J. Williams. 2011. "Caladinho (Redondo, Alto Alentejo) Campanha 1/2010: Relatório de Escavação." Field report. Lisbon: Instituto de Gestão do Património Arquitectónico e Arqueológico.

Mataloto, R., and J. Williams. 2012. "Caladinho (Redondo, Alto Alentejo) Campanha 2/2011: Relatório de Escavação." Field report. Lisbon: Instituto de Gestão do Património Arquitectónico e Arqueológico.

Mataloto, R., and J. Williams. 2015. "Italian Terra Sigillata from Caladinho, Redondo Municipality, Portugal." In Contextos Estratigráficos Romanos na Lusitania, edited by J. Quaresma. Arqueologia e História Monografia: 9–20. Lisbon: Associação dos Arqueólogos Portugueses.

Mataloto, R., J. Williams, and C. Roque. 2016. "Amphorae at the Origins of Lusitania: Transport Pottery from Western Hispania Ulterior in Alto Alentejo." In Lusitanian Amphorae: Production and Distribution, edited by I. Vaz Pinto, R. de Almeida, and A. Martin, 139–51. Archaeopress: Oxford.

Mateo, A. 2001. Observaciones sobre el Régimen Jurídico de la Minería en Tierras Públicas Romanas. Santiago de Compostela: Universidad de Santiago de Compostela.

Mayoral Herrera, V., R. Cazorla Martín, and S. Celestino Pérez. 2010. "The Romanization process of an agrarian landscape: La Serena region." In Corsi and Vermeulen 2010, 263–80.

Mayoral Herrera, V., and S. Celestino Pérez, eds. 2010. Los Paisajes Rurales de la Romanización: Arquitectura y Explotación del Territorio. Madrid: La Ergástula.

Mayoral Herrera, V., and S. Celestino Pérez. 2010. "Romanización, paisaje, arquitectura:

A vueltas con un tema fronterizo." In Mayoral Herrera and Celestino Pérez 2010, 7–8.
Mayoral Herrera, V., R. Mataloto, and C. Roque, eds. 2014. *La Gestación de los Paisajes Rurales entre la Protohistoria y el Período Romano: Formas de Asentamientos y Procesos de Implantación. Anejos de Archivo Español de Arqueologia 70*. Mérida: Instituto Arqueología Mérida.
Mayoral Herrera, V., S. C. Pérez, E. S. Tovar, M. B. Álvarez. 2011. "Fortificaciones e implantación romana entre La Serena y la Vega del Guadiana: El Castejón de las Merchanas (Don Benito, Badajoz) y su contexto territorial." *Archivo Español de Arqueología* 84: 87–118.
Mayoral Herrera, V., J. J. Pulido Royo, S. Walid Sbeinati, S. Celestino Pérez, M. Bustamante Álvarez, A. Pizzo, and L. Sevillano Perea. 2014. "El Castejon de las Merchanas (Don Benito, Badajoz): Un recinto fortificado tardorrepublicano entre la Serena y la Vega del Guadiana." In Mayoral 2014, 65–88.
Millet, M. 2010. "Town and country in the early Roman West—a perspective." In Corsi and Vermeulen 2010, 17–26.
Mitchell, S., and J. A. Arvites, eds. 1983. *Armies and Frontiers in Roman and Byzantine Anatolia: Proceedings of a Colloquium Held at University College, Swansea, in April 1981*. BAR-IS. Oxford: Archaeopress.
Mommsen, T. 1959. *The History of Rome*, vol. 4. Translated by W. P. Dickson. New York: Philosophical Library.
Morais, R. 2003. "Problemàtiques i noves perspectives sobre les àmphores ovoides tardorepublicanes: Les àmphores ovoides de producció lusitana." *Culip VIII i les àmfores Haltern 70. Monografies del Casc*, 5: 36–40.
—. 2010a. "Cerâmica de paredes finas." In Alarcão et al. 2010c, 153–74.
—. 2010b. "Ânforas." In Alarcão et al. 2010c, 181–218.
Morais, R., and C. Fabião. 2007. "Novas produções de fabrico lusitano: Problemáticas e importância económica." In *Actas del Congreso Internacional CRETARIAE. Salsas y salazones de pescado en Occidente durante la Antiguedad. Universidad de Cádiz, noviembre de 2005*, 127–33. Oxford: Archaeopress.
Moret, P. 1990. "Fortins, 'Tours d'Hannibal' et Fermes Fortifiées dans le Monde Ibèrique." *Mélanges de la Casa de Velázquez* 26.1: 5–43.
—. 1995. "Les maisons fortes de la Bétique et de la Lusitanie romaines." *Revue des Études Anciennes* 97: 527–64.
—. 1996. *Les Fortifications Ibériques: De la Fin de l'Âge du Bronze à la Conquête Romaine*. Collection de la Casa de Velázquez 56. Madrid: Casa de Velázquez.
—. 1999. "Casas fuertes romanas en la Bética y la Lusitania." In Gorges and Rodríguez Martín 1999, 55–89.
—. 2000. "L'âge du Fer en Espagne: Réflexions sur quelques travaux récents (1997–1999)." *Documents d'Archeologie Meridionale* 23: 301–304.
—. 2010. "Los tours rurales et les maisons fortes de l'hispanie romaine: Éléments pour un bilan." In Mayoral Herrera and Celestino Pérez 2010, 9–36.
Moret, P., and T. Chapa, eds. 2004. *Torres, Atalayas y Casas Fortificadas: Explotación y control del territorio en Hispania (s. III a. De C.–s. I d. De C.)*. Jaén: Universidad de Jaén.
Morillo, Á., ed. 2002. *Arqueología Militar Romana en Hispania*. Anejos de Gladius 5. Madrid: Ediciones Polifemo.

———. 2003. "Los establecimientos militares temporales: Conquista y defensa del territorio en la Hispania republicana." In *Defensa y Territorio en Hispania de los Escipiones a Augusto*, edited by A. Morillo, F. Cadiou, and D. Hourcade, 41–80. León: Universidad de León, Casa de Velázquez.

Morillo, Á., and J. Aurrecoechea, eds. 2006. *The Roman Army in Hispania: An Archaeological Guide*. León, Spain: Universidad de León Secretariado de Publicaciones.

Morillo, Á., N. Hanel, and E. Morillo, eds. 2009. *Limes XX: Estudios sobre la Frontera Romana/Roman Frontier Studies*. Anejos de Gladius 13. Madrid: Ediciones Polifemo.

Morris, S. P. 2001. "The Towers of Ancient Leukas: Results of a Topographic Survey 1991-1992." *Hesperia* 70: 285–347.

Morris, S. P., and J. K. Papadopoulos. 2005. "Greek Towers and Slaves: An Archaeology of Exploitation." *AJA* 109.2: 155–225.

Ñaco del Hoyo, T., and J. Principal. 2012. "Outposts of Integration? Garrisoning, Logistics, and Archaeology in North-Eastern Hispania, 133–82 BC." In *Processes of Integration and Identity Formation in the Roman Republic*, edited by S. Roselaar, 159–77. Leiden: Brill.

NASA Land Processes Distributed Active Archive Center (LP DAAC). 2001. "ASTER Global DEM Version 2." Sioux Falls, S.D.: USGS/Earth Resources Observation and Science (EROS) Center.

Nelson, K., and B. J. C. McKercher, eds. 1992. *Go Spy the Land: Military Intelligence in History*. Westport, Conn.: Praeger.

Nicolet, C. 1991. *Space, Geography, and Politics in the Early Roman Empire*. Ann Arbor: University of Michigan Press.

Nogales Basarrate, T., L. J. R. Gonçalves, and P. Lapuente. 2008. "Materiales Lapídeos, Mármoles y Talleres en *Lusitania*." In Nogales and Beltrán 2008, 407–66.

Nogales, T., and J. Beltrán, eds. 2008. *Marmora Hispana: Explotación y uso de los materiales pétreos en la Hispania Romana*. Rome: "L'Erma" di Bretschneider.

Ober, J. 1985. *Fortress Attica: Defense of the Athenian Land Frontier, 404-322 B.C.* Leiden: Brill.

OCK = Oxè, A., H. Comfort, and P. Kenrick. 2000. *Corpus Vasorum Arretinorum: A Catalogue of the Signatures, Shapes and Chronology of Italian Sigillata*. 2nd edition. Antiquitas 3, 41. Bonn: Habelt.

Olcese, G. 2003. *Ceramiche Comuni a Roma e in Area Romana: Produzione, Circolazione e Tecnologia (Tarda Età Repubblicana–Prima Età Imperiale)*. Documenti di Archeologia 28. Padua: Società Archeologica Padana.

ORL = *Der obergermanisch-raetische Limes des Roemerreiches*.

Ortiz Romero, P. 1991. "Excavaciones y sondeos en los recintos tipo Torre de la Serena." *Extremadura Arqueológica* 2: 301–18.

———. 1995. "De recintos, Torres y Fortines: Usos (y abusos)." *Extremadura Arqueológica* 5: 177–93.

Ortiz Romero, P., and A. Rodríguez Díaz. 1998. "Culturas indígenas y romanización en Extremadura: Castros, oppida y recintos ciclópeos." In *Extremadura Protohistórica: Paleoambiente, Economia e Poblamiento*, edited by A. Rodríguez Díaz, 247–78. Cáceres: Caja Duero.

Ortiz Romero, P., and A. Rodríguez Díaz. 2004. "La torre de Hijovejo: Genesis, evolucion y

contexto de un asentamiento fortificado en La Serena (Badajoz)." In Moret and Chapa 2004, 31–54.
Osborne, R. 1987. *Classical Landscape with Figures: The Ancient Greek City and its Countryside*. London: George Philip.
Osland, D. K. 2006. *The Early Roman Cities of Lusitania*. BAR-IS 1519. Oxford: Archaeopress.
Ozawa, K., T. Kato, and H. Tsude. 1995. "Detection of beacon networks between ancient hillforts using digital terrain model based GIS." In *Computer Applications and Quantitative Methods in Archaeology 1994*, edited by J. Hugget and N. Ryan, 157–61. BAR-IS 600. Oxford: Archaeopress.
Paço, A., and J. P. Gonçalves. 1962. "Castelo Velho do Degebe (Reguengos de Monsaraz). 1 Reconhecimento preliminar." In *Actas do 26° Congresso LusoEspanhol para o Progresso das Ciências*, 313–16. Porto: Associação Portuguesa para o Progresso das Ciências.
Paço, A., and J. B. Leal. 1966. "Castelo da Lousa, Mourão (Portugal): Una Fortificacíon Romana de la Margen Izquierda del Guadiana." *Archivo Español de Arqueología* 39.113/114: 167–83.
Pamment Salvatore, J. 1997. "Possible Strategic Function for the Location of the Roman Republic Fortress at Cáceres el Viejo in Extremadura, Western Spain." In *Roman Frontier Studies 1995*, edited by W. Groenman-van Waateringe, B. L. van Beek, W. J. H. Willems, and S. L. Wynia, 53–58. Oxford: Oxbow.
Peacock, D., and V. Maxfield. 1997. *Survey and Excavation: Mons Claudianus 1987–1993. Volume 1: Topography and Quarries*. Cair: Fouilles de l'IFAO 37.
Pedroni, L. 2000. "Cerámicas de barniz negro de los niveles republicanos del anfiteatro (Cartagena)." In *La ceràmica de vernís negre dels segles II i I a.C.: Centres productors mediterranis i comercialització a la Península Ibèrica*, edited by X. Aquilué Abadías, J. García Rosello, and J. Guitart Duran, 129–41. Mataró: Museu de Mataró.
Pereira, S. 2005. "A freguesia da Aramenha sob o domínio romano." *Ibn Maruán. Revista Cultural do Concelho de Marvão* 13: 35–61.
Pérez González, C., and E. Illarregui Gómez, eds. 2004/2005. *Arqueologia militar romana en Europa*. Salamanca: Junta de Castilla y León.
Pérez Vilatela, L. 2000. "De la Lusitania independiente a la creación de la provincia." In Gorges and Nogales Basarrate 2000, 73–84.
Pettegrew, D. K. 2001. "Chasing the Classical Farmstead: Assessing the Formation and Signature of Rural Settlement in Greek Landscape Archaeology." *JMA* 14.2: 189–209.
——. 2002. "Counting and Coloring Classical Farms: A Response to Osborne, Foxhall, and Bintliff et al." *JMA* 15.2: 267–73.
Pimenta, J., E. Henriques, and H. Mendes. 2012. *O Acampamento Romano do Alto dos Cacos, Almeirim*. Almeirim: Assoiação de Defesa do Património Histórico e Cultural do Concelho do Almeirim.
Pimenta, J., E. Sepúlveda, J. C. Faria, and M. Ferreira. 2006. "Cerâmicas romanas do lado ocidental do castelo de Alcácer do Sal, 4: Ânforas de importação e de produção lusitana." *Revista Portuguesa de Arqueologia* 9.2: 299–316.
Pina Polo, F., and J. Pérez Casas. 1998. "El oppidum Castra Aelia y las campañas de Sertorius en los años 77–76 a. C." *JRA* 11: 245–64.
Quaresma, J. C. 2006. "Almofarizes béticos e lusitanos: Revisão crono-morfológica de al-

guns tipos." *Revista Portuguesa de Arqueología* 9.1: 149–66.

Quesada-Sanz, F. 2011. "*Guerrilleros* in Hispania? The myth of Iberian guerrillas against Rome." *Ancient Warfare* 2: 46–52.

Queiroga, F. M. V. R. 2003. *War and the Castros: New Approaches to the Northwestern Portuguese Iron Age*. BAR-IS 1198. Oxford: Archaeopress.

Rego, M. 1996. *Mineração no Baixo Alentejo*. Castro Verde: Câmara Municipal de Castro Verde.

Renfrew, C., and M. Wagstaff, eds. 1983. *An Island Polity: The Archaeology of Exploitation in Melos*. Cambridge: CUP.

Richardson, J. S. 1986. *Hispaniae: Spain and the Development of Roman Imperialism, 218–82 BC*. Cambridge: CUP.

— . 1996. *The Romans in Spain*. Oxford: Blackwell.

Robertson, A. S. 1974. "Roman 'Signal Stations' on the Gask Ridge." *Transactions of the Perthshire Society of Natural Science*: 14–29.

Rodà, I. 2013. "Hispania: From the Roman Republic to the Reign of Augustus." In Evans 2013, 522–39.

Rodà de Llanza, I. 1999. "La Explotación de las Canteras en Hispania." In *Hispania, el Legado de Roma*, 123–31. Mérida: Dirección General de Bellas Artes y Bienes Culturales.

Rodriguez, A. R., M. M. Rodriguez, and M. C. Lopez. 1991. "Settlement and Continuity in the Territory of the Guadalquivir Valley (6th Century BC–1st Century AD)." In Barker and Lloyd 1991, 29–37.

Rodríguez Díaz, A. 1998. *Extremadura Protohistorica: Paleoambiente, Economia y Poblamiento*. Cáceres: Caja Duero.

Rodríguez Díaz, A., and P. Ortiz Romero. 2003. "Defensa y território en la Beturia: Castro, *oppida* y recintos ciclópeos." In *Defensa y território en Hispania de los Escipiones a Augusto*, edited by Á. Morillo, F. Cadiou, and D. Hourcade, 219–51. León: Universidad de León.

Roldán, J. M. 1975. *Itineraria Hispana: Fuentes Antiguas para el Studio de las Vías Romanas en la Península Ibérica*. Granada: Universidad de Granada.

— . 1980. "De Numancia a Sertorio: Problemas de la romanización de Hispania en la encrucijada e las guerras civiles." In *Studien zur antiken Sozialgeschichte: Festschrift F. Vittinghoff*, edited by F. Vittinghoff, W. Eck, H. Galsterer, and H. Wolff, 157–78. Köln and Wien: Böhlau.

Romero, F. G. 2002. "Philosophy and historical archaeology: Foucault and a singular technology of power development at the borderlands of nineteenth-century Argentina." *Journal of Social Archaeology* 2: 402–29.

Romero, I. M., and A. Fusco. 2008. "Canteras de *Lusitania*: Un análisis arqueológico." In Nogales and Beltrán 2008, 482–500.

Rossiter, J. J. 1978. *Roman Farm Buildings in Italy*. BAR-IS 52. Oxford: British Archaeological Reports.

Rotroff, S. 2006. *The Athenian Agora, Volume XXXIII: Hellenistic Pottery: The Plain Wares*. Princeton, N.J.: American School of Classical Studies at Athens.

Rowlandson, J. 1996. *Landowners and Tenants in Roman Egypt: The Social Relations of Agriculture in the Oxyrhynchite Nome*. Oxford: Clarendon Press.

RPC = *Roman Provincial Coinage*.

Ruestes, C. 2008a. "A multi-technique GIS visibility analysis for studying visual control of an Iron Age landscape." *Internet Archaeology* 23. http://intarch.ac.uk/
—. 2008b. "Social Organization and Human Space in North-Eastern Iberia during the Third Century BC." *Oxford Journal of Archaeology* 27.4: 359–86.
Ruivo, J. 2010. "Espólio Metálico." In Alarcão et al. 2010c, 481–517.
Ruiz, A., and M. Molinos. 1998. *The Archaeology of the Iberians*. Translated by M. Turton. Cambridge: CUP.
Saavedra Machado, J. L. 1964. "Subsídios para a história do Museu Etnológico Dr. Leite de Vasconcelos." *O Arqueólogo Português* 2.5: 51–448.
Sanmartí, J. 2009. "Colonial Relations and Social Change in Iberia (Seventh to Third Centuries BC)." In *Colonial Encounters in Ancient Iberia: Phoenician, Greek, and Indigenous Relations*, edited by M. Dietler and C. López-Ruiz, 49–88. Chicago: University of Chicago Press.
de Santo António, H. 1745. *Crónica dos Eremitas da Serra d'Ossa*, vol. 1. Lisbon: Officina de Francisco da Sylva.
Schulten, A. 1928. "Campamentos Romanos en España." *Investigación y Progreso* 2.5: 34–36.
—. 1945. *Historia de Numancia*. Barcelona: Barna.
Shackel, P. A. 2003. "Archaeology, Memory, and Landscapes of Conflict." *Historical Archaeology* 37.3: 3–13.
Sheldon, R. M. 2002. "To the Ends of the Earth: Caesar, Intelligence and Ancient Britain." *International Journal of Intelligence and Counterintelligence* 15.1: 77–100.
—. 2005. *Intelligence Activities in Ancient Rome: Trust in the Gods but Verify*. London: Routledge.
Sherk, R. K. 1974. "Roman Geographical Exploration and Military Maps." *ANRW* II.1: 534–62.
Sidebotham, S. E., R. E. Zitterkopf, and J. A. Riley. 1991. "Survey of the 'Abu Sha'ar-Nile Road." *AJA* 95.4: 571–622.
Silva, A. C. 1999. "Salvamento arqueológico no Guadiana." In *Memórias d'Odiana Estudos Arqueológicos do Alqueva*. Beja: Empresa de Desenvolvimento e Estruturas do Alqueva.
Silva, A. C., and J. Perdigão. 1998. *Contributo para a Carta Arqueológica de Arraiolos*. Arraiolos: Câmara Municipal.
Simplício, M. D. V. M. 2003. "*Évora: Origem e Evolução de uma Cidade Medieval*." *Revista da Faculdade de Letras - Geografia* 1.10: 365–72.
Smit Nolen, J. U. 1985. *Cerâmica Comum de Necrópoles do Alto Alentejo*. Lisbon: Fundação da Casa de Bragança.
Smith, J. M. 1997. *Private Matters: In Defense of the Personal Life*. Boston: Addison-Wesley.
Southern, P. 1990. "Signals versus Illuminations on Roman Frontiers." *Britannia* 21: 233–42.
Speidel, M. 1970. "The Captor of Decebalus: A New Inscription from Philippi." *JRS* 60: 142–53.
—. 1983. "*Exploratores*: Mobile Elite Units of Roman Germany." *EpSt* 13: 63–78.
Stanley, F. H. 1984. "Roman Lusitania: Aspects of Provincial Romanization." Ph.D. diss., University of Missouri–Columbia.
Stuiber, A. 1959. "Die Wachhütte im Weingarten." *Jahrbuch für Antike und Christentum* 2: 86–89.
Stylow, A. U. 2005. "Fuentes epigráficas para la historia de la Hispania Ulterior en época

republicana." In *Julio César y Corduba: Tiempo y espacio en la campaña de Munda (49–45 a.C.). Actas del Simposio. Córdoba, 21–25 de abril de 2003*, edited by E. Melchor Gil, J. Mellado Rodríguez, and J. F. Rodríguez Neila, 247–62. Córdoba: Universidad de Córdoba, Servicio de Publicaciones.

Tachikawa, T., M. Kaku, A. Iwasaki, D. Gesch, M. Oimoen, Z. Zhang, J. Danielson, T. Krieger, B. Curtis, J. Haase, M. Abrams, R. Crippen, C. Carabajal, and D. Meyer. 2011. "ASTER Global Digital Elevation Model Version 2—Summary of Validation Results." Report Compiled for NASA Land Processes Distributed Active Archive Center and the Joint Japan-US ASTER Science Team. Sioux Falls, S.D.: USGS/Earth Resources Observation and Science (EROS) Center.

Taelman, D., C. Corsi, M. de Dapper, S. Deprez, L. Verdonck, and F. Vermeulen. 2010. "Geoarchaeological Research in the Roman Town of *Ammaia* (Alentejo, Portugal)." *Bollettino di Archeologia Online Edizione Speciale - Congresso di Archeologia A.I.A.C. 2008* 1: 58–70. http://www.bollettinodiarcheologiaonline.beniculturali.it/

Teichner, F. 2008. *Zwischen Land und Meer: Entre Tierra y Mar.* 2 vols. Studia Lusitana 3. Mérida: Museo Nacional de Arte Romano.

Teichner, F., A. Gradim, G. Grabherr, and K. Oberhofer. 2010. "Castelinho dos Mouros (Alcoutim). Um castelo da epoca republicana." *Xelb* 10: 215–34.

Teichner, F., and T. Schierl. 2009. "Zur Akkulturation des Westens der Iberischen Halbinsel am Beginn der römischen Kaiserzeit: Das Beispiel des Monte da Nora (Terrugem, Portugal)." In Morillo, Hanel, and Martin 2009, 63–75.

Teichner, F., and T. Schierl. 2010. "Nuevos ejemplos de la romanización del paisaje de la posterior Lusitania." In Mayoral Herrera and Celestino Pérez 2010, 89–115.

Terrenato, N., and L. Motta. 2012. "Not Your Run-of-the-Mill Cereal Farmer? The Evidence from Small Rural Settlements in the Cecina valley in Northern Etruria." Paper read at the 2012 Annual Meeting of the Archaeological Institute of America, 5–8 January, Philadelphia.

Tilley, C. 1994. *A Phenomenology of Landscape, Places, Paths and Monuments.* Oxford: Berg.

Tortorella, S. 2005. "Il Repertorio Iconografico della Ceramica Africana a Rilievo del IV-V Secolo D.C." *Mélanges de l'École française de Rome. Antiquité* 117.1: 173–98.

Trousset, P. 1990. "Tours de guet (watch-towers) et système de liaison optique sur le Limes Tripolitanus." In *Akten des 14 Internationalen Limeskongresses 1986 in Carnuntum*, edited by H. Vetters and M. Kandler, 249–77. Wien: Verlag der Österreichischen Akademie der Wissenschaften.

Tschan, A. P., W. Raczkowski, and M. Latalowa. 2000. "Perception and viewsheds: Are they mutually inclusive?" In Lock 2000, 28–48.

Tsirkin, J. B. 1981. "The South of Spain in the Civil War of 50–45 B.C." *Archivo Español de Arqueología* 54: 91–100.

Ulbert, G. 1984. *Cáceres el Viejo: Ein spätrepublikanisches Legionslager in Spanisch-Extremadura.* Mainz am Rhein: Von Zabern.

Van den Hoek, A., and J. J. Herrmann, Jr., 2013. "Thecla the Beast Fighter: A Female Emblem of Deliverance in Early Christian Popular Art." In *Pottery, Pavements, and Paradise: Iconographic and Textual Studies on Late Antiquity*, edited by A. van den Hoek and J. J. Herrmann, Jr., 65–106. Leiden: Brill.

Van Dierendonck, R. M. 2004. "Five Post-Holes and a Ditch: The Valkenburg-Marktveld Timber Watch and Signal Tower." In *Archaeology in Confrontation: Aspects of Roman Military Presence in the Northwest*, edited by F. Vermeulen, K. Sas, and W. Dhaeze, 73–102. Archaeological Reports Ghent University 2. Ghent: Academia Press.

Vasconcelos, J. L. 1895. "'Castelo Velho' e 'Castelinho' do Alandroal." *O Archeologo Português* 1: 212–13.

— . 1913. *Religiões da Lusitânia*, vol. 3. Lisbon: Imprensa Nacional.

Vaz Pinto, I. 2003. *A Cerâmica Comum das Villae Romanas de São Cucufate (Beja)*. Ph.D. diss., Universidade de Lisboa.

Vaz Pinto, I., and R. Morais. 2007. "Complemento de comércio das ânforas: Cerâmica comum bética no território português. In *Actas del Congreso Internacional CRETARIAE. Salsas y salazones de pescado en Occidente durante la Antiguedad. Universidad de Cádiz, noviembre de 2005*, 235–54. Oxford: Archaeopress.

Vaz Pinto, I., and A. Schmitt. 2010. "Cerâmica Comum." In Alarcão et al. 2010c, 27–35.

Vermeulen, F. 2006. "Understanding Lines in the Roman Landscape: A Study of Ancient Roads and Field Systems Based on GIS Technology." In *GIS and Archaeological Site Location Modeling*, edited by M. W. Mehrer and K. L. Wescott, 266–91. London: Taylor and Francis.

Vermeulen, F., and D. Taelman. 2010. "From cityscape to landscape in Roman *Lusitania*: The *municipium* of *Ammaia*." In Corsi and Vermeulen 2010, 311–24.

Viegas, C. 2003. *Terra sigillata da Alcáçova de Santarém—Economia, comércio e cerâmica*. Trabalhos de Arqueologia 26. Lisboa: Instituto Português de Arqueologia.

Wahl, J. 1985. "Castelo da Lousa: Ein Wehrgehöft caesarich-augusteischer Zeit." *Madrider Mitteilungen* 26: 150–76.

Wheatley, D. W. 1995. "Cumulative viewshed analysis: A GIS-based method for investigating intervisibility, and its archaeological application." In Lock and Stančič 1995, 171- 86.

Wheatley, D. W., and M. Gillings. 2000. "Vision, perception and GIS: Developing enriched approaches to the study of archaeological visibility." In Lock 2000, 1–27.

Wheatley, D. W., and M. Gillings. 2002. *Spatial Technology and Archaeology: The Archaeological Applications of GIS*. London: Taylor and Francis.

Williams, J., and R. Mataloto. 2011. "Caladinho 2010: A Preliminary Report on the Excavation of a First-Century BCE Tower in Alto Alentejo, Portugal." *Chronika* 1: 22–26.

Witcher, R. E. 1999. "GIS and Landscapes of Perception." In *Geographical Information Systems and Landscape Archaeology*, edited by M. Gillings, D. J. Mattingly, and J. van Dalen, 13–22. Oxford: Oxbow.

Woodman, P. E. 2000. "Beyond Significant Patterning, Towards Past Intentions: The Location of Orcadian Chambered Tombs." In *Proceedings of the UK Chapter of Computer Applications and Quantitative Methods in Archaeology 1999*, edited by C. Buck, V. Cummings, C. Henley, S. Mills, and S. Trick, 91–105. BAR-IS 844. Oxford: Archaeopress.

Woolliscroft, D. J. 1988a. "The Outpost System of Hadrian's Wall." *Transactions. Cumberland and Westmorland Antiquarian and Archaeological Society* 88: 23–28.

— . 1988b. "The outpost system of Hadrian's Wall: An outer Limes?" *British Archaeology* 6: 22–25.

— . 2000. *The Roman Gask Series Tower at West Mains of Huntingtower, Perth and Kinross*. Edinburgh: National Museums of Scotland.

— . 2001. *Roman Military Signalling*. Stroud and Charleston: Tempus Books.
Yekutieli, Y. 2006. "Is somebody watching you? Ancient surveillance systems in the southern Judean Desert." *JMA* 19.1: 65–89.

INDEX

Alqueva Dam, 2–3, 19, 36, 43, 71
Ammaia, 5, 20–21, 33, 39–40, 110, 114–116, 118–119 (*and see* Figs. 1.3, 2.2, 6.7, and 6.22)
Appian, 1, 13, 23n.21, 23–25, 27–31, 28, 29 33–34, 37, 45, 48, 50
Augusta Emerita, 40–41, 78

Bandits, 1, 5–6, 15, 30–32, 39, 48, 53, 79, 115–117, 119, 122, 128, 130–132, 134–136
Beiçudos, (F2) 60, 113–115 (*and see* Figs. 1.2, 4.1, 6.2, and 6.7)
Border control, 6, 46–49, 123, 125–129, 134, 137–139
Borderless surveillance, 6–7, 49, 119, 121, 125, 130–131, 137

Cabeço de Vaiamonte, 13, 36, 41–42, 110–111, 113–114 (*and see* Figs. 2.2 and 6.1–5)
Caesar, 1, 24, 33–35, 45, 50–51, 104, 115
Caladinho (F9), 10, 13–14, 38, 44, 56–57, 59–60, 64–66, 70, 72–73, 80–107, 110–112, 125, 127, 132–133 (*and see* Figs. 1.2, 4.6, 5.1–9, 5.11–41, 6.10, and 6.13)
Carceral oversight, 7, 123–125, 129–130, 138
Castelinho (F10), 66–67, 106, 117–118 (*and see* Figs. 4.7 and 6.13 14)
Castelinhos do Rosário (F12), 4, 22, 56, 66, 68–69, 74, 78, 118 (*and see* Figs. 4.8–10, 6.15, and 6.19)
Castelo da Lousa, 2, 4, 11, 13, 19–20, 33, 42–43, 51, 63, 68, 71–72, 78, 87, 89, 91, 93, 97–98, 111, 130, 134 (*and see* Figs. 2.2 and 6.15–21)
Castelo da Pena de Alfange (F13), 69–70, 113 (*and see* Figs. 1.2, 6.16, and 6.19)
Castelo do Mau Vizinho (R20), 74–75, 115–116 (*and see* Figs. 1.2, 4.14, and 6.9)
Castelinho dos Mouros, 56, 80
Castelo dos Mouros (R23), 76–77, 115–116 (*and see* Figs. 1.2, 4.15–18, and 6.9)
Castelo Velho de Degebe, 37–39, 71, 110, 119, 130 (*and see* Fig. 6.21)
Castelo Velho de Veiros, 37–39, 71, 110, 114–115, 119, 130 (*and see* Figs. 6.1–5 and 6.7)
Celtici, 17, 29
Column of Trajan, 45–46 (*and see* Figs. 3.1–2)

Cortes (F5), 62–64, 116–117 (*and see* Figs. 1.2, 4.2, and 6.12–13)

Defesinha (F15), 71, 118 (*and see* Figs. 1.2 and 6.18–19)
Digital Elevation Maps, 8, 108–109, 111

Entanglement, 6–7, 12, 102–104, 107–108, 122, 131–139
Estremoz Anticline, 19, 21, 80, 117 (*and see* Figs. 2.2, 6.10–14, and 6.22)
Évora, 18, 20–21, 33, 39–41, 54, 56, 64, 77–78, 101, 110, 115–116, 119 (*and see* Figs. 2.2, 6.8–9, and 6.22)
Évoramonte, 37
Exploratores, 4

Fortins, 3–4, 10–14, 20, 22, 38–39, 40–42, 44, 54–78, 80, 101–108, 109–114, 116–119, 121–122, 124–125, 127–131, 133–135 (*and see* Figs. 1.2 and 6.22)

German-Raetian *limes*, 6, 48–49, 86, 128–129
Guadiana River, 2–3, 17–21, 25–26, 29, 41, 43, 64, 66–67, 69–71, 97, 114–115, 117–119, 125, 134 (*and see* Figs. 6.15–22)

Hadrian's Wall, 6, 48, 121, 123, 125–130
Hispania Ulterior 2, 25–28, 30, 33, 36, 50

Inscriptions, 13, 25–26, 48–49

Jordan, 9, 104, 112, 123, 129, 135

Livy, 1, 13, 23–27, 29–30, 37, 45, 48
Lusitanii (also Lusitanians), 2–3, 17, 23–36, 134–135

Malhada das Penas 1 and 2 (F1), 59, 113, 115 (*and see* Figs. 1.2, 6.1, and 6.7)
Mariano (R17), 72–73, 113–115 (*and see* Figs. 1.2, 4.11–12, and 6.3)
Mesas do Castelinho, 13, 37–38, 55, 87
Military equipment, 11, 41–43, 111
Mines and quarries, 4, 13, 17, 20–22, 68, 78, 104, 111, 115, 123–124, 129–130, 135 (*and see* Figs. 2.3–4)

168 INDEX

Moinho do Tojal (F16), 71–72, 118–119 (*and see* Figs. 1.2 and 6.21)
Mons Claudianus, 101–102, 104–106, 121, 127–128
Monte da Nora, 42, 102, 114–115 (*and see* Figs. 2.2, 6.4–7, and 6.22)
Monte do Almo (F8), 44, 64–65, 116–117 (*and see* Figs. 1.2, 4.8, 6.11, and 6.13)
Monte do Gato (F14), 70–71, 118 (*and see* Figs. 1.2, 6.17, and 6.19)
Monte do Outeiro, 37–38, 78, 116, 125, 130 (*and see* Figs. 2.2 and 6.10–14)

Ostraka, 104–105, 127
Outeiro da Mina (R18), 73, 113–115 (*and see* Figs. 1.2, 4.13, 6.3, and 6.7)
Outeiro Pintado (F6), 63–64, 114–115, 118 (*and see* Figs. 1.2, 4.3, and 6.6–7)

Panopticon, 6–7, 14, 119, 122–124, 127–131, 135–139
Pax Julia (Beja), 13, 20–22, 39–41, 110, 115
Penedo do Ferro (F3), 61, 113–115 (*and see* Figs. 1.2, 6.4, and 6.7)
Pliny the Elder, 21, 33, 42
Pliny the Younger, 13, 45, 48, 50–52
Pottery, African Red Slip, 45–47, 79
Pottery, amphorae, 42–43, 61–63, 65–66, 69–70, 73, 76–77, 80, 88–93, 95, 98–99, 102, 105–106, 133 (*and see* Figs. 4.13, 4.17, 5.1, 5.26–8, and 5.34–6)
Pottery, Baetican, 43, 61–62, 65–66, 69–70, 73, 76, 85, 87–88, 91, 93, 95, 97, 99–100 (*and see* Figs. 4.17, 5.26, 5.29–30, 5.33–37)
Pottery, Campanian black gloss ware, 43, 62, 65, 72, 76, 87, 89, 92, 95, 97–98, 102, 133–134 (*and see* Figs. 5.23–24)
Pottery, cookware, 73, 89–90, 92, 94–95, 98, 102 (*and see* Figs. 5.27–28, 5.33, and 5.37)
Pottery, *dolia*, 65, 90 (*and see* Figs. 5.27–28)
Pottery, local imitations, 72, 85, 87, 89, 92–95, 97–99, 102–103, 133–134, 136
Pottery, Lusitanian, 73, 76, 82, 91, 93, 95, 99, 133 (*and see* Figs. 4.17, 5.29–30, 5.34)
Pottery, prehistoric, 38, 60–61, 67, 80, 82–84, 86, 88, 91–92, 94 (*and see* Figs. 5.1 and 5.6)
Pottery, terra sigillata, 43, 69, 71, 74, 77, 80, 82, 85–87, 89, 95–97, 102, 133 (*and see* Figs. 5.17–22 and 5.29–5.32)
Pseudo-Cyprian, 47, 52, 124

Rocha da Mina, 11, 37–38, 103, 107, 110, 117, 125 (*and see* Figs. 2.5 and 6.10–14)

Rocha de Províncios (F11), 56, 67, 70, 118 (*and see* Figs. 1.2 and 6.19–20)
Recintos-torre, 3–4, 10–14, 20, 22, 38–39, 41–42, 54–58, 62, 65–66, 68, 72–80, 101, 103–105, 107–116, 118–119, 121–122, 124–125, 127, 130–131, 133–134

Santa Justa (R21), 75, 115–116 (*and see* Figs. 1.2 and 6.9)
Santa Susana, 44, 103 (*and see* Fig. 2.6)
Sempre-Noiva (R22), 76, 115–116 (*and see* Figs. 1.2 and 6.9)
Seneca the Younger, 45, 48, 50–51
Serra d'Ossa, 19–20, 37–38, 63–64, 78, 80, 116–118, 121, 124–125 (*and see* Figs. 2.2, 6.7, 6.10–14, and 6.22)
Serra de Segóvia, 37–39, 114–115, 119, 130 (*and see* Figs. 6.6–7)
Sertorius, 15, 24, 27, 32–34, 114, 138
Signaling towers, 45–46, 48–49, 105, 107, 119, 121, 125–128, 130
Skopelarioi, 104–106
Skopeloi, 104–106, 127–128
Slaves, 4, 7, 13, 25–26, 29, 47, 53, 78–79, 106–107, 124, 128–129, 135, 138–139
Speculatores, 4, 49
Societates, 2, 22
Soeiros, (F4) 61–62, 115 (*and see* Figs. 1.2 and 6.8)

Tejo River, 11, 18–20, 25–26, 28–29, 31, 99
Terrugem (R19), 74, 113–115 (*and see* Figs. 1.2, 6.5, and 6.7)
Torre de Palma, 44, 78–79, 113
Três Moinhos (F7), 64, 114–115, 118 (*and see* Figs. 1.2, 4.4, and 6.6–7)

Vale d'El-Rei de Cima (R24), 77, 115–116 (*and see* Figs. 1.2, 4.19, and 6.9)
Vectigalia, 22
Viewsheds, 7–10, 22, 78, 109–110, 112–119, 121, 124–125, 130, 132, 137 (*and see* Figs. 6.1–22 and 7.1)
Villas, 3–5, 13, 15–16, 20, 35–37, 39, 43–48, 50–51, 53, 65, 68–69, 74–79, 103, 107, 110–113, 121, 123–125, 129–130, 134 (*and see* Figs. 2.6, 4.20, and 7.1)
Viriathus, 15, 24, 27–29, 31–33, 35, 135, 138

Watchtowers, 11, 13, 31, 39, 45–50, 52–53, 70, 79, 101, 105, 112, 123, 125–129, 138 (*and see* Figs. 3.1–2)
Wind towers, 45–46

www.ingramcontent.com/pod-product-compliance
Lightning Source LLC
Chambersburg PA
CBHW021759230426
43669CB00006B/125